Reading Walter Benjamin

MANCHESTER
1824

Manchester University Press

Reading Walter Benjamin

Writing through the catastrophe

RICHARD J. LANE

The murky side of Benjamin.

cheers Keith,

Richard lane

2005.

MANCHESTER UNIVERSITY PRESS
Manchester and New York

distributed exclusively in the USA by Palgrave

Published by Manchester University Press
Oxford Road, Manchester M13 9NR, UK
and Room 400, 175 Fifth Avenue, New York, NY 10010, USA
www.manchesteruniversitypress.co.uk

Distributed exclusively in the USA by
Palgrave, 175 Fifth Avenue, New York,
NY 10010, USA

Distributed exclusively in Canada by
UBC Press, University of British Columbia, 2029 West Mall,
Vancouver, BC, Canada V6T 1Z2

British Library Cataloguing-in-Publication Data
A catalogue record for this book is available from the British Library

Library of Congress Cataloging-in-Publication Data applied for

ISBN 0 7190 6436 8 *hardback*
EAN 978 0 7190 6436 4
ISBN 0 7190 6437 6 *paperback*
EAN 978 0 7190 6437 1

First published 2005

14 13 12 11 10 09 08 07 06 05   10 9 8 7 6 5 4 3 2 1

Typeset by SNP Best-set Typesetter Ltd., Hong Kong
Printed in Great Britain
by CPI, Bath

CONTENTS

GLOSSARY OF SELECTED GERMAN WORDS AND EXPRESSIONS

Anschaulichkeit	graphicness, concreteness
Aufhebung	sublation (to take up)
das Jetzt der Erkennbarkheit	the now of recognizability/knowability
Einmalige Erscheinung	unique experience
Flüchtig	fleeing, fleeting, fugitive
Gemeinschaft	community
Geistige Inhalte	spiritual meanings
Jetztzeit	present/now-time
Kugelblitz	ball lightning
Kulturpessimismus	despair of civilization
Offenbarungsglaube	faith/belief via revelation
Rausch	intoxication, euphoria, high, ecstasy, rapture
Trauerspiel	mourning play
Übermensch	Overman
Ursprung	origin
Wahlverwandtschaften	elective affinities
Wahrnehmung	perception
Wandervogel	youth movement (literally 'bird of passage' or 'rolling stone')
Zerstreuung	distraction, scattering, dispersal, diffusion, entertainment, diversion
Zusammenfassung	collecting/holding together; to combine or unite
Zweifalt	'a fold that differentiates and is differentiated' (Deleuze)

ACKNOWLEDGEMENTS

At Manchester University Press thanks go to Kate Fox and Matthew Frost. Discussions concerning Benjamin began for me with Joseph Jones at the University of British Columbia, and continued with the London Network Philosophy and Theory Research Seminar which I directed between 2000 and 2002, and the Critical Theory Group in Vancouver, which I directed between 2003 and 2004. For the London Network Philosophy and Theory Research seminars on *The Arcades Project* special thanks go to my postgraduate students Richard Cope (South Bank University, London) and Judit Szabó (University of Debrecen, Hungary). For research support at the University of Debrecen, thanks go to Tamas Benyei, Nora Sellei, Peter Szaffko and Zoltan Abadi-Nagy. Philip Tew introduced me to the work of B. S. Johnson, which led to many valuable conversations; he was also of inspiration as co-director of the London Network for Modern Fiction Studies. Andrew Bowie introduced me to the work of Manfred Frank, and a welcome new perspective on poststructuralism. For discussions and support, in England and Canada, during the writing of this book, thanks also go to Charles Barbour, John Calder, Robert Eaglestone, Andrew Gibson, Sherrill Grace, Richard Ingram, Torsten Kehler, Thomas Kemple, David Knight, Joy James, Deborah Madsen, Rod Mengham, Ian Ross, Ray Siemens, Steven Taubeneck, John Thieme, Mark Vessey, Jeffrey Weeks, and Gernot Wieland. I would also like to thank the staff of the British Library, London, and the Koerner Library and Main Library of the University of British Columbia, Vancouver. Finally, this book would not have been written without the support of my wife, Sarah.

Early versions of this book were delivered as papers at the Congress of the Social Sciences and Humanities in Toronto in May 2002 ('Aesthetic and Generic Boundary Crossing: Boxed Books and the Avant-Garde'), at the 'Reading Benjamin's Arcades' conference at King Alfred's College, Winchester, in association with *New Formations*, in July 2002 ('The Materiality of the Text: Boxed Books and Portable Archives'), at the 'Faust Conference', at the University of Calgary in April 2003 ('Construction Without Theory: Benjamin's Goethe/Goethe's *Faust*') and at the Eighteenth Century Circle, University of British Columbia, in May 2003 ('Benjamin's "Program of the Coming Philosophy" and the Theory of Experience: Redefining the Subject in Kant').

1

Introduction

A shadow fell across Europe during Walter Benjamin's lifetime (1892–1940). That shadow can be called, variously, National Socialism, the Nazi Party, Fascism, the Holocaust or the Shoah. There are other names, but these are among the most significant. 'Shoah' can be translated as 'destruction' or 'catastrophe': it is the word often used to refer to the Nazis' 'Final Solution' of 1941–45.[1] Walter Benjamin took his own life in the year in which the Nazi euthanasia programme was being rigorously implemented by medical staff and others.[2] Such a programmatic effacement was merely the beginnings of a mass-murder project. For some, the Shoah signals the end of the Enlightenment, as rationality and technology revealed their darkest possibilities in the death camps of Europe, the technological society generated by the Enlightenment project leading directly from mass production to mass destruction. Benjamin called the Second World War a catastrophe, writing in 1939, 'Let us hope that the witnesses to European civilization . . . will survive the murderous rage of Hitler, along with their accounts of it.'[3] Benjamin, a German Jew, had been officially 'expatriated' by the Gestapo in May 1939, although he was already living in Paris. After the outbreak of war, Benjamin was placed in a French internment camp, first at the Stade Colombe in Paris, for ten days, and then at Vernuche.[4] He was released in November of the same year, but his brother was undergoing far worse an ordeal. Georg Benjamin belonged to the Communist Party, and was arrested by the police in 1933, being imprisoned in a police gaol in Alexanderplatz, then in Plötzensee, before being moved to Sonnenburg concentration camp, where he was released at the end of the year. Georg then returned to his duties as a committed Communist, editing and translating 'illegal' materials; he was eventually re-arrested by the Gestapo, sentenced for six years, and then moved to Mauthausen concentration camp.[5] This final move was precisely what Benjamin had feared: 'My brother has been transferred to the prison in Wilsnak, where he is kept busy working on the roads. Life is still supposed to be tolerable there. As I often hear from Germany, the nightmare oppressing people in his situation is not so much the upcoming day in prison as the concentration camp that threatens after years of imprisonment.'[6] The guards at Mauthausen had many favourite sadistic games of torture and murder; one of their games involved throwing an inmate's cap over the wire, whereby the prisoner had to retrieve it, being shot as an 'escapee' in the process.[7] Georg Benjamin died in similar suspicious circumstances, supposedly killing himself by touching a high-voltage power line.[8]

As is well known, Walter Benjamin did finally attempt to flee from Europe as Hitler moved his armies into Paris. Benjamin left Paris for Lourdes, where he eventually acquired an entry permit for the USA, then he moved to Marseilles, where he failed to complete official French formalities for leaving the country. Instead, with a small group of people, he unofficially crossed the Pyrenees into Spain on foot. Overnight, Spanish entry visas had been nullified, meaning that all refugees fleeing from France were to be sent back; Benjamin learnt this news arriving in Portbou and committed suicide during the night of 26 September 1940.[9] In many respects, Benjamin's death was only the beginning of the story, as he slowly became mythologized, turned into an intellectual icon of the twentieth century. In part, in the English-speaking world, this derives from a certain mystique generated by his previously untranslated texts, and the obscurities of his final days. For a long time, only a small number of Benjamin's works were available in translation, and whispers about some huge, but lost, fascinating final manuscript did the rounds. As Broderson notes: 'Much conjecture has also surrounded the fate of the few possessions Benjamin was carrying at the time of his death. The manuscript he was supposedly carrying has acquired almost legendary status.'[10] Jay Parini fictionalizes the loss of the 'manuscript' in his novel *Benjamin's Crossing*, where the child José, who crossed into Spain with Benjamin, accidentally leaves it on a train after being given it for safekeeping:

> José shook his head, letting the tears fall unabashedly now. It didn't matter what his mother said or what anyone thought. That manu-

script had meant so much to him [Benjamin]; indeed, it probably contained everything he had ever thought about, the ultimate formation of his experience as a man. He remembered that Benjamin had asked Frau Fittko to take the manuscript and leave him there, dangling on the precipice, in the Pyrenees. And he was not joking. 'It is more important than I am,' he had said. More important than life.[11]

By fictionalizing this final act of dispossession from the perspective of a child, Parini can expand the legendary manuscript to its largest fantastical possibility: that it contained everything Benjamin 'had ever thought about'. The manuscript becomes converted into something quite alien to the fragments, the essays, the works of newspaper and radio journalism, and so on that Benjamin produced in his lifetime. Benjamin *would* have made sense of it all in this final book, he *would* have given his readers comfort and resolution, perhaps alongside or through a new, bigger theory that could function as a summation and a map to the post-Enlightenment world.[12] Benjamin's manuscript would have helped cancel out, or at least comprehend, the catastrophe of the twentieth century.

Benjamin's 'big book' did still exist, his *Passagen-Werk*, hidden in the Bibliothèque Nationale de France by Georges Bataille during the Second World War, to be retrieved later by Theodor Adorno. It was published in the original in 1982 and in English in 1999 as *The Arcades Project*. Ostensibly a study of the nineteenth-century glass-covered Paris Arcades or passages, this vast labyrinthine text is a collection of comments, quotations, and essay versions – it can be seen as a large notebook or prepatory work, or as a fabulous and insightful montage, but either way, it is *not* the conclusive work of theory that many had hoped for.[13] In fact, in the English-speaking world, Benjamin had long been known not for a book, but for one essay, translated initially in *Studies on the Left* (no. 2, 1960), then in the popular *Illuminations* volume as 'The Work of Art in the Age of Mechanical Reproduction' (1968), with two variants (second and third versions) in the more recent Harvard–Belknap *Selected Writings*, as 'The Work of Art in the Age of its Technological Reproducibility' (2002 and 2003). This essay alone played a significant role in generating Benjamin's iconic status, but other essays in *Illuminations* also became rapidly overdetermined, as scholars hungry for more delved deeply into the volume, although as Hannah Arendt argued, the 'chief purpose of this collection is to convey the importance of

Benjamin as a literary critic.'[14] While *Illuminations* remains excep-
tionally popular and does contain interesting and key essays,[15] it was
not until 1977 that Benjamin's major study, *Ursprung des deutschen
Trauerspiels*, was translated as *The Origin of German Tragic Drama*. As
George Steiner argues:

> The publication of this monograph in English, in 1977, under this
> imprint [Verso], is pregnant with ironies. What English-speaking
> reader has ever glanced at the plays and allegories which Benjamin
> would, though indirectly, resuscitate? Where could he find them?
> The mandarins and aestheticians with whom Benjamin seeks his
> quarrels are long forgotten. The German-Jewish community of
> which he was a late ornament lies in cinders. Benjamin himself died
> a hunted fugitive. Had he lived, Walter Benjamin would doubtless
> have been sceptical of any 'New Left'. Like every man committed
> to abstruse thought and scholarship, he knew that not only the
> humanities, but humane and critical intelligence itself, resides in the
> always-threatened keeping of the very few. *Trauerspiel* is beautifully
> apt: a presentiment of man's suffering and cruelty, made bearable
> through stately, even absurd form. A play of sorrow.[16]

The ironies here are in part to do with the fact that Benjamin as
western cultural icon wrote from a German-Jewish aesthetic and
philosophical background. As Benjamin's status grew in the English-
speaking west, it did so in parallel with an increased interest in structuralist and poststructuralist thought: in other words, an interest in
the (crudely called) 'French' theorists. Benjamin's popularity is in
some ways remarkable because it has survived, or increased, not just
among those who inherit the Marxist-based critical theory project,
but also among those who follow antithetical concepts and/or theories. Thematized, simplified versions of the various 'posts-' (including postcolonialism) reveal shared concerns between theory and
Benjamin, for example, an interest in the fragmentary, the marginal,
the ephemeral, the essay over the treatise, storytelling rather than
system building, the montage form and new visual technologies. As
Adorno puts it: 'The provocative assertion that an essay on the Paris
Arcades is of greater interest philosophically than are ponderous
observations on the Being of beings is more attuned to the meaning
of his [Benjamin's] work than the quest for that unchanging, self-
identical conceptual skeleton which he relegated to the dustbin.'[17]
What thematised series of comparisons between Benjamin and
contemporary critical or theoretical work cannot account for is, say,

Adorno's assertion in the same essay that: 'In all his phases, Benjamin conceived the downfall of the subject and the salvation of man as inseparable.'[18] There is an entire section of the Benjamin industry that in different ways deliberately discounts precisely this inseparability; Peter Osborne, for example, analyses Howard Caygill's approach in his *Walter Benjamin: The Colour of Experience*:[19]

> Setting out from the now generally accepted position that Benjamin's project develops out of the Kantian concept of experience, Caygill's reading is distinctive in four main ways. First, it argues for the 'anti-Hegelian but nevertheless speculative' character of Benjamin's version of this concept. Second, it claims that this is developed out of Kant 'through an extension of a Nietzschean method of active nihilism', as 'an exploration of the ambiguity of nihilism'. Third, it suggests that the paradigm of experience here is not linguistic, as is generally supposed, but rather the intuitive intensities of 'chromatic differentiation'. Finally, and most dramatically, it downgrades the messianic dimension of Benjamin's thought to a dogmatic residue, fit only for critical excision.[20]

While this 'downgrading' in no way impacts upon the originality and vitality of Caygill's study, it is indicative of a discomfort with the theological structural components, if not overall force, of Benjamin's work.[21] While not arguing for Benjamin as theologian *per se*, the following exploration of his work – first in relation to some elements of German and Judaic culture, and second in relation to modern aesthetics – maintains his theological impulse and the persistence of the absolute as a substrate. Reading Benjamin means being aware of a play of forces that were themselves subject to the massively destructive powers of National Socialism, which is *not* to say that the spirit of German-Jewish culture was totally annihilated in the process. Benjamin – at all times – works within the force-field that contemporary theory has relegated to 'metaphysics' or the deconstructed and somewhat dejected domain of transcendental signifiers. Eric Jacobson succinctly defines metaphysics, in relation to his study of Benjamin and Scholem, as 'a highly speculative philosophy of fundamental questions regarding politics and theology, drawing on a near scholastic aptitude for categorial analysis and Talmudic rigor within a conception of divine continuity of meaning. In this way it is in fact a philosophy of divine as well as profane questions.'[22] Thus the chiasmus operative in Benjamin's work – the crossing of the sacred and the profane – is not an attempt to subsume one under the other; and furthermore, Benjamin's 'political theology', as Jacobson puts it, 'is concerned with the profane and consciously addresses itself to it.'[23] The study that follows does not argue for a recuperation of metaphysics, merely that the *'ascertainment of being'*, to use Jaspers's phrase, involves accounting in myriad ways for non-objective thought.[24] Josef Pieper once argued that 'It is a peculiarity of philosophic inquiry, inherent in the matter itself, that it stands from the outset in a fully fledged "contrapuntal" relationship to theology.'[25] It is my argument that Benjamin's intellectual engagement is similarly *contrapuntal* throughout his lifetime, leading to the persistence of the absolute in his work. This book explores, first, a historical-theoretical approach to Benjamin situating him as a 'contrapuntal thinker' in Pieper's sense, and second, the question of form in Benjamin applied to examples in the visual arts (Rachel Whiteread) and literary criticism (B. S. Johnson). The impetus here is to provide an account of Benjamin that continually crosses antithetical critical domains; this necessarily involves a presentation and discussion of some introductory material (Chapters 2 and 3) before moving on to more abstract and theoretical argument.

Notes

1 Jack Miles, *Christ: A Crisis in the Life of God*, London: William Heinemann, 2001, p. 117.
2 See, for example, the discussion of eugenics and euthanasia in section 5 of Michael Burleigh's *The Third Reich: A New History*, London: Macmillan, 2000.
3 Walter Benjamin to Adrienne Monnier, 21 September 1939, letter 320 in *The Correspondence of Walter Benjamin: 1910–1940*, ed. Gershom Scholem and Theodor W. Adorno, trans. Manfred R. Jacobson and Evelyn M. Jacobson, Chicago and London: The University of Chicago Press, 1994, p. 613.
4 Momme Brodersen, *Walter Benjamin: A Biography*, trans. Malcolm R. Green and Ingrida Ligers, London and New York: Verso, 1997, pp. 244–245.
5 Ibid., pp. 208–209.
6 Benjamin to Gretel Adorno, 1 November 1938, letter 305 in *The Correspondence of Walter Benjamin: 1910–1940*, p. 578.
7 Burleigh, *The Third Reich: A New History*, p. 203.
8 Brodersen, *Walter Benjamin: A Biography*, p. 209.
9 Ibid., p. 256.
10 Ibid., p. 259.
11 Jay Parini, *Benjamin's Crossing*, London: Anchor, 1998, p. 301.
12 See the discussion of 'high expectations' in Susan Buck-Morss, *The Dialectics of Seeing: Walter Benjamin and The Arcades Project*, Cambridge, Massachusetts: MIT Press, 1999, pp. 216–217.

13 See the translators' foreword to *The Arcades Project*, trans. Howard Eiland and Kevin McLaughlin, Cambridge, Massachusetts, and London, England: Belknap Press of Harvard University Press, 1999. The quotations from the English translation of *The Arcades Project* are given page numbers and symbols that follow the corresponding text block from which the quotation derives. The symbols place the block in sequential order within a particular sheaf, bundle or *Konvolut* (to use the German word), following Benjamin's arrangement. As the translators of *The Arcades Project* note, Benjamin's handwritten unbound folios 'are gathered into thirty-six sheafs . . . in accordance with a set of themes keyed to the letters of the alphabet. The titles of the convolutes, as well as the numbering of the individual entries, derive from Benjamin. In regard to the ordering, the use of lower-case "a" (as in "A1a, 1") denotes the third page of the folio. The letters without corresponding titles in the Overview may indicate that Benjamin planned further convolutes' (p. 958). The additional material collected in *The Arcades Project* under the title 'First Sketches' comes from a bound notebook; some material from this notebook was transferred to *The Arcades Project* folio by Benjamin. The German editors of the 'First Sketches' have provided the cross-references and numbering, used also by the English translators. See the translators' comments on p. 827. Finally, the translators note in their foreword that 'In an effort to respect the unique constitution of these manuscripts, we have adopted Tiedemann's practice [referring to the German editor of *The Arcades Project*] of using angle brackets to indicate editorial insertions into the text' (p. xiii).

14 Hannah Arendt, 'Editor's Note', in Walter Benjamin, *Illuminations*, trans. Harry Zohn, ed. Hannah Arendt, London: Fontana, 1992 (first published in English in 1968; first Fontana edition 1973), p. 256.

15 'Unpacking My Library', 'The Task of the Translator', 'The Storyteller', 'What is Epic Theatre?', 'On Some Motifs in Baudelaire', 'The Image of Proust', 'Theses on the Philosophy of History'.

16 George Steiner, 'Introduction' to Walter Benjamin, *The Origin of German Tragic Drama*, trans. John Osborne, London and New York: Verso, 1999, p. 24.

17 Theodor W. Adorno, 'A Portrait of Walter Benjamin', *Prisms*, trans. Samuel and Shierry Weber, Cambridge, Massachusetts: MIT Press, 1997, p. 232.

18 Ibid., p. 231.

19 Howard Caygill, *Walter Benjamin: The Colour of Experience*, London: Routledge, 1998.

20 Peter Osborne, 'Philosophizing Beyond Philosophy: Walter Benjamin Reviewed', in Andrew Benjamin and Peter Osborne, eds., *Walter Benjamin's Philosophy: Destruction & Experience*, Manchester: Clinamen Press, 2000, pp. 286–303, at p. 297.

21 See Rainer Rochlitz's discussion of Benjamin's relationship to Judaism, *The Disenchantment of Art: The Philosophy of Walter Benjamin*, trans. Jane Marie Todd, New York and London: Guilford Press, 1996, pp. 5–6.

22 Eric Jacobson, *Metaphysics of the Profane: The Political Theology of Walter Benjamin and Gershom Scholem*, New York: Columbia University Press, 2003, p. 5.

23 Ibid.

24 Karl Jaspers, *Philosophy*, vol. i, trans. E. B. Ashton, Chicago and London: The University of Chicago Press, 1969, p. 63.

25 Josef Pieper, *The End of Time: A Meditation on the Philosophy of History*, trans. Michael Bullock, San Francisco: Ignatius Press: 1999, p. 16.

2

Kulturpessimismus and the new thinking

The decline of the west

Bio-critical accounts of Benjamin rarely begin with Oswald Spengler (1880–1936). Stress (in biographies or critical overviews) is often placed upon intellectual life-phases, such as Benjamin's shift from Messianic to Marxist thought, or stress may be placed upon the connectivity of these phases, which are thereafter explored and explained in their interrelatedness. Key intertexts in either case would be, say, Bloch's Messianic *The Spirit of Utopia* (1923), followed by Lukács's Marxist *History and Class Consciousness* (1923). Going back to more youthful pursuits, the innovative pedagogue Gustav Wyneken (discussed in the next chapter) is of great importance, as well as Benjamin's re-reading of Kant. What would the justification for mentioning Spengler be? His monumental two-volume *Der Untergang des Abendlandes* (1918 and 1922), translated as *The Decline of The West*, is quoted in *The Arcades Project* merely five times, once in convolute C (Ancient Paris, Catacombs, Demolitions, Decline of Paris), twice in convolute J (Baudelaire) and twice in convolute M (Idleness); all the quotations are from a small section of Spengler's second volume. This suggests that Spengler was hardly a key thinker for Benjamin. When it comes to theorizing the city spaces of modernity, Spengler belongs to an entirely other tradition: 'Benjamin's writings on the metropolis . . . clearly reject the simple-minded, reactionary anti-urbanism espoused by critics like Ferdinand Tönnies in *Community and Association* . . . and Oswald Spengler in *The Decline of the West* . . . authors whose sentimental privileging of small-scale communities and peasant life is imbued with parochialism, anti-intellectualism and latent anti-Semitism.'[1] However, Spengler's work *is* indicative to a large extent of the turmoil within German society during the first two decades of the twentieth century. Stirk argues that *The Decline of the West* 'was above all a refutation of the idea of progress, and the climax of that wave of "Kulturpessimismus" which dominated Europe after the Great War.'[2] There were many varieties of *Kulturpessimismus*; Spengler's, regardless of his insistence of total originality, fits into a long line of narratives since Plato, who in turn had portrayed civilization as being merely a degraded copy of ideal Form or Idea.[3] As Popper argues:

> Interpreting existing societies as decadent copies of an ideal state, Plato . . . developed a remarkably realistic historicist theory which found the cause of social change in Heraclitus' disunion, and in the strife of classes in which he recognized the driving as well as the corrupting forces of history. He applied these historicist principles to the story of the Decline and Fall of the Greek city-states, and especially to a criticism of democracy, which he described as effeminate and degenerate.[4]

Spengler advocated a morphological approach to world history, whereby he would generate the 'philosophy of the future', on the West's 'metaphysically exhausted soil'.[5] This exhausted soil would be reinvigorated via his own ensemble or montage effect, whereby disparate cultural notions would be brought together to reveal 'underlying' connections and patterns. For example, early in his introduction to *The Decline of the West* he argues that 'even the humdrum facts of politics assume a symbolic and even a metaphysical character, and . . . things such as the Egyptian administrative system, the Classical coinage, analytical geometry, the cheque, the Suez Canal, the book-printing of the Chinese, the Prussian Army, and the Roman road-engineering can, as symbols, be made *uniformly* understandable and appreciable.'[6] Rejecting Kant's *Critique of Pure Reason*, Spengler argues that the 'essence and kernel of all history' is in fact 'Destiny'[7], in part because he regards historical movements as organic, as being things that grow and eventually decay. Goethe's work is cited here as an inspiration, in particular *Wilhelm Meister* and *Wahrheit und Dichtung*: 'That which Goethe called *Living Nature* is exactly that which we are calling here world-history, *world-as-history*.'[8] The organic, being in the process of becoming, is supremely alive; the inorganic, the system, or the machine, is *the become*, or the dead. Spengler also distinguishes between 'culture' and 'civilization' where the latter is the final development (or destiny/destination) of the former; civilization is, according to Spengler, an external and artificial state of existence, expressed invariably through a city-bound existence.[9] The present epoch, 1800 to 2000, is situated in the ensemble of history in parallel to the transition from the Hellenistic to the Roman age.[10] As such, the present epoch shifts in the nineteenth century from culture to civilization, from becoming to the become, from the organic to the inorganic machine-like existence of the world-cities:

> In place of a world, there is a *city, a point*, in which the whole life of broad regions is collecting while the rest dries up. In place of a type-true people, born of and grown on the soil, there is a new sort of nomad, cohering unstably in fluid masses, the parasitical city dweller, deeply contemptuous of the countryman . . . This is a very great stride towards the inorganic, towards the end – what does it signify? France and England have already taken the step and Germany is beginning to do so.[11]

The 'fluid masses' reject a certain notion of culture, one that is tied up with tradition and hierarchy, with the nobility and the church, and with conservative conventionalism; new modes of popular culture, such as the celebration of sport, become linked by Spengler to archaic, primitive behaviour.[12] As Bloch summarizes it: 'Now there is a "late age" and nothing more, sterile "wakefulness" instead of the once-young "culture-bearing soul" '.[13] A key observation here is that notions of progress generated by Enlightenment thinking are in fact limited, constrained by in-built mortality: 'The future of the West is not a limitless tending upwards and onwards for all time towards our present ideals, but a single phenomenon of history, strictly limited and defined as to form and duration, which covers a few centuries'.[14]

Spengler's 1920 sequel to *The Decline of the West*, called *Preussentum und Sozialismus* (*Prussianism and Socialism*), is rarely mentioned in the English-speaking world, although as Stirk points out 'it is a book which throws much light on Germany's political development since the Great War, and had a much greater effect on German youth than *The Decline of the West*.'[15] In *Preussentum und Sozialismus*, Spengler takes a wide-ranging morphological approach to read the socio-political situation in Germany. Spengler argues for a more authentic Prussian Socialism to replace that of Marx, defining Prussian qualities as being 'a sense of reality, *esprit de corps*, discipline, energy', and that of Prussian Socialism, traced back to the 'Teutonic Knights', being 'fidelity, discipline, denial of self, self-discipline'.[16] In other words, the English individual is compared with the subsumption of the Prussian individual within a wider system of being: 'It was part of the Prussian tradition that the will of the individual should surrender itself to the will of the community. Officers, officials, workers (Spengler's favourite way of dividing up German manhood), the German people in 1813, 1870, and 1914 . . . formed a unity, an entity, which was above the individual ['überpersönlich']. This was not the herd instinct ['Herdengefühl']'.[17] Spengler's notions of 'Socialism' here would be taken up by the Nazis; of interest, also, is the call to youth:

> I count in our struggle on that part of our youth which is deep enough to feel that Germany is strong and unconquered . . . I turn to youth. I call upon all those who have marrow in their bones and blood in their veins. Educate yourselves! Become men! We don't want any more ideologists, no more talk about culture and world-citizenship and the spiritual mission of the Germans. We need hardness, a bold scepticism, a body of socialist supermen ['sozialistische Herrennaturen']. The path to power is clearly marked; the elect of the German workers together with the best representatives of the Old Prussian political spirit, both of them determined to create a truly Socialist state, a democracy in the Prussian sense, firmly united by a common sense of duty, by the consciousness of their great task, by the will to obey in order to rule, by the will to die in order to live, by the strength to make tremendous sacrifices in order to fulfil our destiny . . .[18]

Spengler's call to youth provided further ideological fodder for the Nazi propaganda machine.[19] Destiny is given an apparently rational and logical gloss, but it is actually related by Spengler to something beyond 'rational world-systems', it is something 'passed over in silence by Kant'.[20]

Spengler's notion of destiny is one of the key components of his critique of Kant and German Idealism; his critique relates to a belief that Kant's theory of experience is impoverished. Spengler performs his critique by setting up an opposition between causality and destiny, knowing full well that causality is of great importance to the architectonics of Kant's *Critique of Pure Reason*. In the 'Transcendental Doctrine of Judgment' Kant argues that causality constitutes a law whereby the relation between two states is cogitated: 'it is only because we subject the sequence of phenomena, and consequently all change, to the law of causality, that experience itself, that is, empirical cognition of phenomena, becomes possible; and consequently, that phenomena themselves, as objects of experience, are possible only by virtue of this law.'[21] The latter law is, for Spengler, part of an inorganic logic of understanding that is actually detached from life-experience, which involves '"hope," "happiness," "despair," "repentance," "devotion," and "consolation"'.[22] Of these latter aspects of life, logicians *cannot* speak: 'Causality is the reasonable, the law-bound, the describable . . . But destiny is the word for an inner certainty that is *not* describable. We bring out that which is in the causal by means of a physical or an epistemological system, through numbers, by reasoned classification; but the idea of destiny can be imparted only by the artist working through media like portraiture, tragedy and music.'[23] Spengler is expanding the notion of experience to include non-causal life elements. An essential move here is to disconnect destiny from laws; Spengler argues that all laws are causal and that the recognition of the necessity inherent in the cogitation of causality is paralleled by the necessity of life in terms such as 'destiny', 'dispensation' and 'vocation'.[24] The opposition causality/destiny is therefore functioning in line with the organic/inorganic and logic/aesthetic binaries, which Spengler utilizes to make a direct attack upon Kant's supposed hatred of destiny:

> the thinker in systems, whose whole intellectual existence bases itself on the causality principle . . . [is one of the] 'late' manifestations of an unconscious *hatred* of the powers of incomprehensible Destiny. 'Pure Reason' denies all possibilities that are outside itself. Here strict thought and great art are eternally in conflict. The one keeps its feet, and the other lets itself go. A man like Kant must always feel himself as superior to a Beethoven as the adult is to the child, but this will not prevent a Beethoven from regarding the 'Critique of Pure Reason' as a pitiable sort of philosophy.[25]

In the year in which the first volume of *The Decline of the West* was published, Benjamin wrote 'On the Program of the Coming Philosophy', an essay which offers another, more complex and intellectually dense critique of Kant's concept of experience (see Chapter 6, 'Kant's experience', below). Again, the argument is that Kant has an impoverished notion of experience, but Benjamin argues that this impoverished notion is foundational in the sense of being a low, and limited base for knowledge: 'this is precisely what is at issue: the concept of the naked, primitive, self-evident experience, which, for Kant . . . seemed to be the only experience given – indeed, the only experience possible.'[26] Beyond the fine points of the argument, Benjamin asserts that Kant's concept of experience represents an Enlightenment world view, in other words, one grounded and guided by the desire for scientific principles; the concern is with the development of Kant or future philosophy, and more specifically, Benjamin's critique of the neo-Kantians. In place of this impoverished concept of experience, Benjamin wanted to 'do justice' to what he conceived of as a 'higher experience', that of a future metaphysics, or realm of thought beyond the rational. He is not arguing that metaphysical questions are somehow inoperative in Kant, just that there are 'restrictions' due to two features beyond the impoverished concept of experience: Kant's dualism, and the constant 'relation of knowledge and experience to human empirical consciousness'.[27] Benjamin argues however, that it is precisely at the moment when Enlightenment philosophy 'annihilates' or destroys metaphysical elements that the process mysteriously refers philosophy 'to a deeper, more metaphysically fulfilled experience'.[28] Benjamin argues further that the Kantian grounding in empirical experience is a form of myth, even a mode of 'insane consciousness':

> It simply cannot be doubted that the notion, sublimated though it may be, of an individual living ego which receives sensations by means of its senses and forms its ideas on the basis of them plays a role of the greatest importance in the Kantian concept of knowledge. This notion is, however, mythology, and so far as its truth content is concerned, it is the same as every other epistemological mythology. We know of primitive peoples of the so-called preanimistic stage who identify themselves with sacred animals and plants and name themselves after them; we know of insane people who likewise identify themselves in part with objects of their perception . . . The commonly shared notion of sensuous (and intellectual) knowledge in our epoch, as well as in the Kantian and pre-Kantian epochs, is very much a mythology like those mentioned.[29]

Benjamin is doing two main things here: first, he is rejecting the notion of cognition based upon the sensuous experiences of the subject, and second, he is leading up to his assertion that there are alternative modes of experience that need to be encompassed or embraced by the coming philosophy.[30] These alternative modes are called 'genuine experience' and are founded upon pure, 'epistemological (transcendental) consciousness'.[31] In other words, Benjamin is expanding the concept of experience to include religious, mystical experience that some would simply categorize as 'insane'. Connecting Benjamin's 1916 essay on language with 'On the Program of the Coming Philosophy', Rochlitz notes that Benjamin is writing from 'a German tradition that was itself nourished on mystical and Kabbalistic texts (Jakob Böhme, Hamann, Friedrich Schlegel, Novalis, Humboldt)'.[32] Further, 'It is to that tradition – against the neo-Kantian context within which his studies in philosophy were taking place in Berlin and Freiburg – that he refers to valorize the elements of language and knowledge that could not be reduced to scientific rationality and to the concept of experience that is their correlative.'[33]

Messianic new thinking

There are other modes of *Kulturpessimismus* that intersect with Benjamin's work, other notions of the rejection of progress, and of logical causality. Anson Rabinbach elucidates the realm of Messianic thought which was central for an entire generation of Jewish thinkers at the beginning of the twentieth century: 'Messianism demands a complete repudiation of the world as it is, placing its hope in a future whose realization can only be brought about by the destruction of the old order.'[34] These Messianic thinkers are involved in exploring secular *and* theological concepts that produce a new type of discourse, such as Franz Rosenzweig's *Star of Redemption* (1921).[35] Rabinbach theorizes various axes of Messianic thought, for example: 'Benjamin and Bloch as "theological Messianists"; Landauer/Buber/Scholem as "radical Zionist Messianists," Rosenzweig and Lukács along a critical Hegelian axis; perhaps with Kafka, Brod and the Prague Bar Kochba circle as the antithesis of that constellation.'[36] The four main 'dimensions' of Messianism are sketched out:

> First, there is a restorative aspect which opposes the idea of *restitutio* to reform or any kind of gradual change.
> [. . .]
> Secondly, there is a redemptive *utopian* aspect which conceives of utopia in terms of a new unity and transparency that is absent in all previous ages as its central ideal.

[. . .]

Thirdly, there is a strong *apocalyptic* element which opposes
salvation to historical immanence (evolution, progress, reform,
even some forms of revolution) and conceives of the coming of the
Messianic age as an event which occurs publicly, either historically
or supra-historically.

[. . .]

Fourthly . . . [there is] a profound *ethical ambivalence* in the
Messianic ideal.[37]

The Benjamin–Scholem relationship, which cuts across the axes, is
perhaps the most well-known and long-explored: the correspondence between these two men is rich and deep, marked especially
by the productive tensions of two thinkers whose belief systems
overlapped, but were never entirely shared. Thus, for example,
Steinberg argues that for Scholem 'Zionism was a political answer to
a political predicament', whereas for Benjamin 'this rationalization
of the political begged the question of what in Heideggerian language
is Being.'[38] The well-documented exchange of ideas between
Benjamin and Scholem can be supplemented by the development
of Benjamin's ideas in Scholem's work at a much later date, for
example in texts such as 'The Name of God and the Linguistic Theory
of the Kabbalah' (1973).[39] Franz Rosenzweig (1886–1929) and
Martin Buber (1876–1965) are also crucial to an understanding
not just of Benjamin's individual place in twentieth-century (non-
Christian) Messianic thought, but to the cultural and intellectual
contexts from which he emerged as a thinker. As Britt notes: 'Like
many other Jewish intellectuals in pre-Nazi Germany, Buber and
Rosenzweig worked within the broad context of German intellectual
culture. Like Benjamin, they brought their general philosophical and
philological training to bear on the emerging rebirth of Jewish intellectual culture in Germany.'[40] Buber was the more outwardly polit-
ically engaged of the two, especially in relation to Zionism. At the
Third Zionist Congress of 1899, Buber argued for the importance of
'agitation and propaganda', transmitting cultural values through
education and a re-focus of the movement's journal, *Die Welt*.[41]
Buber, and others, worked towards a notion of Zionism as being a
total world view.[42] A key component in this latter notion or project,
although occurring some time later, was Buber's journal *Der Jude*,
first published in 1916, rapidly to be considered intensely influential within, and expressive of, the new German-Jewish culture. Paul

Mendes-Flohr argues that *Der Jude* not only 'became one of the finest literary and cultural reviews of its day' but also 'marked a new chapter in German-Jewish self-understanding and . . . self-representation'.[43] Buber's position concerning Zionism had been transformed in time into a more comprehensive notion of lived experience, and this found expression in *Der Jude*: 'Buber no longer aimed to gather and present Jewish culture, but rather to sketch the outlines and map the future course of the living Jewish nation as it progressed inexorably to its true spiritual destiny.'[44] A key force in reaching this destiny was that of *Gemeinschaft*, or Jewish belonging/community, which was not just an external affiliation, but an act and process of genuine responsibility, including a 'responsibility for the fate of the community'.[45] Another important project that Buber engaged in was a translation, with Rosenzweig, of the Hebrew Bible into German:

> In Buber's view, the challenge to modern man is to reunite reality with spirit, and the best response to this challenge is a return to the Hebrew Bible as a means of returning religion to reality. The 'man of today' may undertake a program of reading the Jewish Bible 'as though it were something entirely unfamiliar.' The task is a difficult one requiring personal strength of will: 'This terrifying world is the world of God. It lays claim upon you. Prove yourself in it as a man of God!' In this way, Buber claims, the man of today can recover a true understanding of history, beginnings, and personal meaning through the biblical categories of creation, revelation, and redemption.
>
> The Hebrew Bible is thus a restorative for the man of today, reconciling the modern split between spirit (i.e., religion) and reality, with the result that the man of today who encounters the Bible can achieve a meaningful understanding of self and history to replace the spurious idealisms and spurious realisms prevalent in contemporary culture.[46]

As Britt argues, however, 'The details of what accounts for the modern situation remain sketchy, as well as the mechanism whereby the Bible acts on the man of today.'[47] Buber's partner on this translation project, Franz Rosenzweig, is known primarily for his major work, *The Star of Redemption*; this had been preceded by a two-volume study of Hegel, called *Hegel und der Staat* (1920), which had started life as his dissertation in 1912.[48] The main thrust of Rosenzweig's post-Hegel work was a proposed return within German-Jewish thought to the concept of revelation and the concomitant notions of creation and redemption: 'categories that modern religious thought in German had tended to ignore or treat "poetically," that is, as metaphors bereft of genuine theological content'.[49] Ascribing a shift in German-Jewish thought to the inspiration and work of Hermann Cohen (1842–1918), Rosenzweig argued for 'Offenbarungsglaube', or belief attained through revelation:

> Genuine religious belief, he maintained, affirms the reality of revelation – both the factual reality of the historical revelation at Sinai and the possibility of its renewal as an existential event in which God turns to individuals in the here and now and addresses each by his or her 'first and last name' – that is, acknowledges the individual in his or her contingent being – thereby freeing them from the curse of finitude.[50]

Rosenzweig's own 'Offenbarungsglaube' found its most profound expression in *The Star of Redemption*, a complex and deep work. Glatzer argues that the book is a work (and affirmation) of 'new thinking' that 'posits the validity of the concrete, individual human being over that of "humanity" in general; thinking that takes time seriously; fuses philosophy and theology; assigns both Judaism and Christianity distinct but equally important roles in the spiritual structure of the world; and sees in both biblical religions approaches toward a comprehension of reality.'[51] The architectonics of Rosenzweig's book can be thought of as the six points of the Star of David, where the points are God, World, Man and Creation, Revelation, Redemption.[52] The book has a fractal-like synecdochic quality of parts repeating the whole.[53] Rosenzweig opens with an attack upon German Idealism, and indeed the relations with Idealism throughout his book are complex, in part because of the 'infinitesimal' difference between Romanticism and Idealism in the book.[54] Rosenzweig argues that in German Idealism (with Hegel as the main exemplar) 'Philosophy plugs up its ears before the cry of terrorized humanity.'[55] If the cry was heard then, as Rosenzweig suggests, philosophy would have to recognize the *individual*'s relationship with death, which is one of fear. Instead of this singular subject or individual, philosophy posits universal thinking, or the All: 'For idealism, with its denial of everything that distinguishes the singular from the All, is the tool of the philosopher's trade.'[56] Idealism negates the meaning of death, not just in general, but the meaning as experienced by every individual (see the section 'Death's detour' in Chapter 5, 'Goethe and the *Georgekreis*'). Rosenzweig, in a powerful and prophetic phrase, argues that the reality of death 'will not be banished from the world' and that the cry of its victims is 'inextinguishable'.[57] Hegel comes in for direct attack, and the self-reflexive, all-encompassing nature of his dialectic:

> Centuries of philosophical labors were devoted to this disputation between knowledge and belief; they reach their goal at the precise moment when the knowledge of the All reaches a conclusion in itself. For one will have to designate it as a conclusion when this knowledge encompasses completely no longer only its object, the All, but also itself, completely at least according to its own requirements and in its own peculiar manner. This happened when Hegel included the history of philosophy in the system. It seems that reason can go no further than to place itself visibly as the innermost fact known to itself, now as part of the system's structure, and of course as the concluding part. And at the precise moment when philosophy exhausts its furthest formal possibilities and reaches the boundary set by its own nature, the great question of the relationship of knowledge and belief which is pressed upon it by the course of world history seems now, as already noted, to be solved.[58]

Hegel's voracious dialectic sublates all positions of ('false') consciousness, as it moves progressively forward to the point of absolute knowledge or philosophy, which is incorporated or embedded in the system from the start. The embedded and engendering nature of absolute knowledge or philosophy means that all the arguments between Enlightenment thinkers and the theologians are over; like death, belief in the form of religion is in itself sublated and turned into just one more transitional position or phase of thought. As Glatzer argues: 'The existentialist in Rosenzweig posits the priority of being before thought, contesting the Idealist assumption that all of existence, being based upon thought, can be grasped by thought.'[59] Another way of putting this notion of all aspects of a subject's ownmost experience as being 'grasped' by thought is to suggest that religion is an imperfect or more 'rudimentary' form of the Hegelian notion of self-revelation that 'will come in speculative philosophy'.[60] In other words, questions of belief either are part of what Hyppolite calls the 'positive dialectic' of religion,[61] or are resolved by speculative philosophy. For Rosenzweig, this resolution is also a closure and a manifestation of profound deafness or indifference to the finite subject.

Heidegger's later encounter with *The Phenomenology of Spirit* is precisely one of this issue of, and concern with, finitude, and the apparent overcoming in the name of 'in-finitude'.[62] Placing the 'finite' subject in relation to Benjamin's Messianism can be approached in myriad ways, but one key text, the 'Theological-Political Fragment', serves here as an orientation with regard to the German-Jewish 'new thinking'. The debates concerning the dating of this fragment are also of interest, with Scholem placing it in the early 1920s, Theodor Adorno placing it in the range 1937 to 1938, and the editors of the third volume of Benjamin's *Selected Writings* concurring with Adorno and also connecting the text with 'On the Concept of History' (1940).[63] In the light of all of these (and other) competing authoritative critical claims, a case could be made for the fragment as bridging *all* the 'phases' of Benjamin's work, in other words, the bridge revealing the persistence of the absolute as a substrate to his thought. Jacobson regards as a key question here 'whether redemption is initiated prior to or only after the arrival of the Messiah', and, he argues, this question remains unresolved in Benjamin's thought, even given the opening statement of the fragment, that 'Only the Messiah himself completes all history . . .'.[64] Jacobson thus places the fragment firmly 'in the context of Jewish tradition':

> the idea of redemption ending historical time, since predicated by history itself, can be understood within the broader notion of historical completion. The end of historical time, however, is not to be confused with the end of history. History's completion is here expressed not as 'a goal but an end.' While time generates various irreconcilable moments in history, redemption is its only complete and thus true end, rather than a goal set for it as a telos in history. Seen from a negative perspective, neither an earthly kingdom of God, nor the worker's state, nor [sic] bourgeois democracy can be pronounced as the end of a historical telos for Benjamin. Only an understanding approaching history as events that face their end, unmitigated by any external worldly preconditions, reflects a messianic conception, in his view.[65]

The chiasmus operative in the 'Theological-Political Fragment' is between secular and Messianic 'intensity': 'If one arrow points to the goal toward which the secular dynamic acts, and another marks the direction of messianic intensity, then certainly the quest of free humanity for happiness runs counter to the messianic direction. But just as a force, by virtue of the path it is moving along, can augment another force on the opposite path, so the secular order – because of its nature as secular – promotes the coming of the Messianic Kingdom.'[66] The play of secular and Messianic forces is read as a polarity, creating a charge in both realms. As Pieper puts it, 'It is, therefore, this realm of the untemporal-eternal upon which human history, that happens through time, continually and immediately borders.'[67]

Notes

1 Graeme Gilloch, *Walter Benjamin: Critical Constellations*, Cambridge: Polity, 2002, pp. 7–8.
2 S. D. Stirk, *The Prussian Spirit: A Survey of German Literature and Politics, 1914–1940*, London: Faber and Faber, 1951, p. 60.
3 Karl Popper, *The Open Society and its Enemies*, vol. i: *The Spell of Plato*, London: Routledge, 1999, p. 55.
4 Ibid.
5 Oswald Spengler, *The Decline of the West* (complete in 1 vol.), trans. Charles Francis Atkinson, London: George Allen and Unwin, 1926, vol. i: *Form and Actuality*, p. 6.
6 Ibid., p. 7.
7 Ibid.
8 Ibid., p. 25.
9 Ibid., p. 31.
10 Ibid., p. 16.
11 Ibid., p. 32.
12 Ibid., pp. 33–34.
13 Ernst Bloch, *The Principle of Hope*, vol. iii, trans. Neville Plaice, Stephen Plaice and Paul Knight, Cambridge, Massachusetts: The MIT Press, 1995, p. 1360.
14 Spengler, *The Decline of the West*, vol. i, p. 39.
15 Stirk, *The Prussian Spirit: A Survey German Literature and Politics, 1914–1940*, p. 60.
16 Ibid., p. 63.
17 Ibid., p. 65.
18 Ibid., pp. 70–71, from *Preussentum und Sozialismus* (München, 1920; reprinted München: C. H. Becksche Verlagsbuchhandlung, 1925).
19 Robert-Hermann Tenbrock, *A History of Germany*, trans. Paul J. Dine, München: Max Hueber Verlag, 1968, p. 268; see, also, the discussion of 'socialism' in Burleigh, *The Third Reich: A New History*, p. 103.
20 Spengler, *The Decline of the West*, vol. i, p. 119.
21 Immanuel Kant, *Critique of Pure Reason*, trans. J. M. D. Meiklejohn, London: J. M. Dent, 1934, p. 149.
22 Spengler, *The Decline of the West*, vol. i, pp. 117–118.
23 Ibid., p. 118.

24 Ibid.

25 Ibid., p. 120.

26 Walter Benjamin, 'On the Program of the Coming Philosophy', *Selected Writings*, vol. i *1913–1926*, London, England, and Cambridge, Massachusetts: Belknap Press of Harvard University Press, 1996, p. 101.

27 Ibid., p. 103.

28 Ibid., p. 102; in the original: 'Die Entwicklung der Philosophie ist dadurch zu erwarten daße jede Annihilierung dieser metaphysischen Elemente in der Erkenntnistheorie zugleich diese auf eine tiefere metaphysisch erfüllte Erfahrung verweist.' 'Über das Programm der kommenden Philosophie', Walter Benjamin, *Gesammelte Schriften*, vol. ii:1, ed. Rolf Tiedemann, Frankfurt am Main: Suhrkamp Verlag 1982, pp. 160–161.

29 Benjamin, 'On the Program of the Coming Philosophy', *Selected Writings*, vol. i: *1913–1926*, p. 103.

30 Max Pensky, *Melancholy Dialectics: Walter Benjamin and the Play of Mourning*, Amherst: University of Massachusetts Press, 2001, p. 65.

31 Benjamin, 'On the Program of the Coming Philosophy', *Selected Writings*, vol. i: *1913–1926*, p. 104.

32 Rochlitz, *The Disenchantment of Art: The Philosophy of Walter Benjamin*, pp. 20–21.

33 Ibid., p. 21.

34 Anson Rabinbach, 'Between Enlightenment and Apocalypse: Benjamin, Bloch and Modern German Jewish Messianism', *New German Critique*, 34 (winter 1985), 78–124, at 81.

35 Ibid., p. 83.

36 Ibid., p. 84.

37 Ibid., p. 84; p. 85; p. 86; p. 87.

38 Michael P. Steinberg, 'Walter Benjamin Writes the Essays "Critique of Violence" and "The Task of the Translator", Treating the Subject of Messianism he Discussed with Gershom Scholem during the War,' in Sander L. Gilman and Jack Zipes, eds., *Yale Companion to Jewish Writing and Thought in German Culture, 1096–1996*, New Haven and London: Harvard University Press, 1997, pp. 401–411, at p. 402. See, also, Gershom Scholem, *On Jews and Judaism in Crisis: Selected Essays*, ed., Werner J. Dannhauser, New York: Schocken, 1976; Gershom Scholem, *Walter Benjamin: The Story of a Friendship*, trans. Harry Zohn, Philadelphia: Jewish Publication Society of America, 1981; Susan Handelman, *Fragments of Redemption: Jewish Thought and Literary Theory in Benjamin, Scholem, and Levinas*, Bloomington: Indiana University Press, 1991.

39 Jacobson, *Metaphysics of the Profane: The Political Theology of Walter Benjamin and Gershom Scholem*, p. 6.

40 Brian Britt, *Walter Benjamin and the Bible*, New York: Continuum, 1996, p. 74.

41 Michael Berkowitz, *Zionist Culture and West European Jewry before the First World War*, Chapel Hill and London: The University of North Carolina Press, 1996, p. 83.

42 Ibid., p. 84.

43 Mendes-Flohr, *German Jews: A Dual Identity*, p. 22.

44 Mark H. Gelber, 'The First Issue of Martin Buber's German-Jewish Journal *Der Jude* Appears', in Gilman and Zipes, eds., *Yale Companion to Jewish Writing and Thought in German Culture, 1096–1996*, pp. 343–347, at p. 345.

45 Ibid., p. 345.

46 Britt, *Walter Benjamin and the Bible*, p. 77.

47 Ibid.

48 While working on *Hegel und der Staat*, Rosenzweig had discovered a manuscript page in Hegel's hand which he deduced was actually a copy of a work by Schelling which Rosenzweig called 'The Oldest System-Program of German Idealism'. See pp. 20–25 of Ernest Rubinstein's *An Episode of Jewish Romanticism: Franz Rosenzweig's The Star of Redemption*, Albany: State University of New York Press, 1999. For a translation of 'The Oldest System-Program of German Idealism' see Andrew Bowie, *Aesthetics and Subjectivity: From Kant to Nietzsche*, Manchester: Manchester University Press, 1990, appendix.

49 Paul Mendes-Flohr, 'Franz Rosenzweig Writes the Essay "Atheistic Theology", which Critiques the Theology of his Day', in Gilman and Zipes, eds., *Yale Companion to Jewish Writing and Thought in German Culture, 1096–1996*, pp. 322–326, at p. 324.

50 Ibid., p. 323.

51 N. N. Glatzer, 'Foreword' to Franz Rosenzweig, *The Star of Redemption*, trans. William W. Hallo, London and Notre Dame: University of Notre Dame Press, 1985, pp. xiii–xiv.

52 Ibid., p. xvi.

53 See, also, Rubinstein's *An Episode of Jewish Romanticism: Franz Rosenzweig's The Star of Redemption*, p. 26.

54 Ibid., p. 12.

55 Rosenzweig, *The Star of Redemption*, p. 5.

56 Ibid., p. 4.

57 Ibid., p. 5.

58 Ibid., p. 6.

59 Glatzer, 'Foreword' to Rosenzweig, *The Star of Redemption*, p. xiv.

60 Charles Taylor, *Hegel*, Cambridge: Cambridge University Press, 1989, p. 197.

61 Jean Hyppolite, *Genesis and Structure of Hegel's Phenomenology of Spirit*, trans. Samuel Cherniak and John Heckman, Evanston: Northwestern University Press, 1974, p. 537.

62 Martin Heidegger, *Hegel's Phenomenology of Spirit*, trans. Parvis Emad and Kenneth Maly, Bloomington and Indianapolis: Indiana University Press, 1988, p. 39.

63 Jacobson, *Metaphysics of the Profane: The Political Theology of Walter Benjamin and Gershom Scholem*, pp. 22–23 and footnote 5, p. 237; Benjamin, 'Theological-Political Fragment', *Selected Writings*, vol. iii: *1935–1938*, trans. Edmund Jephcott, Howard Eiland and others, ed. Howard Eiland and Michael W. Jennings, Cambridge, Massachusetts, and London, England: Belknap Press of Harvard University Press, 2002, pp. 305–306, at p. 306, footnote 1.

64 Jacobson, *Metaphysics of the Profane: The Political Theology of Walter Benjamin and Gershom Scholem*, p. 25; Benjamin, 'Theological-Political Fragment', *Selected Writings*, vol. iii: *1935–1938*, p. 305.

65 Jacobson, *Metaphysics of the Profane: The Political Theology of Walter Benjamin and Gershom Scholem*, p. 26.

66 Benjamin, 'Theological-Political Fragment', *Selected Writings*, vol. iii: *1935–1938*, p. 305.

67 Pieper, *The End of Time: A Meditation on the Philosophy of History*, p. 69.

3

Metaphysics of youth: Wyneken and 'Rausch'

Wyneken

In October 1913, the radical educator Gustav Wyneken (1875–1964) addressed a major gathering of the youth movement, or *Wandervogel*, at Hohe Meissner mountain. In his wide-ranging speech he argued that 'world history had only just begun' and that 'the younger generation had to help in changing the world permanently.'[1] It was in 1913 that Walter Benjamin also wrote his short essay about youth, called 'Experience', published in *Der Anfang* (*The Beginning*) in 1913–14. Both events – the speech and the essay – appear in retrospect relatively unremarkable; what is essential here is to understand that the very concept of 'youth' was in itself a powerful new phenomenon within German society, and that this phenomenon intersected with notions of destiny and catastrophe. The destiny of the young in Germany prior to the formation of the *Wandervogel* was one of natural progression to adulthood: youth was a mere passing phase, an inferior secondary position to that of adult maturity.[2] As Peter Stachura notes, youth were considered to be 'an integrated junior section of a society dominated and controlled by adults through the major institutions of parental house, school, and church. Denied scope for self expression and self-realisation in natural ways, the younger generation were expected to behave and conduct their lives in miniature versions of their elders'.[3] Benjamin argued that the desire among the young for self-responsibility was always being negated by the notion of experience; in other words, adults always claim to have a superior knowledge based upon not just their experiences, but their realization that youthful *inexperienced* idealism is naïve. Once the young have experienced things, they will realize not only the errors of their ways, but also the ridiculousness of their

ideas and ideals: 'It was all illusion'.[4] Benjamin regards this attitude
as an *a priori* devaluation of youthful life, although in his view this
is in some ways preferable to those pedagogues who do not believe
in youth at all. As Benjamin summarizes: 'our youth is but a brief
night (fill it with rapture!); it will be followed by grand "experience,"
the years of compromise, impoverishment of ideas, and lack of
energy. Such is life. That is what adults tell us, and that is what they
experienced'.[5] The critique of this notion of experience is both
straightforward and powerful: the adult does not realize that there
can be different experiences from that of the puncturing of idealis-
tic beliefs and desires, which in the process reveal a grey common-
place world. Such an adult is 'desolate and without spirit . . . he has
no inner relationship to anything other than the common and the
always-already-out-of-date'.[6] Benjamin argues that this means that
such an adult lives a life 'without meaning or solace'.[7] Youth,
however, 'know something different':

> which experience can neither give to us nor take away: that truth
> exists, even if all previous thought has been an error: Or: that
> fidelity shall be maintained, even if no one has done so yet. Such
> will cannot be taken from us by experience. [. . .]
>   [. . .] Each of our experiences has its content. We ourselves
> invest them with content by means of our own spirit – he who is
> thoughtless is satisfied with error. 'You will never find the truth!'
> he exclaims to the researcher. 'That is my experience.' For the
> researcher, however, error is only an aid to truth (Spinoza). Only
> to the mindless [*Geistlosen*] is experience devoid of meaning and
> spirit. To the one who strives, experience may be painful, but it will
> scarcely lead him to despair.[8]

Youth has access to two types of experience: the disillusioning adult
type and the non-commonplace youthful type; even when the
former occurs, youth has the will to power to overcome disillusion-
ment. The non-commonplace experiences, those not recognized by
philistines, have individual content invested with personal 'spirit' –
they relate to, or express, immediate knowing of the spiritual. In
some ways, this is an early example of Benjamin's desire to expand
the boundaries of experience that he will later bring into play vis-à-
vis Kant, but here the real target is the philistine who 'rejoices in
every new meaninglessness'.[9] For the philistine, spirit simply does
not exist; Benjamin argues that even when adults have spiritual
experiences, they become stripped of value through a negating

attitude. Adult experience overall is in fact considered to be the complete opposite: one of 'spiritlessness'; youthful experience is full of spirit and it is an encounter with spirit: it is beautiful, untouchable and immediate.[10] Benjamin is not only expanding the boundaries of experience *per se*, but he is also wresting the destiny of youth from the world of the philistine: youth's destiny is no longer to be its negation of spirit; youth's destiny is to realize the value of youth in itself and then project those values into an alternative adult future. The destiny of youth lies *outside* the philistine's world. When reading Benjamin's 'Experience' from the beginning of the twenty-first century and the perspective of a thoroughly commodified youth culture (although the frenzied fragmentation of this market is an unwanted implosion from a capitalist perspective), it may be difficult to comprehend the immediacy of youthful spirit, *as spirit*; in part, Benjamin's theorization of youth is dependent on his own interpretation of, and positioning within, the youth movement, and the latter gives a clue to the conceptual and lived nature of youth as a project for Benjamin.[11]

If there was any 'mediating' adult of major importance in Benjamin's life in 1913, it was Gustav Wyneken; writing to his friend Carla Seligson in June of that year, Benjamin describes his new experiences of a professional philosophy group: 'although I do indeed philosophize a lot, I do so in a totally different manner: my thinking always has Wyneken, my first teacher, as its starting point and always returns to him. Even when it comes to abstract questions, I intuitively see the answer prefigured in him'.[12] Benjamin came into contact with Wyneken after being sent to Haubinda boarding school in Thüringen in 1905. Haubinda was one of the earliest 'progressive' schools in Germany, founded by Hermann Lietz and directed from 1904 by Paulus Geheeb and Wyneken.[13] As an educator and thinker, Wyneken championed a new concept of youth culture (*Jugendkultur*) and opposed the over-organized, hierarchical and stuffy state school system, which he believed negated creativity.[14] After breaking with Lietz in 1906, Geheeb and Wyneken founded the Free School Association of Wickersdorf: 'Free communication and exchange of ideas characterised the Wickersdorf system. Education was all about leadership, not ritualistic inculcation of knowledge'.[15] Wyneken also championed the principle of the 'charismatic teacher-leader' forming an erotic bond between himself and the pupils.[16] As Laqueur argues:

[Wyneken] . . . had much affinity with the *Wandervogel* – with its opposition to the mode of life in the big cities, to the progressive mechanization of life, and to the arid intellectualism that made for a degeneration of body and soul. He thought his own school superior to the *Wandervogel*, however, for as he said, the youth movement had a style but as yet no culture of its own. It merely 'organized' the leisure hours of boys and girls, whereas the Free School Association was comprehensive, embracing school life also, combining it with agricultural work, a modified school syllabus, physical education, and life in community, in an attempt to train a new type of man and woman.[17]

Benjamin's stay at Haubinda initiated for him an intense interest in educational reform, expressed through early publications brought into the public domain under the pseudonym 'Ardor', in *Der Anfang*, a journal first published in 1908. Writing under another pseudonym, 'Eckart, Phil.', Benjamin also published an essay called 'Educational Reform: A Cultural Movement' in the widely distributed collection *Student und Schulreform* (1912).[18] Benjamin had gravitated towards the radical wing of the youth movement, joining the 'group for school reform' at Albert Ludwig University in Freiburg im Breisgau, where he had enrolled in April 1912.[19] It was in Freiburg that he listened alongside Martin Heidegger to lectures by the neo-Kantian philosopher Heinrich Rickert. Heidegger would later go on to present his thesis on John Duns Scotus (1266–1308) to Rickert (although he in turn simply passed it on for reading to Engelbert Krebs).[20] Benjamin spent most of his time in Freiburg working on educational reform, rather than on his official studies; his energies were directed by the Free Student Movement, which 'stood for a conception of learning oriented toward Humboldt's ideal of freedom and self-determination . . . Within this loosely organized movement Wyneken's supporters represented the most radical wing. They turned their backs on the debates about the university's political organization, which they deemed futile, and expressed their absolute opposition to Wilhelminian society in the demand for "serving pure spirit" '.[21]

The first stay in Freiburg was short-lived: Benjamin returned to Berlin in the summer of 1912 and enrolled at the Royal Friedrich Wilhelm University, where he attended lectures by Georg Simmel; the return to the city also brought him back into closer contact with Wyneken and his supporters. Brodersen gives a good impression of the intensity of this period for Benjamin:

Benjamin was one of the founder-members of the 'Detachment for
School Reform'. . . . In addition he was elected (in 1912/13) on to the
committee of the Free Students Union. Outside the university he
worked for the Berlin group of the 'League for Free School Communities', taking his turn at chairing meetings and occasionally
giving talks to members and guests. Finally, [he had] . . . frequent
meetings with Wyneken which were by no means restricted to planning and revising various lecture and discussion evenings . . . For
Wyneken also read to his star pupil, in private, from his own works,
which clearly demonstrates the depth of their mutual trust at the
time.[22]

Benjamin was back in Freiburg in 1913 for his second semester at
the institution; he was attending sessions by Rickert again, and
reading a wide range of texts, including works by Bergson, Husserl,
Kant, Kierkegaard, Rilke, Schiller and Spitteler among others.
During 1913–14, he was writing 'The Metaphysics of Youth', an
essay – unpublished during his lifetime – that offers reflections on a
key writing format for young people: the diary.

   After some excruciatingly poor sections on women, prostitution
and so forth, Benjamin turns in 'The Metaphysics of Youth' to the
'unnameable despair that flows in every soul' and the awakening to
that despair in 'the first day of the diary'.[23] The diary poses a central
question: 'In what time does man live?'[24] Benjamin explores in
response to this question a variety of answers: that man occupies a
'timeless realm' in the sense of being a finite being merely awaiting
death; that he is surrounded by 'empty time', not the full time of
immortality; that any access he once had, in youth, to immortal time
is lost, as time slips away from him.[25] The influence of Kierkegaard
is clear, with the notion that subjectivity is measured via the individual's attitude held towards death: 'Lurking even more menacingly
behind the everyday reality was death. [. . .] From day to day, second
to second, the self preserves itself, clinging to that instrument: time,
the instrument that it was supposed to play.'[26] Time is instrumental
(artificially measuring, *apparently* progressing) and, opposed to this,
an opportunity or potentiality (an instrument to play). Benjamin
next describes a mystical experience borne of the despair of finitude:
childhood is recalled and returned to via the loss of adult comprehension and the passing into oblivion: this, again, is part of the
awakening, the first day of the diary, but now it is described as a
redemption and 'the unfathomable document of a life never lived,

the book of a life in whose time everything that we experienced inadequately . . . transformed into experience perfected'.[27] The diary writer becomes a split subject: one who is annihilated by instrumental time, and one who 'stands on the brink of an immortality'[28] into which this transcendental self plunges. The diary is written by the split-subject, although it is at the point of despair, the recognition of annihilation, that the diary comes into being. But what is the experience of the time of the diary? Surely the diary is written in instrumental, incremental time? Benjamin argues that the diary is not written in time; it *is* in a sense immortal time: in other words it can be conceived as an *immediate* experiencing of time, not a chain of experiences. The diary is an overcoming of developmental objective time, and it encompasses and juxtaposes an entire world in each interval (the interval is an early montage assemblage and effect, one not of profane, but sacred, illumination).

In section 2 of 'The Diary' the metaphysics of youth proceeds from time to space. Youth is theorized as a boundary situation, to read Benjamin here through the later work of Jaspers: 'When I imagine a situation, I see it as the relative location of things, as their topographical arrangement in space'.[29] The self dispersed in the immortal time of the diary can be resurrected in the landscape, a description combining the dreams of Romanticism and the *Wandervogel*:

> As landscape all events surround us, for we, the time of things, know no time. Nothing but the leaning of the trees, the horizon, the silhouetted mountain ridges, which suddenly awake full of meaning because they have placed us in their midst. The landscape transports us into their midst, the trembling treetops assail us with questions, the valleys envelop us with mist, incomprehensible houses oppress us with their shapes. We, their midpoint, impinge on them. [. . .] As we advance, the same surroundings sanctify us. Knowing no answers but forming the center, we define things with the movement of our bodies.[30]

The temporality of the dream is confused and confusing: time and space are brought into conjunction, but this is still via the dream of the split-subject, the arrogant youth and the beginner, setting out on a pathway. The landscape is portrayed as 'arbitrary' and as having meaning generated through the subject's wanderings. The wandering youth is the future of the landscape: he or she will give it a form, and a meaning. Alongside this formation there is the collapsing of time and space into an immediacy; Benjamin attempts to sketch multi-temporal space. Thus, the beloved who suddenly appears is a girl and a woman, entering the pages of the diary as *an entire life lived in a moment*. Imagining youth as a boundary situation is to explore the transition from youth to adulthood not as a progression but as a radical break, one which generates the split-subject captured by instrumental time (and desperately losing that time) and transcending instrumental time, through dreams, imagination, love and death. The adult who fails to comprehend the meaning of youth does not even recognize the boundary situation in the first place: 'For consciousness at large a boundary situation is no situation any more, because a knowing, purposively acting consciousness will either take it to be purely objective or else avoid it, ignore it, and forget about it. This type of consciousness remains within the boundaries and cannot even inquire whence they come'.[31] The boundary situation, for Jaspers, is 'something immanent which already points to transcendence'.[32] In 'The Metaphysics of Youth' it is the question of being, surveyed through the temporality of the diary, that leads to an exploration of subjectivity and death: 'Again and again the diary conjures up the death of its writer, if only in the sleep of the reader'.[33]

Death is approached from multiple perspectives by Benjamin in his essay: it is one of the key existentialist boundary situations, of immense importance for Kierkegaard, and later for Heidegger in *Being and Time*.[34] The diary prophesizes death, writes from the perspective of death, mimics through sleep the death of the subject: 'In death we befall ourselves; our deadness releases itself from things. And the time of death is our own.'[35] The central point of the diary is redemption through death: the diary foreshadows death, and it *is* death. Benjamin is attempting to ascertain to what extent meaning resides in the finite individual's life: is meaning something that is potentially accessible, especially to the openness of youth, or is meaning purely to be found at the moment of death and resurrection (through either death or the diary time)? What remains in Benjamin's analysis, at the point of the collapse of time and space, the switch from finitude to immortality, is the self: 'In death we befall ourselves'; this remainder can be observed later in Rosenzweig's work: 'The self is what persists in the face of nothing. Its persistence climaxes at the moment of death, when it no longer even instances its former worldly kind. Here it is pure self-enclosure, the distinctive beyond the grasp of the universal.'[36] The sacred illumination that can be recovered (where recovery means reclaiming past and future time) in the assemblage of the diary form is a fact in and for the subject.[37]

Youth's legacy

The outbreak of the First World War created a permanent rift between Benjamin and Wyneken, owing to Wyneken's turn towards a more nationalistic stance, although Benjamin did not see this rift as an end to his involvement in the youth movement: he took upon himself, indeed, in his own words, wrested, the legacy of youth's *idea* from Wyneken. Benjamin accordingly regarded his break as proof of his 'loyalty'.[38] In a letter of 1915, Benjamin asserts that Wyneken had been one of his main teachers, who had 'pointed the way to a spiritual existence'.[39] Benjamin frames his account by writing that he had wanted to exchange ideas with Wyneken at a meeting in Breslau, where the two main competing student pedagogic groups had failed to come to a consensus shortly before the historic Hohe Meissner meeting which occurred a few days later;[40] unable to even get near to Wyneken at this meeting, Benjamin says that he will share these ideas in his letter instead:

> We who are gathered together here believe that future generations will come to speak your name. Life has no room for this awareness. Yet it should make room for it for a minute's time. We call you the bearer of an idea, and that is how we expressed it to the outside world; it is true. But as the chosen ones, we experienced something altogether different in this era. We experienced that even the spirit, entirely on its own and unconditionally, constrains the living; that the person transcends the personal; we were given to learn what leadership is. We have experienced that there is pure spirituality among people. Something has become true for us that is endlessly more remote for almost everybody else.[41]

The lessons of leadership had been understood: Benjamin had become the new bearer of the idea of youth just as Wyneken was calling for more practical application. But how was the 'pure spirituality among people' to be handled beyond this point? For Benjamin, the idea of youth was problematically, via Wyneken's new stance, sacrificed to the state.[42] Given Wyneken's Hegelianism, perhaps this stance was inevitable. In the First World War, youth would be sacrificed for a 'higher' abstract idea (the state); at the same time, the destruction of youth would 'be' the actual application of (or towards) the attainment of the abstract idea, in other words, a stage of merely imperfect consciousness. This Hegelian notion of progress, regarded from the perspective of the 'new thinking', is predicated upon blindness: the failure to see that each stage of imperfect consciousness is for the individual concerned potentially catastrophic. As Bloch would argue after his experiences of the war: 'one can appreciate how much more violently the self-disclosure of the abstract, and its only apparently negative concretization into the concretely and really total, had to fail before cases of higher reality, in other words before the upper, *existential-moral* limit of the abstractly logical'.[43] The experience of the trenches as a whole was a necessary nightmare given a Hegelian perspective or logical framework, simultaneously being something that, as individual experience, becomes of no account in the grand universal scheme of things. Rosenzweig's cry of humanity is not exactly ignored by philosophy, where philosophy is transformed by Hegel into an 'indiscriminate lawyer' or 'headmaster' representing a higher dimension;[44] rather the cry is predicated as a necessary evil to be passed over in silence. Bloch's exploration of the 'darkness of the lived moment' is returned to by Benjamin, and it is this major component of *The Spirit of Utopia* that feeds into his work, including the later gargantuan *Arcades Project*.[45]

Even though Benjamin had divorced himself from the day-to-day organizational tasks of the youth movement, he wrote that he was the self-appointed successor to Wyneken and that he had no intention in his inheritance of sacrificing youth to the state; inextricably tied to the pedagogic issues of the day were spiritual issues, even if the latter were becoming more and more 'remote' for the people. As Benjamin wrote to Buber: 'I do not believe that there is any place where the word would be more distant from the divine than in "real" action'.[46] The political task in relation to writing was, for Benjamin, not one of motivation or instrumentality; language is not a mere device for influencing human behaviour:

> I can understand writing as such as poetic, prophetic, objective in terms of its effect, but in any case only as *magical*, that is as un-*mediated*. Every salutary effect, indeed every effect not inherently devastating, that any writing may have resides in its (the word's, language's) mystery. In however many forms language may prove to be effective, it will not be so through the transmission of content,

but rather through the purest disclosure of its dignity and its nature.
[. . .] My concept of objective and, at the same time, highly political style and writing is this: to awaken interest in what was denied
to the word; only where this sphere of speechlessness reveals itself
in unutterably pure power can the magic spark leap between the
word and the motivating deed, where the unity of these two equally
real entities resides. Only the intensive aiming of words into the
core of intrinsic silence is truly effective.[47]

Considering that this response came after an invitation to publish in
a new journal, *Der Jude*, the emphasis upon 'speechlessness' and 'the
core of intrinsic silence' is a radical rejection of Buber's project.
Pensky argues that Benjamin's and Buber's work in this period has
a shared goal: 'the formulation of a conception of critical thinking
and writing that, by the purity of its ideas and the rigor of its method,
could represent the purity of a transcendent, messianic truth within
the realm of immanent, historical experience, and further, to direct
this critical energy into the heart of contemporary society in a transformational way'.[48] It would appear foolish to give up the opportunity to publish in what would become a highly influential journal,
under the leadership of one of the period's key theorists of Judaism,
Martin Buber. But Benjamin's rejection of Buber's 'instrumentalism'
was not in fact unique; Rosenzweig was adopting an analogous
position (which also mirrors Benjamin's rejection of Wyneken's
new-found nationalism), expressed in his essay 'Atheistic Theology'
(1914). Buber's *Drei Reden Über das Judentum* (*Three Addresses Concerning Judaism*) had been published in 1911; in the lectures Buber
utilizes a nationalistic discourse of 'blood, community, force' to argue
for an inherent Jewish striving for unity.[49] As Franks and Morgan
summarize: 'According to the *Addresses*, the Jewish people, confronted by psychological and social division and fragmentation, seeks
to bring unity to the world. Its blood harbors a drive to make whole
what is riddled with duality.'[50] The most serious and troubling claim
for Rosenzweig, however, is the notion that God becomes in effect
a human projection designed to deal with division, thus: 'Buber's
racial, biological, and psychological account of the Jewish people
claims that God is part of the mythology that derives from that
people.'[51] In more simple words, there is a collapsing of the distinction between the human subject and God.[52] In his 'Atheistic Theology', Rosenzweig sets out to refute this approach, through a critique
of Christian and Judaic theologies that in turn parallel one another's

'atheism'; he does this by showing how the search for the historical Jesus led to a transition from teacher to personality and to a final mirror-image of the centrality of the Enlightenment human subject. As Miles puts it: 'the skeptical attitude of the eighteenth-century Enlightenment toward the miraculous was joined to the method-ological skepticism of 19th century critical history'.[53] Rosenzweig argues that while for Judaism the cult of personality is of no real consequence, the general thrust of German-Judaic theology does have parallels with the analyses of Jesus, beginning in particular with the work of the neo-Kantian Hermann Cohen (1842–1918):

> Those older religiophilosophical attempts of the 19th century had tried to render this difficult concept [of the Chosen People] unob-jectionable; it had arrived at softenings of a sort similar to those carried out on the figure of Christ in classical German philosophy. Just as the latter had been emptied into the notion of an ideal human being, the idea of nation was reinterpreted among us into the ideal community of mankind – and in both cases the hard feature, of the divine having actually entered into history and being distinct from all other actuality, was blurred.[54]

Rosenzweig argues that one of the problems with German Idealist philosophy for 'Jewish-People' theology is that 'world-historical peoples' necessarily pass away precisely as a condition of their prac-tical fulfilment;[55] with the shift away from pure forms of Idealist philosophy, the self-fulfilling prophecy of 'race' comes to the fore: 'people obtain the right to exist simply from their existence, inde-pendently of their factual achievements'.[56] The opposite of this is of course the equally problematic, catastrophic and devastating 'logic' that people should be destroyed simply because of their (racial) exis-tence. But the scene has been set for Buber's analysis whereby the 'people' become the focal point and constitutive 'actuality' for faith; this deification of the Jewish people and their eternal existence is, for Rosenzweig, a myth. Myth and revelation become opposed, and the latter is sublated via the former: 'it is the highest triumph of a theology hostile to revelation to sublate it entirely in favor of its first term, to show revelation to be mythology'.[57] For Rosenzweig this is the last straw: the divine is no longer regarded as manifestation in the human realm, but virtually the other way round: 'Instead of asserting God's becoming human, one asserted His being human; instead of His descent to the mountain of the giving of the law, the autonomy of the moral law; in general, instead of the history of revelation, an existing human essence, within which history unfolded but which itself was not subjected to history'.[58] In short, Rosenzweig opposes this notion with that of an 'unfillable cleft' between the mysticism and rationalism of atheistic theology and the human subject as a 'receiver of revelation' through faith.[59]

There has been much in-depth debate concerning Benjamin's precise relationship with Judaism; Benjamin's early writings on language and youth reveal that he has a notion of the divine as strongly embedded in his work as is the case with Rosenzweig. The rejection of instrumental notions of language and politics in the letter to Buber is indicative of a concern to resist projecting human desires and goals into the realm of the sacred. Rabinbach argues that in Benjamin's work the 'esoteric language of the intellectual Jew is directed against the language of political instrumentalism. The expressive quality of language carries the promise of redemption from power and judgement, "the absolutely unlimited and creative infinity of the divine word." '[60] Messianic thinking is already present in some of Benjamin's very early writings, such as his correspondence with Ludwig Strauss, which represents and chronicles 'his attempt to find his own path to Judaism'.[61] As Rabinbach suggests: 'These letters [the Strauss correspondence] reveal a side to Benjamin's Jewishness that has been obscured and overshadowed by his later meeting and friendship with Gershom Scholem'.[62] As early as 1912, Benjamin had been engaged in lengthy conversations with Kurt Tuchler concerning Zionism; writing to Herbert Belmore, Benjamin notes how in Stolpmünde 'for the first time I have been confronted with Zionism and Zionist activity as a possibility and hence perhaps as a duty'.[63] While Zionism was ultimately rejected by Benjamin, his intellectual engagement with Tuchler is not without significance. Pensky argues that Benjamin's 'sharp disappointment with the political fate of the youth movement clearly sharpened the messianic and mournful tone of his critical writings', and that this is elucidated by the essay 'The Life of Students'.[64]

Benjamin opens 'The Life of Students' with a critique of a secular notion of history, whereby because it has no concept of an 'end' of time, the measurement of the speed of progress becomes all-important. Instead of this secular notion Benjamin offers the idea that 'elements of the ultimate condition' cannot be perceived as progressive; rather, they 'are deeply rooted in every present in the form of the most endangered, excoriated, and ridiculed ideas and products of the creative mind'.[65] These 'products of the creative mind' are attacked by secular society precisely because they not only have the potential to reveal the absolute in every moment, but because they suggest – and cannot be thought of without – a notion of an apocalyptic end-time. Benjamin creates a utopian or idealized model of students and the university as a metaphor and image of a metaphysical state of history where there is total submission to 'a principle' and identification with 'an idea'.[66] Rejecting vocational training, Benjamin argues that 'a community of learning' should not be directed towards the professions: 'scholarship, far from leading inexorably to a profession, may in fact preclude it'.[67] The state needs a constant replenishment of its functionaries, those professionals who maintain the status quo and who are subsequently awarded by the state. The community of learning, according to Benjamin, should not be directed towards this functional straightjacket, although if the modern state is simply conceived of as a 'given' it will be very difficult to think otherwise, to think of alternative reasons for pedagogy. Thus Benjamin fires off at all and sundry involved in the state-sponsored and state-fulfilling university, including the students: 'nothing has shown more clearly that the students of today as a community are incapable of even formulating the issue of the role of learning, or grasping its indissoluble protest against the vocational demands of the age'.[68] Benjamin's community of learning is a place where the individual can express his or her entire nature: anything else is a society of fragmented and divided beings: 'The socially relevant achievement of the average person serves in the vast majority of cases to repress the original and nonderivative, inner aspirations of the human being'.[69] The university professors and trained individuals are problematically tied in to pedagogy first and foremost via an economic relationship, and then via a supposed societal utility. Benjamin argues that pedagogy should be driven by 'internal' or 'authentic' connections between human beings – for example, between spiritual being and care or concern for the other.[70] Pedagogy, as it is currently experienced, rather than being a direct expression of authentic love is instead mechanical duty: 'This duty is often nothing more than a deflection of purpose, an evasion of the consequences of the critical, intellectual existence to which students are committed.'[71] Benjamin is suspicious of the social work produced as part of the practical manifestation of duty rather than authentic concern; he argues that social work is secondary to the 'problems of spiritual life' and also fails to provide a self-reflexive revolutionizing of 'the conception and value

of such social work in general'.[72] The point being made is that a
genuine service to the poor and the needy involves the transformation of society as a whole, not mere student tinkering in socially useful
work while the students are being trained to serve and reproduce the
hegemonic all-powerful state. Thus the student movements ultimately exclude the essential processes of 'radical doubt', 'fundamental critique' and the constant need for 'reconstruction':

> The modern student body cannot be found in the places where the
> conflicts over the spiritual rebirth of the nation are raging – in the
> controversies about a new art, or at the side of its writers and poets,
> or indeed at the sources of religious life. [The German student body]
> . . . is completely unaware of all these movements; because, as a
> student body, it constantly drifts in the wake of public opinion;
> because it is courted and spoiled by every party and alliance, is flat-
> tered by everyone, and submits to all. [. . .]
>   The perversion of the creative spirit into the vocational spirit,
> which we see at work everywhere, has taken possession of the
> universities as a whole and has isolated them from the nonofficial,
> creative life of the mind.[73]

At a practical level, Benjamin appears to be criticizing a large, diverse
body of student movements for being precisely diverse, and not
focused on the immanent self-reflexive and transformative tasks that
he has in mind; in other words, there is an incommensurability
between these tasks and current cultural forms.[74] The truly creative
metaphysical work comes from people outside the officially sanc-
tioned pedagogic sphere, the 'independent artists and scholars who
are alien and often hostile to the state', a scandalously prophetic
statement given Benjamin's own biographical trajectory.[75] From the
idea of the creative outsider Benjamin thus derives the notion of a
true student who has in effect a parallel existence to his or her official teachers via a non-teleological, non-progressive existence. This
ideal student follows closely his or her teacher without becoming a
teacher or some other state functionary. And what directs such a
parallel existence? The answer is philosophy: 'This philosophy . . .
should concern itself not with limited technical philosophical matters
but with the great metaphysical questions of Plato and Spinoza, the
Romantics, and Nietzsche'.[76] Benjamin is arguing here that
the philosophical question of Being is of vital importance to shape
the transformative energies of 'art and society'; in this sense, the university becomes a rock amid the swirling seas of revolution.

Benjamin's 'The Life of Students' is an essay that reads as contemporary and dated, insightful and naïve; published one year after the outbreak of the First World War, the essay touches upon transformational and revolutionary forces without acknowledging that these forces were soon to be at work most directly and powerfully in the trenches. The centrality of the question of existence or being in 'The Life of Students' was not, however, a side-issue for society at large. Beyond the immediate issue of sheer daily survival, the questioning attitudes unleashed by the First World War would later create a general receptivity to the existential analyses of Karl Jaspers and Martin Heidegger (in *Being and Time*, 1927). Benjamin's opposition between the creative and vocational spirit is not just about individual choice: it concerns the role of the individual in relation to the state, and questions whether the sole function of the individual should be the *maintenance* of the state. The creative spirit is founded upon an oppositional force, one that has the potential to revitalize the state in myriad ways. The conflict of the First World War, the enormous upheaval of society throughout Europe and the concomitant after-effects of the Treaty of Versailles led to a sense of ongoing anxiety and crisis within Germany; rather than a celebration of the state's transformation, the *end* of the state became an overdetermined problematic, addressed by heavyweights such as Oswald Spengler and the political theorist Carl Schmitt. The latter based much of his most famous work on crisis itself, arguing that 'The exception is more interesting than the rule.'[77] The maintenance of the state during crisis, for Schmitt, occurs via the 'suspension of the entire existing order' in favour of unlimited authority: 'In such a situation it is clear that the state remains, whereas law recedes.'[78] Schmitt's work prepares the ground for a radical shift, from crisis to the catastrophe of Nazi power, but the receptivity of youth to that catastrophe can also be read within the very youth movements that had rejected adult society after the First World War. As Bloch argues: 'The federated emotional haze in which young people fought before, without seeing their real opponent, could be easily combined with the intoxicated fascist haze.'[79]

'Rausch' – or youth's intoxication

The rapturously filled night of youth – and indeed the intoxication of the uncontrolled or uncontrollable transcendent experience of

youth in itself – serves proleptically or can be regarded as a projection of later Benjaminian experiences. As such, youthful 'Rausch'
is temporally complex, being an experience that adults deplore,
deny or simply deflate retrospectively, and one that is constantly
sought after for its ecstatic nature – its *ecstasis* – in terms of taking
the subject both beyond himself or herself and also into the future
of Benjamin's critical and conceptual world. In an experiment with
hashish in 1930, Benjamin focuses on the imagistic transformations
involved:

> Some attempt to characterize the image zone. [. . .] . . . there can be
> an absolutely blizzard-like production of images, independently of
> whether our attention is directed toward anyone or anything else.
> Whereas in our normal state free-floating images to which we pay
> no heed simply remain in the unconscious, under the influence of
> hashish images present themselves to us seemingly without requir-
> ing our attention. Of course, this process may result in the produc-
> tion of images that are so extraordinary, so fleeting, and so rapidly
> generated that we can do nothing but gaze at them simply because
> of their beauty and singularity.[80]

In the 'image zone' of intoxication, a rapid flurry of multiple fleeting images present themselves as singularities; these images are
involuntarily made present, or, present themselves as such. Much
later, just prior to his death, Benjamin theorizes an analogous
process whereby the dialectical image is conceived of as an 'involuntary memory' of a redeemed humanity.[81] When he is intoxicated
in his experiment, Benjamin's concern is with the speed of the
ungraspable images: they have to be reconstructed via imitation (just
as children do with their weak remnant of mimetic power),[82] and
they turn out to be images of objects 'with strongly ornamental features. Objects easy to ornament are the best: walls, for instance, or
vaulting, or certain plants.'[83] These increasingly baroque images are
explained via linguistic analysis and with reference to Surrealist
paintings producing a blend of interpretation and nonsense (which
Benjamin's small audience find amusing). The existential state of
'Rausch' is not, however, one of the passive observer being over-
whelmed by the rapid succession of these images; instead, there is
an alternation and oscillation of 'totally different worlds of consciousness', a flipping back and forth between dreaming and waking
states.[84] This circuit describes or models the different positions of narrative production and interpretation, although the reader appears to

be fairly secure in judging when (and where) narrative production *per se* lies and when interpretation of that narrative should begin, as with Freud's masterful interpretation of dreams.[85] Benjamin *appears* to be offering the rapture of a drug-induced dream state as an experimental process that he is merely describing and decoding for the reader; that is, the intoxicated texts are clearly riddled with interpretive clues that are, apparently, immediately followed up within the texts themselves. But in the case of another presentation of intoxication, 'Myslovice – Braunschweig – Marseilles', the situation is not quite so crystalline, especially when the text starts with a disclaimer that casts suspicion on all that follows: 'This story is not mine'.[86] 'Myslovice – Braunschweig – Marseilles' is narrated by 'Eduard Scherlinger', a name that signifies, by a whisker, the poison hemlock: '*Schierling*, of course, is a poison'.[87] This hairline fracture, or etymological gap, is a spacing that opens the text to further ambiguity and difficulty. Derrida opens his 'Plato's Pharmacy', or discussion of the *pharmakon* as poison and/or cure, with a statement about the difficulty of the perception and interpretation of texts: 'A text is not a text unless it hides from the first comer, from the first glance, the law of its composition and the rules of its game. A text remains, moreover, forever imperceptible. Its laws and its rules are not, however, harboured in the inaccessibility of a secret; it is simply that they can never be booked, in the present, into anything that could rigorously be called a perception'.[88] Benjamin, utilizing the *pharmakon* and converting it into the proper name of his narrator – the etymological gap taunting the reader – quotes his own experiences of 'Rausch', displacing them and recovering them at the same time, via the publication of the text. Without the possibility of the *ecstases* of intoxication, of the experience beyond the norm, his text remains impenetrable, flaunting its riddling, but also locating and advertising its 'secret', to use Derrida's word, in a multi-temporal process of perception. In this chain of hashish-smoking texts, one of the essential secrets is the manipulation of language to produce images and jokes: the password in 'Myslovice – Braunschweig – Marseilles' remains as silent as one of the etymological components of the name (*Braunschweig* = brown and silent), whereas in 'Hashish, Beginning of March 1930', the placement of an unusual word in a different context generates humour: 'My "Decline of the *pâtissier's* art" unleashed a gale of laughter in the others.'[89] Jacobs notes that with the opening of 'Myslovice – Braunschweig – Marseilles', even given the more serious narrative frame, 'it is impossible to miss an already reverberating laughter. "Then my friend, the philosopher Ernst Bloch, let fall a proposition, in some connection or other which I have never learned, that there was no one who had not once in his life already come within a hair of becoming a millionaire. We laughed". [. . .] This is a warning, the inner story tells us: "For it is with . . . laughter . . . that the intoxication begins" [. . .].'[90] The generation of humour via 'Rausch' appears less a spontaneous affair, and more a manipulation of signifying systems: the pseudo-scientific 'report' or experiment is written as if a Freudian document. In 'Myslovice – Braunschweig – Marseilles', the failure to make a fortune is presented via the achievement of negotiating and interpreting the state of intoxication; such negotiation and inter-pretation appear to have greater value than the lost cash. It is prob-ably not coincidental that both 'Hashish, Beginning of March 1930' and 'Myslovice – Braunschweig – Marseilles' are texts from 1930, the year of the French translation of Freud's book on jokes, *Der Witz und seine Beziehung zum Unbewussten*, originally published in Vienna in 1905. The Surrealists would eventually take over the joke form in the process of developing 'black humour' which 'undercuts the representation of the world'.[91] 'Rausch', as a *pharmakon*, is respon-sible paradoxically for complex narrative production *and* the replace-ment of language with images through a form of humour that is both a denial of the 'reality principle' and the intoxication of will to power.[92] This denial as such becomes focused on death, as Breton makes clear with reference to Freud's condemned man who shouts, on the way to his execution, 'This week is getting off to a good start!'[93]

Youth as a concept is one that is caught in a double bind: it has the immediacy and authenticity of an experience that cannot be apprehended or negated by philistines, *and* it is a state of intoxica-tion that denies the 'reality principle' (yet also creates a complex interplay of word and image). The writings on youth and intoxica-tion reveal further, however, a central preoccupation for Benjamin: that of time. From the 'diary time' to the slowing down or freezing of time in a hashish trance, through the various texts and approaches to history across his entire writing career, Benjamin proposes an alternative to Martin Heidegger's works, in particular *Being and Time* (1927). Howard Caygill charts the overall parallels between Benjamin and Heidegger:

Both were critical to the point of hostility of prevailing neo-Kantian and Hegelian liberal progressive philosophies of history, and both engaged with a constellation of themes which included 'tradition', 'origin', 'technology' and 'art'. Both explored these themes within the context of an analysis of the grain of everyday experience in modernity: Heidegger in the analyses of Division 1 of *Being and Time* and Benjamin in the 'Arcades Project'. Finally, both sought to comprehend the changes in the modern political occasioned by what Benjamin described as the 'tremendous shattering of tradition' and its 'intimate connection with the contemporary mass movements' ... Their accounts of these changes stressed the role played by technology in the emergence of a political realm riven by the opposition between the mass movements of the left and the right.[94]

Two unpublished fragments from 1916, Benjamin's '*Trauerspiel* and Tragedy' and 'The Role of Language in *Trauerspiel* and Tragedy', critique Heidegger's positions on time. Caygill argues that the main difference revealed between the two thinkers is the 'distinction between fulfilment *in* historical time and the fulfilment *of* historical time', where 'Benjamin identifies Heidegger's understanding of historical time as tragic, one in which past, present and future can be gathered in time, whereas for him fulfilled time is Messianic, a gathering *of* time which is not *in* time'.[95] In effect, the placing of redemption within, or outside, time, is a marker of essential difference, and this is also revealed in the notion of *moment* as ecstatic (Heidegger) versus the moment as Messianic (Benjamin).[96] Caygill argues that Benjamin rejects the decisionism implicit in Heidegger's account of the subject, especially in the opposition between tragedy and *Trauerspiel*, where the latter reveals an empty, meaningless death of 'indecision and accident in the face of catastrophe'.[97] While the later hashish experiments generate visual images that destabilize the order and logic of rational linguistic communication, the *Trauerspiel* fuses indecision with play, expressed as a type of sound or music: 'here, on the question of form, is the point where the crucial distinction between tragedy and mourning play emerges decisively. The remains of mourning plays are called music. Perhaps there is a parallel here: just as tragedy marks the transition from historical to dramatic time, the mourning play represents the transition from dramatic time to musical time.'[98] Further, the mourning play 'is the site of the actual conception of the word and of speech in art; the faculties of speech and hearing still stand equal in the scales, and ultimately everything depends on the ear for lament, for only the most profoundly heard lament can become music. Whereas in tragedy the eternal inflexibility of the spoken word is exalted, the mourning play concentrates in itself the infinite resonance of its sound'.[99] Tragedy is coterminous with dialogue; that is to say, it is the form and possibility of the expression or existence of human dialogue; sadness emerges and fills language in the mourning play, representing not a 'pure' mode of expression but one subject to change: 'Words have a pure emotional life cycle in which they purify themselves by developing from the natural sound to the pure sound of feeling. For such words, language is merely a transitional phase within the entire life cycle, and in them the mourning play finds its voice'.[100] The dissolution of words into music is part of a redemptive process whereby 'feelings' are reborn 'in a suprasensuous nature'.[101] While the time of tragedy is focused and recovered through the ultimate decisional moment, in the mourning play time is cyclical and repetitious, ultimately abandoned or destroyed via the musical completion of the form, the 'infinite resonance' of sound. Heidegger's philosophy is a rejection of the suprasensuous, and a working out of the possibility of an authentic mode of being-in-the-world; Benjamin's conception of youth is one that remains open to a multiplicity of forms that signal and transform themselves at the end of time.

The metaphysics of youth

As Philip Tew writes: 'Youth is not an innocent category; it exists within complex social and ideological forms such as imperialism, oppression, nationalism, religious fervour and overarching all of them, modernity itself'.[102] Tew challenges the conflation or equation of youth 'with romanticism and struggle' in favour of a contextualization, following Lefebvre and Merleau-Ponty, 'within theoretical and social relations'.[103] Benjamin's hyperbolic and at times romanticized youth-movement assertions are tempered by his study of Romantic criticism and his severe critique of late Romanticism in his 'Concept of Criticism' essay. The concept of experience is also developed and modified, replacing the Kantian scientific world view with that of the 'immediate thinking of reflection' of early Romantic thought, which penetrates 'into the absolute'.[104] A decade after the 'Concept of Criticism' essay Benjamin argued that 'There is no greater error than the attempt to construe experience . . . according to the model on which the exact natural sciences are based'.[105] Rejecting Kantian causality once again, Benjamin posits instead lived 'similarities' which he links with the doctrine of 'romantic observation' ('Beobachtung').[106] This doctrine, with its synonym of 'experiment', is a mystical process of reflection whereby the subject evokes 'self-consciousness and self-knowledge in the things observed',[107] leading to an interpenetration of subject and object, or a collapsing of both into one another: 'The medium of reflection of knowing and that of perceiving coincide for the Romantics. The term "observation" alludes to this identity of media . . .'.[108] Philosophy's Enlightenment task is thus revealed to be an impossibility,[109] and perhaps even more essentially for Benjamin, art and a reconfigured philosophy also here coincide. The lived experiences of youth can be equated with 'observation' in a way that 'most people' have no wish to learn from.[110] Convictions can be overturned, however, by a return to the experiential openness of 'the new', which in turn becomes the antithesis to the planned and a lifetime of ennui – the 'new' is the moment of awakening.[111] In *The Arcades Project*, youth is projected as the attempt to 'free ourselves from the world of our parents through cunning'[112] – which is also analogous to the 'wholly unique experience [*Erfahrung*] of dialectic'.[113] The experience of Youth – or childhood, which is evocative of even more openness towards creativity and difference – is analogous to that of dream experience: now the individual's experience is repeated by an entire generation and each epoch.[114] In the spacetime ('Zeitraum') and dreamtime ('Zeit-traum') of the nineteenth century, the specific overall focus of *The Arcades Project*, Benjamin posits another childhood.[115] This childhood has a task: 'to bring the new world into symbolic space ['Symbolraum']',[116] since 'The child, in fact, can do what the grownup absolutely cannot: recognize the new once again.'[117] But this is not a passive recognition: it has transformative potential and adds to the 'Symbolraum': 'There is no more insipid and shabby antithesis than that which reactionary thinkers like Klages try to set up between the symbol-space of nature and that of technology. To each truly new configuration of nature – and at bottom, technology is just such a configuration – there correspond new "images".' Every childhood discovers these new images in order to incorporate them into the image stock of humanity'.[118] Benjamin is careful here to distinguish between the transformative potential as occurring within a 'zone of transition' or 'threshold experience' of which the adult world has grown poor, except perhaps in an erotic economy which Benjamin playfully traces in convolute O, 'Prostitution, Gambling': 'A *Schwelle* [threshold] is a zone. Transformation, passage, wave action are in the word *schwellen*, swell, and etymology ought not to overlook these senses'.[119] Benjamin charts the zones of potential – in his essays on youth, the 'Berlin Childhood' and the Paris Arcades – their transformative energies recognized by those young minds always open to the new.

Notes

1 Walter Z. Laqueur, *Young Germany: A History of the German Youth Movement*, London: Routledge, 1962, p. 36.
2 Peter D. Stachura, *The German Youth Movement 1900–1945*, London: Macmillan, 1981, p. 15.
3 Ibid.
4 Benjamin, 'Experience', *Selected Writings*, vol. i: *1913–1926*, p. 3.
5 Ibid.
6 Ibid., p. 4.
7 Ibid.
8 Ibid.
9 Ibid.
10 Ibid., p. 5.
11 For a related discussion concerning the 'concept of youth' see Philip Tew, '*The Lexicon of Youth* in MacLaverty, Bolger, and Doyle: Theorizing Contemporary Irish Fiction via Lefebvre's *Tenth Prelude*', *Hungarian Journal of English and American Studies*, 5:1 (1999), 181–197.
12 Benjamin to Carla Seligson, 5 June 1913, letter 15 in *The Correspondence of Walter Benjamin: 1910–1940*, p. 29.
13 Laqueur, *Young Germany: A History of the German Youth Movement*, p. 53; see Bernd Witte, *Walter Benjamin: An Intellectual Biography*, trans. James Rolleston, Detroit: Wayne State University Press, 1997, pp. 18–19.
14 Stachura, *The German Youth Movement 1900–1945*, p. 25.
15 Ibid., pp. 25–26.
16 Ibid., p. 26.
17 Laqueur, *Young Germany: A History of the German Youth Movement*, p. 54.
18 'Chronology, 1892–1926', in Walter Benjamin, *Selected Writings*, vol. i: *1913–1926*, p. 494.
19 Witte, *Walter Benjamin: An Intellectual Biography*, p. 23; Brodersen, *Walter Benjamin: A Biography*, p. 37.
20 Rüdiger Safranski, *Martin Heidegger: Between Good and Evil*, trans. Ewald Osers, Cambridge, Massachusetts, and London: Harvard University Press, 1999, p. 63.
21 Witte, *Walter Benjamin: An Intellectual Biography*, p. 23.
22 Brodersen, *Walter Benjamin: A Biography*, p. 47.

23 Benjamin, 'The Metaphysics of Youth', *Selected Writings*, vol. i: *1913–1926*, p. 10.
24 Ibid.
25 Ibid., p. 11.
26 Ibid.
27 Ibid.
28 Ibid.
29 Jaspers, *Philosophy*, vol. ii, p. 177.
30 Benjamin, 'The Metaphysics of Youth', *Selected Writings*, vol. i: *1913–1926*, pp. 12–13.
31 Jaspers, *Philosophy*, vol. ii, p. 179.
32 Ibid.
33 Benjamin, 'The Metaphysics of Youth', *Selected Writings*, vol. i: *1913–1926*, pp. 13–14.
34 Martin Heidegger, *Being and Time*, trans. John Macquarrie and Edward Robinson, Oxford: Blackwell, 1990; see pp. 279–311 ('Dasein's Possibility of Being-a-whole, and Being-towards-Death').
35 Benjamin, 'The Metaphysics of Youth', *Selected Writings*, vol. i: *1913–1926*, p. 15.
36 Rubinstein, *An Episode of Jewish Romanticism: Franz Rosenzweig's The Star of Redemption*, p. 78.
37 See the discussion concerning the construction and discovery of the 'self' in Arnold B. Come, *Kierkegaard as Humanist: Discovering My Self*, London, Buffalo, Montreal and Kingston: McGill-Queen's University Press, 1995.
38 Benjamin to Gustav Wyneken, 9 March 1915, letter 39 in *The Correspondence of Walter Benjamin: 1910–1940*, p. 75.
39 Ibid., p. 76.
40 Brodersen, *Walter Benjamin: A Biography*, p. 59.
41 Benjamin to Gustav Wyneken, 9 March 1915, letter 39 in *The Correspondence of Walter Benjamin: 1910–1940*, p. 76.
42 Ibid.
43 Ernst Bloch, *The Spirit of Utopia*, trans. Anthony A. Nassar, Stanford, California: Stanford University Press, 2000, p. 184.
44 Ibid., p. 185.
45 See Benjamin, *The Arcades Project*, p. 883, <h°,2>: 'What Proust intends with the experimental rearrangement of furniture, what Bloch recognizes as the darkness of the lived moment, is nothing other than what here is secured on the level of the historical, and collectively. There is a not-yet-conscious knowledge of *what has been*: its advancement has the structure of awakening. <See K1,2.>'
46 Benjamin to Martin Buber, July 1916, letter 45 in *The Correspondence of Walter Benjamin: 1910–1940*, p. 80.
47 Ibid.
48 Pensky, *Melancholy Dialectics: Walter Benjamin and the Play of Mourning*, p. 42.
49 Paul W. Franks and Michael L. Morgan, in Franz Rosenzweig, *Philosophical and Theological Writings*, trans. and ed., with notes and commentary, by Paul W. Franks and Michael L. Morgan, Indianapolis and Cambridge: Hackett, 2000, pp. 5–6.
50 Ibid., p. 6.

51 Ibid.

52 Ibid., p. 5.

53 Miles, *Christ: A Crisis in the Life of God*, p. 284.

54 Franz Rosenzweig, 'Atheistic Theology', in *Philosophical and Theological Writings*, pp. 15–16.

55 Ibid., p. 16.

56 Ibid., p. 17.

57 Ibid., p. 18.

58 Ibid., p. 19.

59 Ibid., p. 24.

60 Rabinbach, 'Between Enlightenment and Apocalypse: Benjamin, Bloch and Modern German Jewish Messianism', p. 107.

61 Ibid., p. 91.

62 Ibid.

63 Benjamin to Herbert Belmore, 12 August 1912, letter 9 in *The Correspondence of Walter Benjamin: 1910–1940*, p. 17.

64 Pensky, *Melancholy Dialectics: Walter Benjamin and the Play of Mourning*, p. 43.

65 Benjamin, 'The Life of Students', *Selected Writings*, vol. i: *1913–1926*, p. 37.

66 Ibid., p. 38.

67 Ibid.

68 Ibid., p. 39.

69 Ibid., pp. 39–40.

70 Ibid., p. 40.

71 Ibid.

72 Ibid.

73 Ibid., pp. 41–42.

74 Pieper, *The End of Time: A Meditation on the Philosophy of History*, p. 37.

75 Benjamin, 'The Life of Students', *Selected Writings*, vol. i: *1913–1926*, p. 42.

76 Ibid., p. 43.

77 Carl Schmitt, *Political Theology: Four Chapters on the Doctrine of Sovereignty*, trans. George Schwab, Cambridge, Massachusetts, and London, England: MIT Press, 1985, p. 15.

78 Ibid., p. 12.

79 Bloch, *The Principle of Hope*, vol. ii, p. 586; for an excellent analysis of the pressures on youth movements to Nazify, in this case Catholic youth, see John Cornwell's *Hitler's Pope: The Secret History of Pius XII*, London: Viking, 1999.

80 Benjamin, 'Hashish, Beginning of March 1930', *Selected Writings*, vol. ii: *1927–1934*, ed. Michael W. Jennings, Howard Eiland and Gary Smith, trans. Rodney Livingstone and others, Cambridge, Massachusetts, and London, England: Belknap Press of Harvard University Press, 1999, pp. 328–329.

81 Benjamin, 'Paralipomena to 'On the Concept of History'', *Selected Writings*, vol. iv: *1938–1940*, ed. Howard Eiland and Michael W. Jennings, trans. Edmund Jephcott and others, Cambridge, Massachusetts, and London, England: Belknap Press of Harvard University Press, 2003, p. 403.

82 Benjamin, 'Berlin Childhood around 1900', *Selected Writings*, vol. iii: *1935–1938*, p. 374.

83 Benjamin, 'Hashish, Beginning of March 1930', *Selected Writings*, vol. ii: *1927–1934*, p. 329.

84 Joël and Fränkel, 'Der Haschisch-Rausch', quoted in Walter Benjamin, 'Hashish in Marseilles', *Selected Writings*, vol. ii: *1927–1934*, p. 673.

85 See Sigmund Freud, *The Interpretation of Dreams*, trans. James Strachey, Harmondsworth, Middlesex: Penguin, 1986; see, also, Mikkel Borch-Jacobsen's extended critique of Freud's 'mastery' in *The Freudian Subject: Language, Discourse, Society*, trans. Catherine Porter, Basingstoke and London: Macmillan, 1989.

86 Benjamin, 'Myslovice – Braunschweig – Marseilles', *Selected Writings*, vol. ii: *1927–1934*, p. 386.

87 Carol Jacobs, *In the Language of Walter Benjamin*, Baltimore and London: The Johns Hopkins University Press, 1999, p. 61.

88 Jacques Derrida, *Dissemination*, trans. Barbara Johnson, Chicago and London: The University of Chicago Press, 1981, p. 63.

89 Benjamin, 'Hashish, Beginning of March 1930', *Selected Writings*, vol. ii: *1927–1934*, p. 329.

90 Jacobs, *In the Language of Walter Benjamin*, p. 62.

91 Jacqueline Chénieux-Gendron, *Surrealism*, trans. Vivian Folkenflik, New York: Columbia University Press, 1990, p. 88.

92 Ibid., p. 89.

93 Ibid., p. 91.

94 Howard Caygill, 'Benjamin, Heidegger and the Destruction of Tradition', in A. Benjamin and Osborne, eds., *Walter Benjamin's Philosophy: Destruction and Experience*, pp. 1–30, at p. 2.

95 Ibid., p. 10.

96 Ibid., p. 15.

97 Ibid., p. 19.

98 Benjamin, '*Trauerspiel* and Tragedy', *Selected Writings*, vol. i: *1913–1926*, p. 57.

99 Benjamin, 'The Role of Language in *Trauerspiel* and Tragedy', *Selected Writings*, vol. i: *1913–1926*, p. 61.

100 Ibid., p. 60.

101 Ibid., p. 61.

102 Tew, '*The Lexicon of Youth* in MacLaverty, Bolger, and Doyle: Theorizing Contemporary Irish Fiction via Lefebvre's *Tenth Prelude*', p. 182.

103 Ibid.

104 Benjamin, 'The Concept of Criticism', *Selected Writings*, vol. i: *1913–1926*, p. 130.

105 Benjamin, 'Experience', *Selected Writings*, vol. ii: *1927–1934*, p. 553.

106 Ibid.; 'The Concept of Criticism', *Selected Writings*, vol. i: *1913–1926*, p. 147.

107 Benjamin, 'The Concept of Criticism', *Selected Writings*, vol. i: *1913–1926*, p. 148.

108 Ibid.

109 Andrew Bowie, *Aesthetics and Subjectivity: From Kant to Nietzsche*, p. 76.

110 Benjamin, 'Experience', *Selected Writings*, vol. ii: *1927–1934*, p. 553.

111 Ibid.; Benjamin, *The Arcades Project*, pp. 916–917, no. 23 and no. 24.

112 Benjamin, *The Arcades Project*, p. 908, no.9.

113 Ibid., p. 838 <F°,6>.

114 Ibid., p. 388 [K1,1].

115 Ibid., p. 389 [K1,4] and p. 390 [k1a,2].
116 Ibid., p. 390 [K1a,3], and p. 855 <M°,20>.
117 Ibid., p. 390 [K1a,3].
118 Ibid.
119 Ibid., p. 494 [O2a,1].

4

History: surreal Messianism

Eternal return

Nietzsche once said that if existence had a goal, it would have been reached by now.[1] The context of this statement is his theory of the 'eternal return': that a measure of one's life can be gained by the ability to affirm the repetition of each and every element of that life. In Nietzsche's *Zarathustra*, the eternal return becomes an overpowering of past, present and future, as Berkowitz suggests: 'For if all things are knotted firmly together, then mastery of any moment would result in mastery of the whole; if all things are knotted firmly together, then successfully willing the moment becomes the supreme expression of the will to power.'[2] Deleuze, in *Nietzsche and Philosophy*, briefly examines two aspects here: first, the eternal return as cosmological and physical doctrine, and second, the eternal return as ethical and selective thought. With the first aspect, the eternal return is regarded as a synthesis: 'a synthesis of time and its dimensions, a synthesis of diversity and its reproduction, a synthesis of becoming and the being which is affirmed in becoming, a synthesis of double affirmation.'[3] The second aspect of the eternal return, according to Deleuze, is, in part, a test: that of the subject, to see if he or she has the ability to negate reactive forces.[4] Benjamin explores the theory of the eternal return in convolute D of *The Arcades Project*, on 'Boredom, Eternal Return'. He begins with selections from *L'Eternité par les astres* (1872) by Louis-Auguste Blanqui (1805–81), arguing that the counterpart to Blanqui's 'view of the world' is that of the universe as a 'site of lingering catastrophes'.[5] The selections from Blanqui's *L'Eternité par les astres* in convolute D form a bridge between the materials on boredom and those on Nietzsche; Blanqui's is a cosmic infernal vision of the world, a 'terrible indictment of a society that projects this image of the cosmos – understood as an image of itself – across the heavens.'[6] Discussing his work on Baudelaire, in a letter to Horkheimer in 1938, Benjamin projected a three-part study which intersected or converged with this particular set of *Arcades Project* material.[7] The three parts of this study were to be 'Idea and Image', 'Antiquity and Modernity' and 'The New and the Immutable'. The second part of the Baudelaire study, where a chiasmus between antiquity and modernity is revealed, is suggestive of the dialectical shocks created by the critical constellations of *The Arcades Project* as a whole: put simply, old appears new, and the new is fractured and placed under critique by the old: 'Benjamin's gaze [with *The Arcades Project*] focused on the afterlife of these fantastical "dream" forms – the ruined arcade, the obsolete object, outmoded fashions – with the goal of disenchanting them and redeeming their utopian promise. As they are ruined, ridiculed and demolished, the enslaving forms of yesteryear yield their critical potential, their revolutionary energy, their truth.'[8] The projected third part of the Baudelaire study theorizes that the new is nothing but the 'halo of the commodity' where the concept and experience of the immutable are 'exploded' by this discovery: 'The third part deals with the historical configuration, where the *Flowers of Evil* joins Blanqui's *Éternité par les astres* and Nietzsche's *Will to Power* [*Der Wille zur Macht*] (the eternal return) by virtue of the idée fixe of the new and the immutable.'[9] This projected third part was never written, although it remains in fragmentary form as such, or as a critical constellation (the two ways of describing the section being radically different), in *The Arcades Project*. Witte reads the Baudelaire study, and its unwritten third part, as an analysis of the political situation with Hitler's rise to power in Nazi Germany:

> the epistemological grounding of Benjamin's critique turns into an assessment of the actual political situation. The parallel between Louis Bonaparte and Hitler, between Baudelaire and Benjamin, appears legitimate because the social conditions between 1848 and 1851, and between 1918 and 1933, remained fundamentally the same. [. . .] Benjamin's historico-philosophical construction is based on the experience that history, once it has entered the stage of the commodity-producing society, can no longer generate anything qualitatively new, but, in the sense of Blanqui and Nietzsche, perpetuates itself as a fashionable renewal of a corrupt and forever unchanging world condition.[10]

Benjamin regarded the eternal return and the belief in progress, the latter 'an infinite perfectibility understood as an infinite ethical task', as 'indissoluble antinomies' which generate the need for a 'dialectical conception of historical time'.[11] A dialectical conception of this antinomy leads to the notion that the eternal return is rational and the belief in progress mythical.[12] Both models of history – eternal return and rational progress – are ultimately undermined and fundamentally questioned by Benjamin's dialectical thinking.

Readers of Benjamin are familiar with his last work – 'On the Concept of History' – which not only appears to offer as a series of aphorisms or propositions a potential synthesis of Messianic and materialist thought, but also most emphatically and repeatedly rejects the notion of history as progress. The first of the propositions constructs an image of historical materialism that can only be successful by enlisting the 'services of theology';[13] the second proposition deals with redemption and a '*weak* Messianic power';[14] propositions 3, 4 and 6 also explore redemption; proposition 9, the most famous of them all (and probably the most critically contested), describes the Klee painting *Angelus novus*, depicting the angel of history with his face turned to the past: 'Where a chain of events appears before *us*, *he* sees one single catastrophe, which keeps piling wreckage upon wreckage and hurls it at his feet.'[15] Rolf Tiedemann, in his 'Historical Materialism or Political Messianism? An Interpretation of the Theses "On the Concept of History"',[16] argues that Benjamin 'makes obvious use of the theological terminology of his earlier writings: he sees "redemption" as the Other of history, cites the true believers' "Judgment Day," and speaks of both the Antichrist and the Messiah.'[17] In prefacing his analysis of the apparent oddity of the conjoining of materialist and Messianic thought in this work, Tiedemann foregrounds the fact that the *concept* of history is actually replaced by that of an *image*: 'The basis for Benjamin's image of the pile of debris growing up into the skies and the basis for the catastrophic concept of history in the Theses goes beyond its linguistic conceptualization. It is in essence an image, one that the observer can only stare at, condemned to silence, unable to differentiate or to identify details.'[18] The image of the ever-increasing pile of debris is replaced by Benjamin's commentary upon Klee's *Angelus novus*. Tiedemann argues that ultimately the angel is an allegorical image standing in for the historical materialist, not the Messiah; the angel has seen through the usual human illusions (precisely those myths of progress or the eternal return) and desires to fix the damage before him. Tiedemann is sceptical of the theological recovery implicit in certain readings of 'On the Concept of History'; he argues, through his own allegorical account, that 'It is only for the historical materialist that writing history is inextricably linked to "making" history. He should possess a theory of history that itself becomes historical praxis, a part of the class struggle.'[19] Benjamin's 'On the Concept of History' may enlist the services of theology, but historical materialism is in control;[20] reading Benjamin's text as 'a handbook for urban guerillas'[21] allows Tiedemann to explore the relationship between Marxist thought and events current to the essay such as the rise of Fascism and the increasingly obvious and dangerous totalitarianism of Soviet Russia, *and* Benjamin's fragmentary approach to meditating upon the future of materialist thought and praxis. In the process of Tiedemann's reading, not only is theology subordinated, but it is effectively transposed or transmogrified as the sign of materialism: for example, the angel stands for the historical materialist,[22] the secret agreement between the generations 'may sound mystical' but 'has a materialistic intent',[23] and the Messiah in the traditional religious sense is replaced, in effect, by the materialist.[24] As the sign of the materialist's opposite, theology remains throughout 'On the Concept of History', according to Tiedemann, 'unreal':

> Whenever Benjamin's language in the historico-philosophical theses invokes anew the theological origin of Marxian concepts, the secularized content of these ideas is always maintained. The Messiah, redemption, the angel and the Antichrist are all to be found in the Theses only as images, analogies, and parables, and not in their real form. Benjamin does not for a moment contemplate a representation of what Marx had at long last achieved in terms of theory and what the working class movement preserved in practice.[25]

What would the 'real form' of these theological concepts be? An idea of the forces involved through revelation, suggesting why only 'images, analogies, and parables' are utilized by Benjamin, can be found in an unpublished fragment from 1919–20 called 'World and Time'.[26] Like Rosenzweig in his 'Atheistic Theology' from 1914, in 'World and Time' Benjamin is concerned with revelation as a separate power, countering the idea that revelation is a force that can be contained and controlled by organized religion. Revelation, according to Benjamin, is a massively destructive force: 'In the revelation of the divine, the world – the theater of history – is subjected to a great process of decomposition, while time – the life of him who represents it – is subjected to a great process of fulfillment.'[27] This massive decomposition, literally the 'end of the world', is simultaneously a 'liberation', as Benjamin puts it, 'of a (dramatic) representation'.[28] The history represented here is that of Biblical history, which is, as Pieper writes: 'a single stream of historical happening – starting with the Creation, the beginning per se, ending with the Judgment on the Last Day, and between beginning and end the history of the Fall of Man, the awaiting, the Logos made flesh, the agony on the Cross, the Resurrection, the Ascension of the God-man.'[29] Benjamin critiques Catholicism because it admits of divine power in the world in a non-destructive sense; the crossing of the secular and divine worlds in the Catholic theocracy is thus regarded as problematic as it is only after the day of Judgment that divine power can manifest itself constructively as such: 'That is why in this world nothing is constant and no organization can be based on divine power, let alone domination as its supreme principle.'[30] 'World and Time' is also written as a series of propositions: the first proposition presents history as understood via the Holy Bible and revelation, while the second proposition rejects theocracy; the third and fourth propositions deal with the differences between divine laws and the profane realm of politics, the latter defined by Benjamin as 'the fulfillment of an unimproved humanity'.[31] Divine power, given its destructive force, is related by Benjamin to anarchy and revolution: theocracy leads to instability, whereas within the community the revolutionary force of the divine is manifested: 'Such manifestations are to be sought not in the sphere of the social but in perception oriented toward revelation and, first and last, in language, sacred language above all.'[32] The fifth proposition is the most fragmentary of them all: it deals with the rejection of a 'realization' of divine power, because it is only through the manifestation of the divine (as other, as entirely non-human) that a glimpse of its destructiveness can be had; Benjamin suggests that there is a division between such a glimpse, which is a moment of 'supreme reality', and the self-enclosed nature of the divine, that is, the realm of the fulfilled world which for human beings can come into existence as such only after the Last Judgment. 'World and Time' reveals

an awareness of divine power that pervades, at whatever level, later
Benjaminian notions such as profane illumination and the revolutionary force of dialectics at a standstill. In other words, even a
cursory examination of 'World and Time' reveals that we should not
read Benjamin's use of theological components in the later 'On the
Concept of History' as mere semiotic ciphers, that is to say, empty
or unreal signs that stand in for the otherwise absent 'real thing';
rather, we should regard theology as the key which will unlock the
destructive forces in Benjamin's work.[33]

Profane illumination

How did Benjamin's task shift from the precisely defined 'perception
oriented toward revelation and, first and last, in language, sacred
language above all'[34] to that of dialectics at a standstill, even where
the latter may be considered to release explosively a potentially
Messianic force? Intriguingly, three fragments that form part of
Benjamin's original *Habilitation* plans survive, revealing once more
a number of strong theological interests in the philosophy of language.[35] In his 'Outline for a *Habilitation* Thesis' Benjamin constructs
a series of 'Theorems on Symbolism' where there is an absolute division between 'material objects', 'symbols' and God. It is only through
'objective intention' that certain objects can 'point' to God, where
objective intentions are defined via a multiplicity: '(Memory –
remembrance, fidelity (in portraying something) – copy, philosophy
– truth, penance – purification, and so on.).'[36] In parallel with this
theorem Benjamin writes: 'Remembrance = Holy Communion'.[37]
The 'fulfilment' of material objects in pointing towards God can
occur through the objective intention of remembrance; conversely,
remembrance is the Eucharist, where the 'objects' involved are
simultaneously acts of remembrance *and* the body and blood of
Christ. The work of history as holy remembrance and the analysis
of works of art all requires a comprehensive theory of language,
sketched via the three fragments. Yet Benjamin did not write this
particular thesis or develop much further such a theory of language;
instead, he switched under guidance to the idea of German studies,
in particular that of the largely forgotten format of the German
mourning play or *Trauerspiel*.[38] The *Habilitation* was not all that
Benjamin was writing at this time: he was also composing during
1923 to 1926 the radically playful, aphoristic montage text 'Ein-

bahnstrasse' or 'One-Way Street', to be published in 1928. George Steiner takes a critical view, calling the completed *Habilitation* 'an uncomfortable hybrid':

> Benjamin laboured to reconcile the technical demands and tonal manners of a *Habilitationsschrift* with those of an uncompromisingly personal, even lyric statement. From the academic point of view, the German baroque horror-dramas and emblem-books were the object of dispassionate investigation. From an epistemological-formal point of view . . . these cobwebbed texts were the occasion for a chain of reflections on the nature of aesthetic objects, on the metaphysical presumptions of allegory, on language in general, and on the problem, obsessive to Benjamin, of the relations between a work of art and the descriptive-analytic discourse of which it is the target. To these must be added the very nearly private status of the *Erkenntniskritische Vorrede* [the 'Epistemo-Critical Prologue'] . . . The product of these intentional and methodological disparities is, undoubtedly, a major work. But it is also a work which is flawed and difficult to place in focus.[39]

The *Habilitation*, or *The Origin of German Tragic Drama*, has been called by Max Pensky a text 'thoroughly taken up with the specter of history and historical time' as well as being about a genre, the mourning play, that 'is embedded thoroughly within historical time'.[40] Tragedy, Benjamin observes, is concerned with myth, whereas the mourning play is about catastrophic politico-historical events. As Pensky notes: 'the experience of historical catastrophe itself is incorporated into the structure and the content of the work, becoming the controlling premise of dramatic action, the fixed metaphorical referent for the generation of dramatic language.'[41] In the 'Epistemo-Critical Prologue', Benjamin develops a new, histori-cal notion of 'origin' with which he performs a number of tasks, not the least of these being to remain faithful to 'perception oriented toward revelation'. 'Origin' is reconfigured, away from Nietzsche's eternal return, and away from the neo-Kantian development of a scientific history:

> Origin [*Ursprung*], although an entirely historical category, has, nevertheless, nothing to do with genesis [*Entstehung*]. The term origin is not intended to describe the process by which the existent came into being, but rather to describe that which emerges from the process of becoming and disappearance. Origin is an eddy in the stream of becoming, and in its current it swallows the material

involved in the process of genesis. That which is original is never revealed in the naked and manifest existence of the factual; its rhythm is apparent only to a dual insight. On the one hand it needs to be recognized as a process of restoration and re-establishment, but, on the other hand, and precisely because of this, as something imperfect and incomplete.[42]

Hanssen argues that the 'Epistemo-Critical Prologue' creates an over-layering of 'Greek and Judaic conceptions of nature and history respectively'.[43] What this means is that profane and theological realms converge in the 'Epistemo-Critical Prologue', manifested in Benjamin's 'reinterpretation of the doctrine of Ideas along cabalistic lines – which defined the Idea not as *eidos* but as the divine Word, suggesting that the profane origin must be thought in relation to a divine Origin.'[44] Benjamin's use of Platonic 'Ideas' in the 'Epistemo-Critical Prologue' should not be thought of as a simple, problematic return to Platonism; rather, the convergence of two systems of thought leads to an overcoming of 'the dualism between historical contingency and the ahistorical, transcendent Ideas'.[45] The 'origin' is a theological-dialectical notion: it is the 'process of becoming and disappearance',[46] thus facilitating the study of development and decomposition not, as with Spengler, in a simplistic linear sense, but in a synchronous sense (an act of simultaneous development and decomposition). Thus, the 'original' is embedded for Benjamin in a dual process of restoration and revealed incompletion: 'There takes place in every original phenomenon a determination of the form in which an idea will constantly confront the historical world, until it is revealed fulfilled, in the totality of its history.'[47] Benjamin appears to distance the critic at this point: the critic does not uncover or dis-cover the idea – instead, the entire history, or constellation of con-frontations of the idea, is self-determining. As Rochlitz argues: 'what matters more in Benjamin's view of truth is both that it is absolutely revelational, independent of human knowledge, and that it depends on an irreducible plurality of idea-forms or "monads," which present a complete vision of the world each time. Every "idea" – tragedy, tragic-drama, story – presents a "part" of truth that has to be inte-grated into an enumerable totality.'[48] Benjamin goes on to describe how the immanent history of an idea is constituted by 'essential being' or the 'past and subsequent history of this being'; further, this 'essential being' and historical life of the idea is non-human and non-humanist and is called by Benjamin 'natural history':[49]

With this term, he [Benjamin] first of all referred to a process of transience and to a logic of decay that radically undermined Enlightenment and post-Enlightenment conceptions of human history, anchored in categories of human freedom and historical teleology. [. . .] Benjamin's positive validation of natural history was meant to overcome the limitations of historical hermeneutics, whose category of 'meaning' (*Sinn*) remained grounded in the understanding of a human subject. [. . .] Benjamin's profound reformulation of the term ['origin'] sought to merge the premises of transcendental philosophy with what traditionally is said to fall outside its boundaries: the contingency, singularity, transcience, or alterity of history.[50]

Benjamin's *The Origin of German Tragic Drama* compares two literary forms: tragedy and *Trauerspiel* (mourning play). The 'Epistemo-Critical Prologue' reveals that Benjamin intends to proceed using immanent criticism, whereby his critical discourse inhabits the same epistemological field as that of the artwork.[51] Such a procedure creates a 'resonance in history'[52] otherwise missing from the studies of the *Trauerspiel*. It would be a mistake to read this 'resonance' as an effect of empathy, as the latter may simply be regarded as a manifestation of re-reading history in the light of, and as, present-day concerns. Benjamin regards this 'empathic' approach as characteristic of the present age: 'there is no new style, no unknown popular heritage to be discovered which would not straight away appeal with the utmost clarity to the feelings of contemporaries.'[53]

Surrealism

Two conceptual journeys taken by Benjamin – through Surrealism and Marxism – could quite reasonably be assumed to reduce, if not completely efface, the centrality of Messianic thought in his work; the 'perception oriented toward revelation' becomes undoubtedly focused more closely upon – or shifted into a writing that is mimetic of – the experiences of the transformational city-spaces and wider political upheavals of twentieth-century Europe. While critics have long since moved away from the simplistic notion of 'phases' in Benjamin's work, this move does not always recuperate or account for the theological material previously consigned to his youth. Franz Rosenzweig's call for a new type of thinking 'situated between theology and philosophy'[54] is useful in elucidating the transformation of Benjamin's work since the new type of thinking bridges what

Rosenzweig calls 'maximum subjectivity' and 'maximum objectivity';[55] such a bridge is charged or made possible by the concept of revelation, whether acknowledged or not: 'From theology's point of view, what philosophy is supposed to accomplish for it is thus by no means to reconstruct the theological contents, but to anticipate them or rather . . . to supply them with a foundation, to demonstrate the preconditions on which it rests.'[56] The cul-de-sac of the historical approach to Christ, for example, would be replaced, following Rosenzweig's account, by the authority of a new prophetic philosophy that is also restorative: 'philosophy is the Sybilline Oracle which, by predicting the miracle, turns it into a "sign," the sign of divine providence.'[57] Rosenzweig's vision of the new philosophy's task is revolutionary (philosophy has the power to counteract the *catastrophe*, for theology, of historical empiricism);[58] whether it could be implemented, via profane illumination and dialectics at a standstill, is another matter entirely. The two latter processes, thought of as developing from the profound boundary experiences of Marxism and Surrealism, need to be brought into relation with Benjamin's Messianic thought to gauge his alignment with the 'new philosophers'. Surrealist categories, functioning as discrete processes *and* collectively as a more powerful critical constellation, were seen by Benjamin as being an existential pushing at the limits of the 'poetic life'.[59] To read the categories as purely aesthetic or pseudo-revolutionary attempts at more radical change is to negate the power of Surrealism; for example, Hal Foster, noting that the marvellous is in effect the uncanny, argues that the marvellous is 'projected, at least in part, away from the unconscious and repressed material toward the world and future revelation.'[60] Poetry, for the Surrealists, is to be 'exploded from within';[61] the explosive energies released or unleashed function not just in space (marks, writing, language), but in time, for example the experiments with automatic writing are as much to do with temporality as with graphic production. Further, the explosion is not a subjective event, but a revelation of truth, not as some timeless universal, but rather as a truthful horizon or necessary possibility for the existing subject: 'truth is not – as Marxism would have it – a merely contingent function of knowing, but is bound to a nucleus of time lying hidden within the knower and the known alike.'[62] The circuit between knower and known was interlaced anew after Surrealism to create what Benjamin calls profane illumination; Benjamin suggests, however, that this state of being, reached existentially through lived experiences, not theoretical knowledge, 'did not always find the Surrealists equal to it'.[63] The constellation creates the conditions of profane illumination, but that does not mean that the full revolutionary potential is discharged. One of the potentially explosive categories that fascinated Benjamin was that of the 'outmoded':

> [Breton] . . . was the first to perceive the revolutionary energies that appear in the 'outmoded' – in the first iron constructions, the first factory buildings, the earliest photos, objects that have begun to be extinct, grand pianos, the dresses of five years ago, fashionable restaurants when the vogue has begun to ebb from them. The relation of these things to revolution – no one can have a more exact concept of it than these authors. No one before these visionaries and augurs perceived how destitution – not only social but architectonic, the poverty of interiors, enslaved and enslaving objects – can be suddenly transformed into revolutionary nihilism.[64]

Things conceal 'immense forces' which must be brought to realization, the 'point of explosion';[65] at the centre of the Surrealist world of things is the city of Paris: 'But only revolt completely exposes its Surrealist face (deserted streets in which whistles and shots dictate the outcome). And no face is surrealistic to the same degree as the true face of a city.'[66] To become equal to profane illumination means to switch from contemplation to 'revolutionary opposition',[67] but as long as this opposition remains purely in play, the 'intoxicating component'[68] of all revolutionary acts, the profane illumination, also remains a form of constant anarchism (a constructive phase is never reached). Inspired by Surrealism, yet also noting limitations in Surrealist methodology, Benjamin began his own study of the outmoded Paris Arcades; the complex architectonics of *The Arcades Project*, a new way of doing history and philosophy, attempts to 'find the constellation of awakening',[69] via materialism: 'It may be considered one of the methodological objectives of this work to demonstrate a historical materialism which has annihilated within itself the idea of progress. Just here, historical materialism has every reason to distinguish itself sharply from bourgeois habits of thought. Its founding concept is not progress but actualization.'[70] As Benjamin notes, 'Overcoming the concept of "progress" and overcoming the concept of "period of decline" are two sides of one and the same thing.'[71]

The annihilation of the idea of progress is simultaneously the erasure of the false traces of bourgeois living, as with the work of the new architects who turned their backs on the stuffy nineteenth-century interiors which 'look as overcrowded as halls full of funerary urns'.[72] The architects of modernity used glass and steel, those materials that were the 'enemies' of secrets and possessions.[73] It is necessary to distinguish between the glass-milieu of modernism, an environment for those who had experienced the destruction and impoverishment of the First World War, and the archaic glass-milieu of the nineteenth-century Paris Arcades.[74] Benjamin's obsession with the Paris Arcades brought together two impulses: to present philosophy via aphorisms and montage form, and to unleash the revolutionary potential of the task or work as a collection of convolutes (the configuration of dialectical images): 'Benjamin recalled that the conception for the *Passagen-Werk* was inspired by reading Louis Aragon's Surrealist novel, *Le Paysan de Paris*, in which the Paris Arcades figure centrally.'[75] As Buck-Morss writes, concerning Breton and Aragon:

> André Breton's novel *Nadja* (1928), Benjamin notes, is a book more about Paris than about the elusive heroine named in the title. Breton includes photographs of Paris empty of people that mark the narrated events as if transient experience could be made present within the material spaces of cafés and street-corners known to the reader. Louis Aragon's novel, *Le Paysan de Paris*, describes in detail one arcade, the Passage de l'Opera, just before this material space itself disappeared . . . In both books the ephemeral quality of the material world is charged with meaning. The early *Passagen-Werk* notes speak of a 'crossroads' in 'the development of thinking' where, in regard to 'the new gaze at the historical world,' a decision must be made concerning 'its reactionary or revolutionary evaluation. In this sense, the same thing is at work in Surrealism and Heidegger.'[76]

After the annihilation of the idea of progress, the mythological is also reconstituted: Aragon's Surrealist categories are reversed (dream becomes, or is realized by, awakening; mythology becomes, or is realized by, history); the process is constituted by 'the awakening of a not-yet-conscious knowledge of what has been'.[77] History works not just on the collective in this account, but on the existential subject: the non-reflective subject is immersed in the sensuous experience of the Arcades without being awakened, just as the non-reflective modern subject is immersed in the hyperreal world of even more sophisticated media-based commodity relations (in effect, *virtual* arcades). But what is awakened? Through the construction of dialectical images, Benjamin argues that 'what has been within a particular epoch is always, simultaneously, "what has been from time immemorial."'[78] The so-called materialist reconstitution of dream and mythology, to take two Surrealist obsessions, becomes a deformation of Enlightenment rationality and technology, radical enough to encompass the metaphysical; the awakening, it is contended in this study, is also a potential return 'to a deeper, more metaphysically fulfilled experience'.[79] Benjamin conceives of the Arcades as an intermingling or 'communication' of contradictions: 'Organic world and inorganic world, abject poverty and insolent luxury . . . the commodity intermingles and interbreeds as promiscuously as images in the most tangled of dreams.'[80] The Arcades are a 'Primordial landscape of consumption'.[81] Benjamin calls this intermingling an 'energy' or 'dialectics' that works within the Arcades; he imagines the dialectic as being a ferocious manifestation passing through the Arcades, 'ransacking them, revolutionizing them . . . [turning] them upside down and inside out, converting them, since they no longer remain what they are'.[82] In the 'Materials for the Exposé of 1935', Benjamin places his ideas concerning this dialectical force into schematic form:

> First dialectical stage: the arcade changes from a place of splendor to a place of decay
> Second dialectical stage: the arcade changes from an unconscious experience to something consciously penetrated
> Not-yet-conscious knowledge of what has been. Structure of what-has-been at this stage. Knowledge of what has been as a becoming aware, one that has the structure of awakening.
> Not-yet-conscious knowledge on the part of the collective
> All insight to be grasped according to the schema of awakening. And shouldn't the 'not-yet-conscious knowledge' have the structure of dream?[83]

The awakening is not just related to the past; the new way of doing history awakens the collective, that is to say, what is now seen is what was 'the nearest' or the 'most obvious'.[84] The history of the twentieth century involved a contradictory blindness and insight into catastrophe as it unfolded; to remember is also to be aware of the absence of a person who disappeared a day before, a family who boarded a train with no apparent destination the previous week, a ghetto cleared of its inhabitants on a certain day of the month. The 'genuine historical object'[85] is the most ephemeral; Benjamin compares this ephemerality with that of the 'fixity of the philological object'; the two come together in theology via revelation, leading to the formula: 'The idea of a history of humanity as idea of the sacred text.'[86] Note that these formulae and fragments are gathered together during 1934–35, forming part of the Surrealist-Marxist boundary experience. Benjamin appends to his idea of humanity the notion that the 'history of humanity – as prophecy – has, at all times, been read out of the sacred text.'[87] There is a certain circularity at this point in the Arcades materials: the most ephemeral and the most fixed come together at the point of dissolution and remembrance, the conjoining being also a gathering guided in this instance by revelation and sacred text, which *is* history as prophecy. The dialectic being developed in *The Arcades Project* is here extremely close to Rosenzweig's notion of philosophy as 'the Sybilline Oracle which, by predicting the miracle, turns it into a "sign," the sign of divine providence.'[88] Rolf Tiedemann sees Benjamin's theological arguments as belonging very much to the earliest phases of *The Arcades Project*, being influenced in particular by Ernst Bloch:

> At the time of the first *Arcades* sketch, Benjamin was concerned less with a mediation of theological and political categories than with their identity. In this he was very much like Ernst Bloch in *Geist der Utopie* (Spirit of Utopia), which he explicitly took as his model. [. . .] At this stage, Benjamin conceived of the *Passagen-Werk* as a mystical reconstitution: dialectical thinking had the task of separating the future-laden, 'positive' element from the backward 'negative' element, after which 'a new partition had to be applied to this initially excluded, negative component so that, by a displacement of the angle of vision . . . , a positive element emerges in it too – something different from that previously signified. And so on, ad infinitum, until the entire past is brought into the present in a historical apocatastasis'.[89]

Tiedemann also argues for a visible movement away from the Blochian project, with the additional layers of research, or convolutes, added to *The Arcades Project* after discussions with Adorno and others. This reintroduction of intellectual 'phases' is in fact the removal of a key component of Benjamin's thought *yet again*; now the 'theological phase' is allowed further scope (into, or up to, the earliest sketches of *The Arcades Project*), only to be curtailed (once more) at a later date. The indeterminacy of the 'central categories'[90] of *The Arcades Project*, along with the palimpsest nature of its architectonics, both allows for and disallows the reintroduction of strict 'phases'. Tiedemann, while arguing for a lack of 'terminological consistency',[91] introduces into a footnote the centrality of the Messianic:

> Benjamin never brought himself to define these categories at length, yet they are the basis of all his thoughts on the *Passegen-Werk*, which he identified with the 'world of dialectical images' and for which dialectic at a standstill was to be 'the quintessence of the method' (P°,4). He apparently developed the theory of dialectical images mainly in conversations with Adorno. Although both concepts are absent from Benjamin's publications during his lifetime, the 'dialectical image' appears – with reference to its Benjaminian origins – in Adorno's *Habilitationsschrift* on Kierkegaard, which was published in 1933 . . . The difference [between Adorno's and Benjamin's notion of dialectical image] might be found in the connection Benjamin made between the dialectical image and elements of messianism – a connection to which Adorno, the more scrupulous Marxist, could not accede. One may try to put it this way: the phantasmagorias of the arcade or the collector as such are not dialectical images in Benjamin's sense; both the arcades and the collector become dialectical images only when the materialist *deciphers* them *as* phantasmagorias. *But in Benjamin's opinion, the key that allows the historical materialist to unlock the code remains connected to the discovery of a messianic force in history.*[92]

The Messianic force is dangerously unstable and negates the conventional materialist notion of progress, the latter perceived instead as 'endlessness', to use Rosenzweig's phrase.[93] Benjamin's historical materialism is not an attempt to uncover the constructedness of history, its fictional status as theorized by postmodernists, but is instead a destruction of the 'fictions' of a commodified or hyperreal world, an unleashing of forces which occur simultaneously with 'the birth of authentic historical time'.[94] Benjamin famously formulates the relation of his thinking as a whole to theology: 'My thinking is related to theology as blotting pad is related to ink. It is saturated with it. Were one to go by the blotter, however, nothing of what is written would remain.'[95] The analogy itself reads as curiously antiquated in the current realm of digital technology, which has moved far beyond the fountain pen, the ink bottle and blotting paper.[96] In fact the latter objects have almost been withdrawn from everyday use by so-called 'technical progress'.[97] Benjamin includes in convolute N a letter from Adorno, where he theorizes how the 'vitiation' of an object's use-value leads to a hollowing out and transformation of the object into a 'cipher' which in itself forms a vacuum that draws in meanings.[98] As 'ciphers' objects can be thought of as elements composing a secret-writing that in fact signifies far beyond the limited functioning of hyperreality, where an object or sign is completely commutable. As Adorno puts it: 'Subjectivity takes possession of them [the "ciphers"] insofar as it invests them with intentions of desire and fear. And insofar as defunct things stand in as images of subjective intentions, these latter present themselves as immemorial and eternal.'[99] Benjamin's thinking/writing is 'saturated' in or by theology; the antiquated image of the blotting-pad introduces a 'defunct' thing into the formulation and converts it into a 'cipher' – as cipher, all of Benjamin's writing is a secret-writing in its 'present instant' or 'Aktualität.'[100] Notions of progress are replaced by notions of 'danger': 'What is even more decisive is that the dialectician cannot look on history as anything other than a constellation of dangers which he is always, as he follows its development in his thought, on the point of averting.'[101] The secret-writing may merely be a constant re-emergence of the notion that 'Man is neither a phenomenon nor an effect, but a created being.'[102]

Rolf Tiedemann sketches the ways in which the early components of *The Arcades Project* were affected by Benjamin's discussions concerning Marxism, with Adorno and Horkheimer: 'In all probability, both . . . insisted in discussions of the submitted texts – mainly the 'Early Drafts' published with the *Passagen-Werk* – that it was impossible to speak sensibly about the nineteenth century without considering Marx's analysis of capital'.[103] In relation to the architectonics of the project, Tiedemann notes that:

> None of the old motifs were abandoned, but the building was given stronger foundations. Among the themes added were Haussmann's influence, the struggles on the barricades, railways, conspiracies, *compagnonnage*, social movements, the Stock Exchange, economic history, the Commune, the history of sects, and the Ecole Polytechnique; moreover, Benjamin began assembling excerpts on Marx, Fourier, and Saint-Simon.[104]

In some ways this additional material only serves to make *The Arcades Project* more labyrinthine, more mysterious a structure, moving from a reasonably light, to a darker world, with warning signs of the dystopian Fascist regime under way in Benjamin's time.[105] Convolute V, for example, on 'Conspiracies, *Compagnonnage*', charts the murky world of political allegiances in secret societies and other trade or guild organizations. The convolute gathers together a series of quotations which offer minute glimpses into this underground world, as with a small torch shone into a large cave. The convolute begins with a quotation from Daniel Halévy's *Décadence de la liberté*: 'Those *agents provocateurs* who, during the Second Empire, often mingled with rioters were known as "white smocks"',[106] and ends with reference to Filippo Buonarroti, from André Monglond's *Le Préromantisme français*: 'In 1828 *The Conspiracy of Equals*, by Buonarroti, appears in Brussels. "Very quickly, his book becomes the breviary of conspirators." Title: [*History of Babeuf's*] *Conspiracy for Equality*, 60,000 copies sold in only a few days.'[107] The interpenetration of revealed and concealed identities in convolute V leads to a destabilization of the notion of homogenous organized political groups: the very authenticity of individuals within these groups, and questions concerning their allegiances, becomes more and more problematic. Gathered together here we find, among others, agents provocateurs, secret police files and police spies, catacombs, barricades, insurgents, worker associations, proletarian conspiracies and conspirators, the Communist League, socialist utopians, secret societies, student societies, popular societies, agitators, impostors, conspiracy theories and theorists, propaganda, disguises, freemasonry, *compagnons* (trade guilds), secret reports, Jesuits, Assassins and Blanquists. Entire secret armies can be paraded on the Paris streets without being recognized:

> January 1870, after the murder of Victor Noir: Blanqui has the Blanquists, presented by Granger, file by before him, without letting the fact be known. 'He went out . . . and took up his post on the Champs-Elysées. It was there, as Granger had announced to him, that he would find, parading before him, the army of which he was the mysterious general. He recognized the squadron leaders, as they came into view, and, behind each of them, he saw the men grouped geometrically and marching in step, as though in regiments. It was all done according to plan. Blanqui held his review – strange spectacle – without arousing the slightest suspicion. Leaning against a tree, surrounded by the crowd of onlookers, the vigilant old man saw his comrades pass by, orderly amid the surging of the people, silent amid the steadily mounting uproar.[108]

Blanqui's permanent revolution is simultaneously invisible and made manifest: the spectacle of the Parisian streets not only holds historical traces and contains explosive forces, but encompasses parallel existences. Buck-Morss regards the key figure of the flâneur as undergoing metamorphosis in Benjamin's work, being indicative of how the interpenetrative spectacle of the Paris streets can be appropriated: 'Flâneur – sandwichman – journalist-in-uniform. The latter advertises the state, no longer the commodity.'[109] The flâneur who once took a turtle for a walk in the Paris Arcades, allowing the creature to set his pace, is transformed from a person of utmost leisure to one of trade;[110] the intellectual flâneur becomes likened to the reporter or photojournalist, and his most reductive and explicit form is that of the 'sandwichman': 'paid to advertise the attractions of mass culture'.[111] The transformation continues: 'While condemning the contents of modern culture . . . [Fascism] found in the dreaming collective created by consumer capitalism a ready-at-hand receptacle for its own political phantasmagoria. The psychic porosity of the *un*awakened masses absorbed the staged extravaganzas of mass meetings as readily as it did mass culture.'[112] The 'innervations of the collective' can take place in the service of myriad different revolutions.[113] One of these revolutions is not the liberation of mankind, but the encouragement of race-hatred and the debasement, if not ultimately the destruction, of life.

Messianic time

Theology keeps 'out of sight' in Benjamin's later work, but that is not to say that the Messianic is not still an ongoing concern.[114] The abandonment of simplistic causality (in historicism) and the recognition of a short-circuit between past and present, or history as the subject 'of a construction whose site is not homogeneous, empty time, but time filled full by now-time [*Jetztzeit*]',[115] is also to concede that the present thus understood is 'shot through with splinters of messianic time'.[116] This is quite different from the notion of the state, as Rosenzweig theorizes the process, attempting 'to give nations eternity within the confines of time'.[117] To live in the realm of Messianic hope, Rosenzweig argues, is to step outside the world of contradiction and the constant or continual resolution of contradiction which defines the activities of people within the secular state:

In order to keep unharmed the vision of the ultimate community it must deny itself the satisfaction the peoples of the world constantly enjoy in the functioning of their state. For the state is the ever changing guise under which time moves step by step toward eternity. So far as God's people is concerned, eternity has already come – even in the midst of time! For the nations of the world there is only the current era. But the state symbolizes the attempt to give nations eternity within the confines of time, an attempt which must of necessity be repeated again and again.[118]

The loosely veiled reference to Hegel reveals that the ultimate progression to Absolute Spirit is undermined by constant repetition: it is a 'false' eternity as such, an *eternal return to eternity*. The state 'must transform the constant alternation of their [the peoples'] life into preservation and renewal'.[119] The natural life-force of the peoples, one which is theorized here as being ultimately bound through time to motion, places 'an irreconcilable conflict between preservation and renewal'.[120] History, under these conditions, simply fades away 'in unobstructed alternation and transformation'.[121] But then the state intervenes to impose a structure (the law) which *dams* constant change: 'Now of a sudden there exists something which endures.'[122] Rosenzweig portrays the life-force as being temporarily swayed, temporarily constrained by the vision of the enduring state, until 'boisterous life' once again breaks the dam and overflows. However, this reveals the 'true face' of the state when, in an attempt to regain control of the situation, law is replaced by 'coercion'.[123] For Rosenzweig, coercion in the state is an aporia: coercion is presented not as a denial of law, but as a process that institutes new law, where the latter is eventually revealed to be, in actuality, 'old law'.[124] The state is thus portrayed as providing refuge to a fixed notion of itself, and thus rises above the constant flux and arbitrariness of the people: 'The living people allows the living moment to transpire naturally, as the multiplication of customs and the alternations of law show, while the state opposes to this its mighty assertion of the moment.'[125] The now-time of the state is the force of coercive law, creating a simulacrum of eternity. The problem here is how to distinguish that this is indeed a simulacrum. Rosenzweig opposes to the aporia here the 'eternal people' – indeed, this opposition is of necessity, as he could already be describing in the loosest terms such a theology. He argues that Jewish custom and law is unalterable (and thus eternal) and that this is a concluded concept; the state, however, grapples with its aporia in each moment, and shapes each moment 'according to its desires and capacities'.[126] In other words, the state constantly re-creates the simulacrum of eternity only to utilize this simulacrum for its own ends. 'Progress' here is not the outcome of a resolution, but the necessity to be always in the process of solving contradiction; Rosenzweig abandons abstract Hegelian terminology to name two key processes: war and revolution. Thus, he argues that the state 'would cease to be a state at the moment where neither the one nor the other were to take place – even if it be only in the form of a thought of war or revolution.'[127] Benjamin's dialectics at a standstill is designed to dislodge the process of revolution from its role in creating the simulacrum of progress which is also the inauthentic eternity. However, this can be interpreted in two main ways: either as the constitution of a new notion of the state, or as the construction of a new conceptuality which is also the interpenetration of the sacred and the profane. The 'threat' which hangs over dialectics at a standstill is that of 'becoming a tool of the ruling classes'.[128] Benjamin argues that 'Every age must strive anew to wrest tradition away from the conformism that is working to overpower it. The Messiah comes not only as the redeemer; he comes as the victor over the Antichrist.'[129] There are two parallel levels of understanding here working to subsume and cancel out each other: the 'eras' of the state are capable of being wrested away from the control of the ruling classes, but ultimately, the very notion of 'eras' *per se* belongs to the simulacrum of eternity. The latter is cancelled out by the arrival of the Messiah. As Tiedemann argues: 'As a "messianic cessation of the event," it would have devolved upon the dialectic at a standstill to bring home in the *Passagen-Werk* the very insight Benjamin had long assimilated when he began that project: "the profane . . . although not itself a category of this [messianic] Kingdom, is at least a category, and one of the most applicable, of its quietest approach." Benjamin's concept of profane illumination would remain "illuminated" in this way to the end; his materialist inspiration would be "inspired" in the same way, and his materialism would prove theological in the same way, despite all "recasting processes."'[130]

Notes

1 Benjamin, *The Arcades Project*, p. 115 [D8,1].
2 Peter Berkowitz, *Nietzsche: The Ethics of an Immoralist*, Cambridge, Massachusetts, and London, England: Harvard University Press, 1996, pp. 198–199.
3 Gilles Deleuze, *Nietzsche and Philosophy*, trans. Hugh Tomlinson, London: Athlone, 1983, p. 48.
4 Ibid., p. 70.
5 Benjamin, *The Arcades Project*, p. 111 [D5,7].
6 Ibid., p. 112 [D5a,6].
7 Benjamin to Max Horkheimer, 16 April 1938, letter 297 in *The Correspondence of Walter Benjamin: 1910–1940*, p. 556.
8 Gilloch, *Walter Benjamin: Critical Constellations*, p. 23.
9 Benjamin to Max Horkheimer, 16 April 1938, letter 297 in *The Correspondence of Walter Benjamin: 1910–1940*, p. 557.
10 Witte, *Walter Benjamin: An Intellectual Biography*, p. 186.
11 Benjamin, *The Arcades Project*, p. 119 [D10a,5].
12 Ibid.
13 Benjamin, 'On the Concept of History', *Selected Writings*, vol. iv: *1938–1940*, p. 389; 'Theses on the Philosophy of History', *Illuminations*, p. 245.
14 Benjamin, 'On the Concept of History', *Selected Writings*, vol. iv: *1938–1940*, p. 390; 'Theses on the Philosophy of History', *Illuminations*, p. 246.
15 Benjamin, 'On the Concept of History', *Selected Writings*, vol. iv: *1938–1940*, p. 392; 'Theses on the Philosophy of History', *Illuminations*, p. 249: 'Where we perceive a chain of events, he sees one single catastrophe which keeps piling wreckage upon wreckage and hurls it in front of his feet.'
16 Rolf Tiedemann, 'Historical Materialism or Political Messianism?' An Interpretation of the Theses "On the Concept of History", in Gary Smith, ed., *Benjamin: Philosophy, Aesthetics, History*, Chicago and London: University of Chicago Press, 1989, pp. 175–209.
17 Ibid., p. 176.
18 Ibid., p. 177.
19 Ibid., p. 184.
20 Ibid., p. 190.
21 Ibid., p. 202.
22 Ibid., p. 181.
23 Ibid., p. 184.
24 Ibid., pp. 185–186.
25 Ibid., p. 188.
26 Benjamin, 'World and Time', *Selected Writings*, vol. i: *1913–1926*, pp. 226–227.
27 Ibid., p. 226.
28 Ibid.
29 Pieper, *The End of Time: A Meditation on the Philosophy of History*, p. 23.
30 Benjamin, 'World and Time', *Selected Writings*, vol. i: *1913–1926*, p. 226.
31 Ibid.
32 Ibid., p. 227.
33 Rochlitz argues: 'Just as the philosophy of art was in Benjamin's early works linked to a theological critique of myth and violence, the philosophy of history is, in Benjamin's late works, placed under the sign of "theology".' *The Disenchantment of Art: The Philosophy of Walter Benjamin*, p. 231.

34 Benjamin, 'World and Time', *Selected Writings*, vol. i: *1913–1926*, n. 227.

35 These are 'According to the Theory of Duns Scotus', 'Outline for a *Habilitation* Thesis' and 'Language and Logic', Benjamin, *Selected Writings*, vol. i: *1913–1926*, pp. 228, 269–271 and 272–275.

36 Benjamin, 'Outline for a *Habilitation* Thesis', *Selected Writings*, vol. i: *1913–1926*, p. 270.

37 Ibid.

38 Witte, *Walter Benjamin: An Intellectual Biography*, p. 68.

39 George Steiner, 'Introduction' to Benjamin, *The Origin of German Tragic Drama*, p. 15.

40 Pensky, *Melancholy Dialectics: Walter Benjamin and the Play of Mourning*, p. 74.

41 Ibid., p. 75.

42 Benjamin, *The Origin of German Tragic Drama*, p. 45.

43 Beatrice Hanssen, *Walter Benjamin's Other History: Of Stones, Animals, Human Beings, and Angels*, Berkeley, Los Angeles and London: University of California Press, 1988, p. 25.

44 Ibid.

45 Ibid.

46 Benjamin, *The Origin of German Tragic Drama*, p. 45.

47 Ibid., pp. 45–46.

48 Rochlitz, *The Disenchantment of Art: The Philosophy of Walter Benjamin*, p. 40.

49 Ibid., p. 47; see Hanssen, *Walter Benjamin's Other History: Of Stones, Animals, Human Beings, and Angels*, p. 10.

50 Ibid., p. 3.

51 Gilloch, *Walter Benjamin: Critical Constellations*, p. 33.

52 Benjamin, *The Origin of German Tragic Drama*, p. 48.

53 Ibid., p. 53.

54 Rosenzweig, *The Star of Redemption*, p. 106.

55 Ibid.

56 Ibid., pp. 107–108.

57 Ibid.

58 Crudely put, the so-called 'progress' of the historical project, a weeding away and exposure of proven facts, undermines the very system of belief that was supposed to be strengthened by the project; progress, in this case, merely turns into *embarrassment*. See Rosenzweig, *The Star of Redemption*, p. 93.

59 Benjamin, 'Surrealism', *Selected Writings*, vol. ii: *1927–1934*, p. 208.

60 Hal Foster, *Compulsive Beauty*, Cambridge, Massachusetts, and London, England: The MIT Press, 1993, p. 20.

61 Benjamin, 'Surrealism', *Selected Writings*, vol. ii: *1927–1934*, p. 208.

62 Benjamin, *The Arcades Project*, p. 463 [N3,2].

63 Benjamin, 'Surrealism', *Selected Writings*, vol. ii: *1927–1934*, p. 209.

64 Ibid., p. 210.

65 Ibid.

66 Ibid., p. 211.

67 Ibid., p. 213.

68 Ibid., p. 215.

69 Benjamin, *The Arcades Project*, p. 458 [N1,9].

70 Ibid., p. 460 [N2,2]. In the original: 'Es kann als eines der methodischen Objekte dieser Arbeit angesehen werden, einen historischen Materialismus zu demonstrieren, der die Idee des Fortschritts in sich annihiliert hat. Gerade hier hat der historische Materialismus alle Ursache, Sich gegen die bürgerliche Denkgewohnheit scharf abzugrenzen. Sein Grundbegrift ist nicht Fortschritt sondern Aktualisierung.' *Gesammelte Schriften*, vol. vi, ed. Rolf Tiedemann, Frankfurt am Main: Suhrkamp Verlag, 1982, p. 574 [N2,2].

71 Ibid. [n2,5].

72 Benjamin, 'Short Shadows (II)', *Selected Writings*, vol. ii: *1927–1934*, p. 701.

73 Benjamin, 'Experience and Poverty', *Selected Writings*, vol. ii: *1927–1934*, p. 734.

74 'A generation that had gone to school in horse-drawn streetcars now stood in the open air, amid a landscape in which nothing was the same except the clouds and, at its center, in a force field of destructive torrents and explosions, the tiny, fragile human body.' Benjamin, 'Experience and Poverty', *Selected Writings*, vol. ii: *1927–1934*, p. 732.

75 Buck-Morss, *The Dialectics of Seeing: Walter Benjamin and The Arcades Project*, p. 33.

76 Ibid., pp. 33–34.

77 Benjamin, *The Arcades Project*, p. 458 [N1,9].

78 Ibid., p. 464 [N4,1].

79 Benjamin, 'On the Program of the Coming Philosophy', *Selected Writings*, vol. i: *1913–1926*, p. 102.

80 Benjamin, *The Arcades Project*, 'First Sketches, Paris Arcades ⟨I⟩', p. 827, ⟨A°,5⟩.

81 Ibid.

82 Ibid., p. 833, ⟨D°,4⟩.

83 Ibid., 'Materials for the Exposé of 1935', p. 907, No. 8.

84 Ibid.

85 Ibid., p. 917, No. 25.

86 Ibid.

87 Ibid., p. 918, No. 25.

88 Rosenzweig, *The Star of Redemption*, p. 108.

89 Rolf Tiedemann, 'Dialectics at a Standstill: Approaches to the *Passagen-Werk*', in Benjamin, *The Arcades Project*, pp. 929–945, at p. 936 [N1a,3].

90 Tiedemann, 'Dialectics at a Standstill: Approaches to the *Passagen-Werk*', p. 942.

91 Ibid.

92 Ibid., pp. 1,014–1,015; my emphases.

93 Rosenzweig, *The Star of Redemption*, p. 227.

94 Benjamin, *The Arcades Project*, p. 463 [N3,1].

95 Ibid., p. 471 [N7a,7].

96 Perhaps an analogy could be made with the temporary files that are created in various computer operating systems each time a 'save' is made of work in progress; these temporary files appear to be 'erased' when a file is closed, but in fact they still exist on the computer's storage media. Further, an archive of so-called 'deleted' files exists on magnetic storage media, and this material can be retrieved unless it is overwritten to such an extent that it becomes in effect illegible. We are not so far from the blotting-pad after all.

97 Benjamin, *The Arcades Project*, p. 466 [N5,2].

98 Ibid.

99 Ibid.

100 Ibid., p. 470 [N7,7].

101 Ibid., p. 470 [N7,2].

102 Benjamin, 'Types of History', *Selected Writings*, vol. I: *1913–1926*, p. 115.
103 Rolf Tiedemann, 'Dialectics at a Standstill: Approaches to the *Passagen-Werk*', p. 937.
104 Ibid.
105 Buck-Morss, *The Dialectics of Seeing: Walter Benjamin and The Arcades Project*, p. 304.
106 Benjamin, *The Arcades Project*, p. 603 [V1,1].
107 Ibid., p. 619 [V10,3].
108 Ibid., p. 617 [V9,1].
109 Benjamin, Notes to *Charles Baudelaire, Gesammelte Schriften*, vol. i, p. 1174, quoted in Buck-Morss, *The Dialectics of Seeing: Walter Benjamin and The Arcades Project*, p. 307.
110 Benjamin, 'On Some Motifs in Baudelaire', *Illuminations*, p. 193, footnote 6.
111 Buck-Morss, *The Dialectics of Seeing: Walter Benjamin and The Arcades Project*, pp. 306–307.
112 Ibid., p. 312; see also p. 470, footnote 89.
113 Benjamin, *The Arcades Project*, p. 652 [X1a,2].
114 Benjamin, 'On the Concept of History', *Selected Writings*, vol. iv: *1938–1940*, p. 389; 'Theses on The Philosophy of History', *Illuminations*, p. 245.
115 Benjamin, 'On the Concept of History', *Selected Writings*, vol. iv: *1938–1940*, p. 395.
116 Ibid., p. 397.
117 Rosenzweig, *The Star of Redemption*, p. 332.
118 Ibid.
119 Ibid.
120 Ibid.
121 Ibid., p. 333.
122 Ibid.
123 Ibid.
124 Ibid.
125 Ibid.
126 Ibid.
127 Ibid., pp. 333–334.
128 Benjamin, 'On the Concept of History', *Selected Writings*, vol. iv: *1938–1940*, p. 391.
129 Ibid.
130 Tiedemann, 'Dialectics at a Standstill: Approaches to the *Passagen-Werk*', p. 945.

5

Goethe and the *Georgekreis*

The struggle with an angel

Significant episodes in Benjamin's life – such as the withdrawal of his *Habilitation* thesis – have led many commentators to note how the role of 'outsider' dominated his fortunes and writings. One such episode concerns Benjamin's critique of the Stefan George circle, with the publication of his essay on Goethe's *Die Wahlverwandtschaften* (*Elective Affinities*).[1] In view of the fact that Benjamin was a follower of the charismatic leader of youth Gustav Wyneken, it may come as a surprise that he should so violently critique and reject an analogous set of followers of an even more influential charismatic leader, in other words, the circle of thinkers or disciples known as the *Georgekreis*. The self-confessed task of Stefan Anton George (1868–1933) was to transform Germany's cultural world-standing: he would offer no less than a new spiritual leadership.[2] While George's model for his role was drawn partly from Mallarmé's 'Mardi soirs', the connection with the Symbolists is not as straightforward as some critics have suggested.[3] George's new journal, *Blätter für die Kunst* (*Pages for Art*), established in 1892, was the primary vehicle for the writers and thinkers who would eventually be known as the *Georgekreis*, but in contrast with the Symbolists' work, in this work traits such as 'the mystic, oracular, and reflective tendencies of symbolism are absent.'[4] The fact was that George's ambitions stretched way beyond those of the Symbolists: 'The cult of artistic perfection, the erudition which evokes different periods of history or elements of the artistic national heritage, and which preceded the Symbolist movement in France, were what George saw as the foremost needs of the German poetic language.'[5] Artistic perfection manifested itself in the figure of the genius: the critic would bathe in the light of that genius, and would perhaps attempt to approach or come near to the brilliance. The obsession with perfection also indicates an awareness of – if not an obsession with ferreting out – the 'second rank'; for example, George's definition of 'form' is a highly divisive one in terms of aesthetic production: '[form is] . . . that deeply moving element in rhythm and sound, by which at all time the originators, the Masters, have distinguished themselves from the epigones, the artists of second rank.'[6] The biography of Goethe by Gundolf (Friedrich Gundelfinger, 1880–1931) was an exemplary piece of idolatry, an attempt to approach in George's terms a 'Master'; Benjamin had planned a far wider attack on the *Georgekreis* and this notion of singular self-present genius, not simply through individual (and at times indirect) essays, but via the establishment of his own doomed and unpublished journal, the *Angelus novus*. George's emphasis upon a national cultural and spiritual rebirth guided by a new poetic language is indicative of the importance of translation, another key focus of Benjamin's; the most infamous comparison to be made here is between George's and Benjamin's translations of Baudelaire's *Fleurs du mal*, where both base their resulting texts on wider artistic and philosophical programmes. George at times practises a mode of censorship: 'the translation is . . . pithy and apodictic, and, at times, syntactically overcomplicated . . . the translation – parts of which are indeed brilliantly skillful – often does violence to the images of the original in such a manner that sense is sacrificed for the sake of sound.'[7] George's translation was not something that had appeared in isolation: his official, published version, called *Blumen des Bösen*, had appeared in 1901 and reached its sixth edition by the time of Benjamin's translation in 1922.[8] Other translations of Baudelaire included those by: 'Paul Wiegler (1900), Camill Hoffmann and Stefan Zweig (1902), Graf Wolf von Kalckreuth (1907), Fritz Grundlach (1909) and Mario Spiro (1913).'[9] Benjamin acknowledges George, in 'The Task of the Translator', as having 'extended the boundaries of the German language'.[10] But the overall superiority of George's translation ultimately fails to convey the essentially urban modernity of Baudelaire's work:

> At the points where the modernity of Baudelaire's poems was most tangible, Benjamin gave a far more faithful rendering than George. This becomes clear when their versions of the poem 'Paysage' [Landscape] are compared. In a certain respect George transfigures and naturalizes the typical features of the modern age – technology,

social unrest, the city – and even allows them on occasion to disappear completely. The city, which is the focal point of the 'Tableaux parisiens' cycle, does not appear in George's translations, or is not recognizable as such. He archaizes 'Les tuyaux, les clochers, ces mâts de la cité' to become 'Den rauchfang den turm und die wolken weit' [The chimney, the tower and the clouds afar]: the city is simply avoided, so that its specific profile melts into the physiognomy of a rural centre in this German version. How differently this reads in Benjamin's 'Auf Turm und Schlot, die Masten von Paris' [To the tower and smokestack, the masts of Paris]![11]

The subsuming of the city in the 'physiognomy of a rural centre' is paralleled by George's censorship of bodily and erotic images found in Baudelaire's original.[12] The spiritual poet will appear in control of his aesthetic and his destiny.

Some time after George's private copies of his *Blumen des Bösen* had been circulated among friends and followers, he published in 1900 *Der Teppich des Lebens und die Lieder von Traum und Tod, mit einem Vorspiel* (*The Tapestry of Life and the Songs of Dream and Death, with a Prelude*). Unlike Benjamin's exploration of the relationships between the human subject and the absolute in 'On the Concept of History', in George's *Prelude* cycle there is a struggle with an angel which firmly places humanity in control. The 'naked angel' is first seen through a gate, approaching the poet as a messenger of the noble, beautiful life;[13] the angel asserts that the poet's desire to be at one with him, recovering the fires of youth and creativity, cannot be attained by force, but the poet counters that *unless he is blessed he will not release the angel*: 'Ich lasse nicht · du segnetest mich denn.' In effect, the poet has argued that 'I will not release you (from *my* power) unless you bless me.' As Goldsmith says:

> The sudden appearance, in the first poem, of the messenger from *das schöne leben* suggests that the concept is something the poet had known before and is not a new revelation; it is his own formulation. God, or a god, as the source of the angel's authority is not mentioned in the *Vorspiel*. The absence of any invocation before the messenger's appearance indicates the fact that he represents the poet's alter ego. The biblical image of Jacob wrestling with the angel is used to express the poet's possessing himself of spiritual power and enthusiasm for his mission: 'I will not let you go unless you bless me'.[14]

The image of this struggle with an angel is extremely powerful, resonating with its Biblical intertext; in Genesis 32: 28, Jacob, who prevails against the angel, is re-named: 'And he said, Thy name shall be called no more Jacob, but Israel: for as a prince hast thou power with God and with men, and hast prevailed.' The act of naming here is multiple: a subject is named as having 'power with God', but also an entire people are named; George is appropriating not just the Biblical image of the struggle with an angel but also God's power of naming (or bringing into being) found in Genesis.

For contemporary theorists, the approach to Genesis 32 usually occurs indirectly via Roland Barthes's rich structural analysis in his essay 'The Struggle with the Angel: Textual Analysis of Genesis 32: 22–32'.[15] Barthes, resisting interpretation, fills his essay with interpretive suggestions generated by the abrasion, friction or 'grating of readability' in turn generated by the contradictions, redundancies or indeterminacies of this passage in the Bible;[16] once again, the power of naming is stressed, this time in relation to the mark: 'And when he saw that he prevailed not against him, he touched the hollow of his thigh; and the hollow of Jacob's thigh was out of joint, as he wrestled with him.'[17] As Barthes puts it: 'By marking Jacob (Israel), God (or the Narrative) permits an anagogical development of meaning, creates the formal operational conditions of a new "language" . . . God is a logothete, a founder of a language, and Jacob is here a "morpheme" of the new language.'[18] Benjamin would clearly reject the simple or straightforward carrying-over of the Biblical power of naming into the modern poet's world as George asserts in his *Prelude*; Benjamin's stated project in his early essays was to recover sacred language, not to construct or transform it anew.[19] As Benjamin notes: 'before God no privileged value can be ascribed to the poetic life.'[20] In fact Benjamin's technical approach to interpretation, after his encounter with Surrealism, is closer to Barthes's notion of 'metonymic montage': 'the themes (Crossing, Struggle, Naming, Alimentary Rite) are *combined*, not "developed".'[21] George brings about the transfer of the power of naming via fiat, an act of will which combines self-promotion and assertion of power with that, through allusion, of an apparent official sanctioning: George takes or carries over into his poem the struggle as transaction and as sanctioning (yet again) Jacob and Israel. To put this another way, rather than *sanctus* we see in the *Prelude* the power of *sanctiō*, the inviolable decree being the poet's word. Benjamin, however, utilizes a technical approach, one that is in tune with the power of *combination*, to use Barthes's term; Benjamin thinks of this technical approach as generating a force-field where there is an interpenetration of historical and present time.[22] George takes over the power of ancient or historical text in a process of fulfilment, giving a 'sense of fulfilled expectation, of satisfactory closure'[23] from an authoritative and authorizing text, one that is more usually retroactively interpreted in this way in relation to the New Testament. Naming continues with the closure of this section of Genesis: Jacob asks the name of the one whom he has struggled with and receives a blessing. He realizes that he has struggled with God: 'And Jacob called the name of the place Peniel: for I have seen God face to face, and my life is preserved.'[24] Not only is the place named, but Jacob is now permanently marked; the marking is transformed into a law, whereby the people of Israel will not eat of the hollow of the thigh touched by God.[25] In between Jacob's naming of the place as event, and the transformation of the touch into law (which Barthes has great fun in interpreting as a wrestling 'dodge', 'ploy' or 'blow'[26]), the sun strikes Jacob's marked flesh. From a Kabbalistic perspective, Jacob has engaged with 'the full might of cosmic energy',[27] and this cosmic energy is now shining onto the sign of his success, his passing the test being something in his power only because it has been *granted to him*, not because he is a self-sufficient subject. The latter brings us to the core issue concerning George's poet, his autonomy, which generates his demand-as-assertion to the angel. From Benjamin's Biblical perspective, this autonomy would not represent progress or even a recovery and transformation of sacred power; instead, it is a sign of the Fall. As Bonhoeffer argues: 'This fact of the captivity of human thinking within itself, that is to say, of its inevitable autocracy and self-glorification as it is found in philosophy, can be interpreted theologically as the corruption of the mind, which is caused by the first fall.'[28] Even more damagingly, Bonhoeffer asserts that such an autonomous, self-centred subject 'does violence to reality'; in other words, the self-centred subject 'makes himself God.'[29]

The essay form

Benjamin chose the essay form to attack the intellectual and aesthetic pretensions of the *Georgekreis*, taking Gundolf's biography of Goethe, as noted, as his indirect highly critical route or rout. A fragment from 1917, Benjamin's 'Comments on Gundolf's *Goethe*', sets the stage for later published works. Benjamin succinctly sums up his feelings about Gundolf's *Goethe* in his oft-quoted final sentence: 'His book is a veritable falsification of knowledge.'[30] The object of this direct statement is two-fold: not just that Gundolf fails to have anything meaningful or profound to say about Goethe, but that his methodological approach as a system of biographical and conceptual interpretation is faulty. Gundolf constructs his biography, primarily and principally, from Goethe's works, thus stripping away all other contextual materials, creating a 'false exclusivity and monumentality'[31] of the works themselves in the portrayal of the subject as genius. In essence, this is history *'in a vacuum'*:[32]

> He goes on to create an apparently powerful but in reality entirely vacuous portrait of Goethe. For does Gundolf actually have an image of Goethe – that is, an idea – in mind? Anything but. He is simply attempting to use him to verify a methodological idea whose conceptual implications he is incapable of grasping. Furthermore, the actual verification is a cheat as well, since he does not apply his idea to Goethe. That would be impossible in the absence of concepts.[33]

The image of Goethe constructed out of the *Georgekreis*'s notion of the originary genius is an 'optical illusion'.[34] This leads to a deeper problem, for 'language itself' must somehow be capable of enabling the optical illusion *and* its contestation: Benjamin suggests that the 'semblance' is objectively real and that this leads 'From the philosophy of language as well as epistemology' into questions 'about the objective possibility of semblance and error'.[35] Benjamin returns, in his review of Max Kommerell's *Der Dichter als Führer in der deutschen Klassik: Klopstock, Herder, Goethe, Schiller, Jean Paul Hölderlin*, to the way in which the *Georgekreis* build a pre-programmed notion of history.[36] He argues that for them 'history is never a subject of study; it is only an object of their claims. They attempt to coopt the past as the seal of their origins or as paradigm.'[37] The concern here is the way in which the *Georgekreis* attempted to build a 'secret Germany' upon the basis of their readings of 'classicism' and as a reaction against modernity. In his review Benjamin parodies and wittily responds to not just Kommerell's book, but the entire worrying ideology of Teutonic recovery: 'Stefan George's theory of the hero should be counted among these occult disciplines. Here it throws light on the principal figures in the Weimar court of the Muses –

sometimes on a prophetic aspect, other times on a Pan-like aspect, still others on a satyr-like or centaur-like aspect. You become aware of just how at ease the classical writers were on horseback.'[38] In searching for the source of the 'dynamism' in these figures, Benjamin argues that Kommerell constructs an imaginary past, one guided more by vision than by reality in the production of 'an esoteric history of German literature'.[39] Benjamin goes on to argue that Kommerell is actually involved in 'a salvation history of the Germans',[40] one 'that risks collapsing at every moment into the apocryphal, the ineffable, and the meretricious'.[41] Inevitably, the Germans must be compared by the *Georgekreis* to the Greeks, being shown to be the heirs of the Greek mission: 'the birth of the hero'.[42] The *Georgekreis* are responsible for generating a 'mythological force field' into which bizarre and fictitious notions can be inserted.[43] Benjamin calls the writings of the *Georgekreis* 'the clanking of steel runes, the dangerous anachronism of sectarian language'.[44] However, the most extended attack upon the 'depraved categories of the George circle', as Benjamin puts it in *The Arcades Project*,[45] is Benjamin's essay on Goethe's *Elective Affinities*.

In a letter written to Scholem in 1921 we read Benjamin worrying about depression and the need to complete various urgent projects: 'I have to complete writing my critique of the *Elective Affinities*. This is just as important to me as an exemplary piece of criticism as it is as a prolegomena to certain purely philosophical treatises – what I have to say about Goethe is located somewhere between these two.'[46] Benjamin correctly assesses the essay's 'exemplary' status: like his work on the German mourning play, his essay on Goethe's novel continues to be studied today, either as an important piece of Goethe interpretation to be critically encountered in itself, or as one to be overcome. The essay opens with an assertion concerning methodology, that critique will be utilized rather than mere commentary alone: 'Critique seeks the truth content of a work of art; commentary, its material content.'[47] There is a dialectical relationship between critique and commentary, one that develops as the work of art becomes famous or exposed/consumed. What is meant here by 'truth content'? We can think of truth as the attained knowledge of the work, or the 'absolute validity' of the work:[48]

> The philosophical problem of the work of art's validity is linked to the idea of truth defined in theological terms. This idea is incarnated

in the true work of art, but it is not made conceptually explicit, for it is inaccessible to philosophy; only criticism, in deciphering the work of art, can help philosophy obtain it. Within the work of art itself, the subject matter and the truth content have to be distinguished. The artist approaches the subject matter through his technique and receives the truth content in the completed form of the work; the exegete addresses the subject matter in the form of commentary and the truth content in the form of criticism.[49]

The dialectic of the commentator and critic is enhanced with the simile of the development of the work 'as a burning funeral pyre'.[50] The commentator is regarded here as a chemist, the critic as an alchemist, where 'only the flame itself [of the work's burning or destruction] preserves an enigma: that of what is alive'.[51] The dialectic is developed even further when it comes to the thematic of marriage. Kant's definition of marriage from *The Metaphysics of Morals* is quoted, and dialectical thinking utilized to try and apprehend how beneath the seemingly antiquated notions of this bachelor-philosopher there is something 'infinitely deeper' than that found in 'sentimental ratiocination'.[52] Benjamin argues that the definition of marriage cannot be deduced from the facts of life-long fidelity; rather the 'content' of marriage is the 'seal' of this matter:

> Just as the form of the seal cannot be deduced from the material of the wax or from the purpose of the fastening or even from the signet (in which one finds concave what in the seal is convex) . . . so the content of the matter cannot be deduced by means of insight into its constitution or through an exploration of its intended use or even from a premonition of its content; rather, it is graspable only in the philosophical experience of its divine imprint, evident only to the blissful vision of the divine name.[53]

The reflections on marriage refer not just to Goethe's novel, but also to its enclosed novella; with the latter, Benjamin performs an allegorical reading which leads him to conclude that it is a portrayal of ideal marriage in the face of God.[54] There are two obvious problems for the contemporary reader here: first, Benjamin's critical approach is largely theological; second, the significance of the 'institutions' being explored may not be entirely clear (the heterogeneous but related institutions are marriage, law, Goethe and the *Georgekreis*). Criticism here examines the interference patterns generated between the dialectic of novel and novella, not to arrive at a sublation, but rather to generate a schema bringing into clear outline the alchemist's 'flame'. And what the alchemist sees is a little figure, a *sigillum*, an authentic sign or seal. The seal is not the wax, or the engraved object (a ring or a stamp), or the mark: it is the efficacious process in its entirety, which is also to say the result that goes *beyond* the process, interpreted here in theological terms.[55] This non-sublatory dialectics could be theorized as an early version of dialectics at a standstill, and it is no mere coincidence that Benjamin's later assertion in *The Arcades Project* that 'construction' presupposes 'destruction' is in fact an allusion to Heidegger.[56]

The institutions being critiqued in Benjamin's essay are also measured in relation to the absolute authority of God; as the artwork undergoes critical decomposition, or 'the processual disclosure of the truth content of the work of art'[57] the ultimate revelation of truth occurs with the work's destruction. In relation to contemporary literary-theoretical approaches to texts, this type of reading has virtually ceased to exist (or if it does, has ceased to have validity), except in the sense that a text's destruction may now occur via the worshipping of a particular theoretical or ideological configuration against which, and via which, all autonomous artworks are measured and re-shaped. Surprisingly, as the essay continues, and given the notion that Benjamin's theological approach is murky to contemporary secular readers, he asserts that 'The subject of *Elective Affinities* is not marriage.'[58] In fact the protagonists, rather than forming the basis of an ethical criticism of individual failings within marriage (or a critique of the institution itself), fall mute. They are 'Deaf to God and mute before the world'.[59] What does Benjamin mean by this muteness, this silence? He links language, once again, with naming, and suggests that Goethe's novel has few names (a bizarre but relevant observation), in fact and in interpretation (Benjamin strips away several names as being degrading, fake and arbitrary). The characters are culpably exposed to fate, their destinies foreshadowed by the all-pervasive death symbolism. In other words, superstition holds sway as religious tradition is abandoned.[60] Benjamin reaches this surprising conclusion about the subject of *Elective Affinities* only through the process of immanent critique, a process which can lead to a genuine renewal of critical discourse and ingrained habits of judgment: 'For the function of great criticism is not, as is often thought, to instruct by means of historical descriptions or to educate through comparisons, but to cognize by immersing itself in the object. Criticism must account for the truth of works, an exaction just as essential for literature as for philosophy.'[61] Benjamin claims that this exaction is precisely the one avoided by the *Georgekreis*; the central issue here is the melding of works and life, so that the former are subsumed by a (false) concept of the latter. Benjamin carefully works his way through what he sees as the erroneous process of melding, the first falsehood or *proton pseudos*, in part 2 of his essay, to arrive all the more convincingly at his refutation. He begins by arguing that the traditional notion, that the work sheds light on the life of an author, always already contains the first falsehood; it is also easier to begin with study of the author rather than the 'content and essence' of a work.[62] Benjamin asserts in contradistinction that works and deeds are 'non-derivable'.[63] In other words, while it is wrong to simply find the 'meaning' of life or work in the opposite, it is still essential to comprehend life and work via an immanent critique of both:

> What in this way escapes banal representation is not only insight into the value and mode of works but, equally, insight into the essence and life of their author. All knowledge of the essence of the author, according to his totality, his 'nature,' is from the outset rendered vain through neglect of the interpretation of the work. For if this, too, is unable to render a complete and final intuition of the essence, which for various reasons is indeed always unthinkable, then, when the work is disregarded, the essence remains utterly unfathomable. But even insight into the life of the creative artist is inaccessible to the traditional biographical method.[64]

The question becomes one of 'origin' and the false certainties involved in anchoring or fixing meaning according to the originary chiasmus, where the meaning of a life is located in the work, and the meaning of the work is located in the life. Benjamin suggests that the place of biographical information is realizable or utilizable only 'where knowledge of the fathomlessness of the origin excludes each of his works, delimited according to their value and their content, from the ultimate meaning of his life.'[65] The illusion of the originary chiasmus is revealed through a thorough knowledge of the works: the author 'function'[66] can then be understood as being composed through fragmentary, incomplete knowledge as such. Gundolf's *Goethe* asserts the unified, mythic status of the life: 'The canonical form of mythic life is precisely that of the hero.'[67]

The superhuman hero undertakes the task: in fact the latter is the distinguishing feature of the superhuman contra the human. With the *Georgekreis* the poet is also (inappropriately) assigned the task, a divine mandate. Again, Benjamin theologically refutes this: 'From God, however, man receives not tasks but only exactions, and therefore before God no privileged value can be ascribed to the poetic life.'[68] Benjamin re-works this point in relation to rank: 'Since the mission of poetry seems, for the George circle, to stem directly from God, not only does this mission grant to the poet an inviolable though merely relative rank among his people, but, on the contrary, it grants to him a thoroughly problematic supremacy simply as a human being and hence grants problematic supremacy to his life before God, to whom, as a superman, he appears to be equal.'[69] The 'true' literary work is one liberated from the notion of the task: it is an upspring or up-welling from within the subject.[70]

Benjamin distinguishes between poet and saint; the latter stands in a relationship with God, the former in a relationship with (human) community. The poet and the saint, as representatives of 'types', determine the relationship schema. The *Georgekreis* thus falsify the definitions of work and poet, and at the point in which they are attempting to build a new community, they divorce the subject from his or her community and mistake the poet for the saint. Put more simply, the *Georgekreis* are being charged with a misunderstanding of corporate identity, where the subject 'both wills, decides, and *acts* as an individual, responsible person at the same time as living in basic modes of corporate *being*.'[71] The *Georgekreis* are misappropriating what it means to define being, as being-in-a-community through the sacred, where the poet now functions as Creator, the 'second error':

> a second, no less important error adheres confusingly and fatally to the heroizing attitude of the members of the George circle, as they supply the basis for Gundolf's book. Even if the title of 'creator' certainly does not belong to the poet, it has already devolved upon him in that spirit which does not perceive the metaphorical note in it – namely, the reminder of the true Creator. And indeed the artist is less the primal ground or creator than the origin or form giver [*Bildner*], and certainly his work is not at any price his creature but rather his form [*Gebilde*]. To be sure, the form, too, and not only the creature, has life. But the basis of the decisive difference

between the two is this: only the life of the creature, never that of
the formed structure [*des Gebildeten*], partakes, unreservedly, of the
intention of redemption.[72]

The poet organizes the work, and the work has organization; both
the poet and the work have life, autonomous life (including death,
and an afterlife), but only the poet is a creature redeemed in Christ.
It is Christ who 'does for human beings what they cannot do themselves',[73] and thus the work itself cannot be given this role by the
human subject. For Benjamin, poet and work are ambiguous and
labyrinthine: anyone who claims otherwise is merely conjuring up
a fantasy, or following dogma. The poet, regarded as a hybrid form
of 'hero and creator', is the nadir of misunderstanding. Benjamin's
attack upon Gundolf's *Goethe* appears to be remarkably contemporary, but it is important to attend closely to his text to continue with
his theological immanent critique. Gundolf asserts that Goethe's
greatest work is his life, which leads to a blurring of life and works:
'This position achieves two things . . . : it eliminates every moral
concept from the horizon, and, at the same time, by attributing to
the hero-as-creator the form which goes to him as victor, it achieves
the level of blasphemous profundity.'[74] In other words (simplify-
ing again), Goethe is a masterful self-creation of Goethe. Goethe's
greatest work is himself, and this work is produced as self-sufficient
creator-creation. Benjamin is not arguing that a correctly isolated
biography and work would lead to correct interpretation; rather,
that the truth content of the life of the subject, even given the
biographical, material, archive, is in itself not *open* to interpretation
or decoding. The totality of the subject is infinite.[75] Such a theological notion of the subject is at odds with contemporary notions of
the constructed 'subject' or 'assemblage', where life-as-work is
voided or evaded in the argument that the life is a work of pure
fiction or fictionalizing.[76] In other words, while contemporary critics
would tend to agree with Gundolf that the life is a construct, or
work, they would disagree that this was an intentionally manufac-
tured product that stood above all others. Further, while contemporary critics would tend to agree with Benjamin that it is a mistake
to locate the meaning of the work in the life, and the meaning of
the life in the work, the theological 'blasphemy' of regarding the
poet as creator is no longer, generally, a relevant or even meaningful notion.

Goethe as critical constellation

Benjamin's *Elective Affinities* essay is often read either purely as a major piece of Goethe criticism, or as an example of his method of immanent critique; we need to retain the concept of the critical constellation, that is, the method of the montage form, to comprehend why Goethe is central in Benjamin's criticism of the *Georgekreis*. Taking *The Arcades Project* as the overall model, it becomes clear that it is not just a case of *why* Goethe is constantly being quoted, referred to, alluded to, consigned to footnotes, and so on in Benjamin's work; it is also a case of where Goethe is used in relation to what other juxtapositions and textual and/or conceptual organizations. We can see the importance of the latter in an unpublished fragment from 1932, 'On Ships, Mine Shafts, and Crucifixes in Bottles'. In this three-sentence fragment, Benjamin quotes Franz Glück on Adolf Loos: ' "While reading Goethe's rebuke to philistines and many other art lovers who like to touch copper engravings and reliefs, the idea came to him that anything that can be touched cannot be a work of art, and anything that is a work of art should be placed out of reach." '[77] The problematic definition of the artwork here is later developed by Benjamin with the suggestion that it is technological and societal change that leads to a radically different definition of the work of art, stripped of its aura. This fragment, in other words, can be read as an incredibly dense earlier version of 'The Work of Art in the Age of its Technological Reproducibility'. But what of the form of the fragment itself? The fragment consists of a list, a quotation and a question; the list in its entirety is: 'On ships, mine shafts, and crucifixes in bottles, as well as panopticons', and the question that comes after the quotation: 'Does this mean that these objects in bottles are works of art *because* they have been placed out of reach?'[78] Benjamin draws together here outmoded objects and the architecture of surveillance that converts human subjects into isolated objects; in both cases, the objects are physically out of reach, but clearly are not works of art. The form of the fragment functions via the shock-tactics of montage: Benjamin juxtaposes Goethe's rebuke with reflections upon modernist architecture, art, imprisonment and surveillance. The montage is a powerful reminder of what is at stake for the subject with the necessary possibility of the aesthetic being forced into the service of the repressive state. How far is this use of dialectics at a standstill, in the fragments and major essays on Goethe, mere coincidence? Ernst

Bloch, in volume 3 of *The Principle of Hope*, finds parallels between the Hegelian dialectic and Goethe's *Faust*:

> Faust's dialectical world-tour, with its continual corrections, has only one parallel: Hegel's 'Phenomenology of Mind'. Faust changes with his world, the world changes with its Faust, a test and an essentiation in ever new layers until ego and Other could harmonize purely. In Hegel this is the ascending mutual determination of subject by object, of object by subject until the subject is no longer tainted with the object as with something alien.
> [. . .]
> . . . the dynamic of Faust is closest to that in Hegel's 'Phenomenology of Mind'. The movement of the restless consciousness through the spacious gallery of the world, the inadequate as Becoming the event: this stormy *history of work and formation* between subject and object connects Faust with the Phenomenology.[79]

The major difference between Benjamin's and Bloch's notions of dialectics *at work in Goethe* is that of competing interpretations of entelechy; Bloch's reading of *Faust* is tied up with a systematic *recovery* of progressive utopian thought, whereas Benjamin's reading involves another project entirely. In his 'Goethe' essay Benjamin looks at Goethe's relationship with Kant:

> While . . . [Goethe] could not find any point of contact with Kant's main critical oeuvre – the *Critique of Pure Reason* and the *Critique of Practical Reason* (i.e., ethics) – he held the *Critique of Judgment* in the greatest possible esteem. For in that work Kant repudiates the teleological explanation of nature which had been one of the chief supports of enlightened philosophy and of deism. [. . .] Kant's definition of the organic as a purposiveness whose intent lay inside and not outside the purposive being was in harmony with Goethe's own concepts. The unity of the beautiful – natural beauty included – is always independent of purpose. In this, Goethe and Kant are of one mind.[80]

Tied in with Benjamin's reading of *Faust*, the process is seen in fact not as a simple reversal or inversion as such of the teleological, but is in fact a *folding*. In relation to *Faust* Benjamin argues that Goethe:

> creates at the end of his life, in the setting of an ideal Baroque Germany, a screen on which he projects a magnified image of the world of the statesman in all its ramifications, and at the same time shows all its defects intensified to the point of grotesqueness.

Mercantilism, Antiquity, and mystical scientific experiments: the perfection of the state through money, of art through Antiquity, of nature through experiment. These provide the signature of the German Baroque which Goethe here invokes.[81]

The folding in question is that of the Enlightenment into the Baroque. *Faust* is of significance for Benjamin not just because of its pushing at the boundaries of possible existence,[82] but also because of its presentation of the realm of human experience as a series of dialectical images. That is to say, Enlightenment components do not sublate all other experiences; rather, they are aspects of the 'boundlessness' of what Benjamin calls 'the journey of the soul'.[83] Benjamin's folding here is part of a proposal whereby Kant's notion of experience is widened to such an extent that the Kantian project itself is called into question, and the supremacy of the sciences is deconstructed in favour of a philosophy of language. This is not a 'linguistic turn' as commonly understood in its contemporary post-structuralist sense; rather it is a strategic move in 'The Program of the Coming Philosophy'. Benjamin's folding of the Enlightenment into the Baroque is in itself mimetic of Baroque aesthetics and thought, as sketched by Deleuze in his *The Fold: Leibniz and the Baroque*. It is worth picking up on one key concept, that of the 'ideal fold' or '*Zweifalt*', 'a fold that differentiates and is differentiated'[84]: 'When Heidegger calls upon the *Zweifalt* to be the differentiator of difference, he means above all that differentiation does not refer to a pregiven undifferentiated, but to a Difference that endlessly unfolds and folds over from each of its two sides, and that unfolds the one only while refolding the other, in a coextensive unveiling and veiling of Being, of presence and of withdrawal of being.'[85] The architectonics of the monad is sometimes thought of as a purely isolated, immanent space; according to Deleuze, through the process of the fold, the 'totality' of monadic time and space is shown to be simply working through a different circuit, the 'two vectors' and the 'coexistence' of the *Zweifalt*.[86]

Benjamin proposes his own *Zweifalt*: that of the combination of the otherwise 'double task' of the creation of 'a new concept of knowledge and a new conception of the world'.[87] This rather grand project is in other words the Baroque folded back upon or into Kant:

Kant's epistemology does not open up the realm of metaphysics because it contains within itself primitive elements of an unpro-

ductive metaphysics, which excludes all others. In [Kant's] epistemology every metaphysical element is the germ of a disease that
expresses itself in the separation of knowledge from the realm of
experience in its full freedom and depth. The development of philosophy is to be expected because each annihilation of these metaphysical elements in an epistemology simultaneously refers it to a
deeper, more metaphysically fulfilled experience.[88]

Reading Benjamin's essay on Goethe's *Elective Affinities*, Howard
Caygill puts this another way, relating the grand project to the task
of critique: 'The absolute is *folded* into experience in complex and
often inconspicuous ways, which it becomes the task of critique not
at the outset to judge, but first to delineate and map.'[89] In convolute
N of *The Arcades Project*, 'On the Theory of Knowledge, Theory of
Progress', there is a related reference to Goethe's *Faust*. The
reference itself is in a section which re-writes Benjamin's modest
proposal 'for the cultural-historical dialectic' where instead of split-
ting any particular epoch into positive and negative elements, that
is, progressive and obsolete elements, he argues that the so-called
negative grounds that charge or fuel the dialectic need to be re-
divided or subdivided by a 'new partition' which will give a new perception of the 'abortive, retrograde, and obsolescent'.[90] The latter is
an infinite process that brings the past into the present (the compli-
cation of a bound 'infinity' being best explored via Fichte).[91] The
Faust reference re-writes this notion with 'the indestructibility of the
highest *life* in all things'.[92] Benjamin asks: 'Consider though: Isn't it
an affront to Goethe to make a film of *Faust*, and isn't there a world
of difference between the poem *Faust* and the film *Faust*? Yes, certainly. But again, isn't there a whole world of difference between a
bad film of *Faust* and a good one? What matter are never the 'great'
but only the dialectical contrasts, which often seem indistinguish-
able from nuances. It is nonetheless from them that life is always
born anew.'[93] This quotation completes a convolute cluster or triad
which begins with the Baroque folding of the past into the present,
and ends with Benjamin pondering the differences not only between
productions of *Faust*, but between the technological forms of those
productions. Production here is a *Zweifalt*, which enables the critic
to reflect not just on the 'original' work *per se*, but on the decomposition and renewal of the work in the process of dialectics at a
standstill.

Death's detour

Howard Caygill notes how Benjamin approaches the process of critique not with the Kantian certainty of 'a philosophically secured concept of truth and value' which is then applied in the act of critical judgment, 'but rather philosophy itself is risked in the critical encounter.'[94] Philosophy is risked as such by holding it open to transformation via the encounter:

> In the case of Romanticism, a movement which emerged as a response to the limitations of Kant's concept of critique, it is first subjected to critique in Kantian terms, but then transforms those terms in the critical encounter. The object of critique reflects the limitations of the given doctrine of criticism back upon the critic, who then approaches the object anew. In this way Benjamin repeats the Hegelian critique of the finite character of Kantian critique – its narrow notion of experience that banished the absolute from thought – but without the collateral of a progressive philosophy of history. The absolute is folded into experience . . .[95]

In part 3 of the *Elective Affinities* essay, the object of critique is the work of art, which is regarded as a 'construction' having an affinity with 'the ideal of the problem' of philosophy: the 'nonexistent question seeking the unity of philosophy'.[96] Philosophy is the guide for critique, yet, as noted, will be transformed in the process. The character of Ottilie in Goethe's novel comes into focus for Benjamin, consummated in her death, but of significance more for the intersection of death and/in life.[97] To follow Ottilie's character is to follow the 'nonexistent' question, and here it is shown to be a complex schema where the 'immanence of death in life cannot be symbolically expressed, but can only be shown; Ottolie does not *symbolise* death in life, but the shape of her character shows that it is being undergone: the absolute as death is not abstract and removed but is present and leaves its mark on finite existence.'[98] The 'absolute folded into experience' is a schema which, again, jars not only with the quarantine of questions concerning the absolute but also with the entire problematic of contemporary notions of death. How is death thought today, and how does the quarantine or bracketing of issues central to Benjamin's essay impact upon readings of the essay?

In *The Spirit of Utopia*, Bloch notes how death can create legal inconveniences: while modern society prefers a cause of death, so that it can rationalize it, even rational death is perceived as something that wastes the time of the living, especially as legal inconveniences also cost money to process and pass over. Death is not only an inconvenience for modern society, but it is an inconvenience for poststructuralism and/or postmodernism. In *Symbolic Exchange and Death*, Jean Baudrillard argues that within modern society the dead 'cease to exist', that the dead 'are thrown out of the group's symbolic circulation . . . [and are exiled] further and further away from the group of the living.'[99] Thus:

> In the domestic intimacy of the cemetery, the first grouping [of the dead] remains in the heart of the village or town, becoming the first ghetto, prefiguring every future ghetto, but are thrown further and further from the centre towards the periphery, finally having nowhere to go at all, as in the new town or the contemporary metropolis, where there are no longer any provisions for the dead, either in mental or physical space. Even madmen, delinquents and misfits can find a welcome in the new towns . . . Only the death-function cannot be programmed and localised. Strictly speaking, we no longer know what to do with them, since, today, *it is not normal to be dead*, and this is new. To be dead is an unthinkable anomaly; nothing else is as offensive as this. Death is a delinquency, and an incurable deviancy. The dead are no longer inflicted on any place or space-time, they can find no resting place; they are thrown into a radical utopia. They are no longer even packed in and shut up, but obliterated.[100]

Baudrillard suggests that the inconvenient dead have gone from being ghettoized to being obliterated; from this perspective, death as being equals a 'radical utopia'. If Baudrillard's critique of poststructuralism is correct, in particular his notion of the hyperreal, but also the transition from the structuring principles of the symbolic to those of the semiotic, images of death in contemporary society need to be made self-sustaining, and world-forming; more crudely put, death needs to be commodified, so that it can be traded. Is death a structuring principle which can be accounted for via Benjamin's fold? If death is radically utopian, it is outside modern society; if death is outside the structure, then death is material *and* metaphysical. To put this another way: death is extrastructural. As Manfred Frank notes in his discussion concerning centred and de-centred structures: 'Should meaning . . . which, like a principle, or . . . like a woven pattern, [that] organizes the texture of structure/text indeed be *central*, then it would be impossible to think it, i.e., to distinguish it. It would thus not participate in the distinctions of structure itself: as extrastructural place it would be a nonplace, an *ou topos*, a utopia.'[101] From a poststructuralist perspective, there are a number of problems here, and a number of critical arguments, one of which is the now familiar Derridean accusation of a metaphysics of presence. Frank summarizes:

> Derrida, following Heidegger, emphasizes that the succession of interpretations of Being was always accomplished within the framework of a rule, never blindly or by chance. He emphasizes further that the chain of placeholders of the highest principle . . . developed within a continuity. They all have in common that they comprehend the meaning of Being as *presence* . . . as either a sensual or conceptual being-accessible, being-graspable, or being-attainable of the principle.[102]

Death as an inconvenience, an interruption, and as a reminder, is also thus extrastructural and locates being via presence. The familiar Derridean reading implies that this metaphysical notion of death also needs deconstructing. Is the deconstruction, or desire for deconstruction, of symbolic, material and metaphysical death merely another version of death's 'obliteration', to use Baudrillard's phrase? If death as being is a reminder, then its obliteration is disastrous, if not catastrophic: to obliterate the living is a crime; the extra horror arises when the dead, and all their traces, are also obliterated.

In *Symbolic Exchange and Death*, Jean Baudrillard argues that while the possibility of the revolutionary change of the system known as postmodernism has passed, the irruption of the symbolic within the world of the semiotic has potential, radical consequences. Baudrillard argues that the system of postmodernism feeds on the energy of resistance or contradiction, for a number of reasons, one of which is that the system constructs the real and that to fight back as such, either at the level of philosophical critique or at some other more physical level, is to engage in the constructed real's terms and conditions, one of which is that there is no genuine engagement or critique that cannot be recycled.[103] The recycling is not a dialectical process. Critique is constructed, according to Baudrillard, by engaging not with signs or 'energy' but with the symbolic, for example the gift.[104] As he argues: 'We must therefore displace everything into

the sphere of the symbolic, where challenge, reversal and overbid-
ding are the law'.[105] Even though there is an argument here for an
extension of the boundaries of death as being within postmodernity,
so that it is a material *and* metaphysical event, it is still not clear how
death can be considered as *not* being a sign in the poststructuralist
sense. One of the problems of the extension of the boundaries of
death is that it can go too far into the realm of speculative philosophy and become disengaged from the ownmost human experience.
Both Kierkegaard and Heidegger, in different ways, argue this.
Simon Critchley rejects the existential and phenomenological analyses of death: 'In phenomenological terms, death is not the object or
meaningful fulfilment of an intentional act . . . Death is ungraspable
and exceeds both intentionality and the correlative structures of phenomenology, whether the latter is understood in its Hegelian,
Husserlian or Heideggerian senses.'[106] From a poststructuralist perspective, Critchley is undoubtedly right. But just as death from a
poststructuralist perspective is ungraspable, there is a sense that this
can also be transformed into a critique of poststructuralism's inade-
quacies. For example, Hegel argues in *The Phenomenology of Spirit* that
death as pure being, while immediate in the course of nature, and
not an individual's conscious decision, *is* recuperated by the family,
retrieved from nature and *made* a retrospectively rational decision.[107]
This is so for the ethical community, and if the ethical community
is itself missing, then this does not mean that such a recuperation of
death is negated for all time; there is no way in which Critchley's
position could be 'transformed' via rational (or irrational) argument
into Hegel's position: they are fundamentally opposed. But Baudrillard argues that the impossible transformation of the former position into the latter position is in itself an ethical necessity. This still
has not answered the question concerning how death can be considered as not being a sign in the structuralist and poststructuralist
sense. For this a brief detour via Heidegger's work is productive,
where death is conceived of as 'an existential phenomenon' which
'must be understood as a possibility – as the fundamental and constitutive possibility of Dasein's end.'[108]

As George Hunsinger points out, for Heidegger 'The possibility
of my death is . . . ownmost because it is non-relational.'[109] The
notion of death as non-relational is the point at which death can be
theorized as symbolic. Heidegger calls the same retrospective recuperation of death in Hegel, in the section on 'The Ethical Order', 'tar-

rying alongside', 'in a mode of respectful solicitude'.[110] But this description causes problems, because it is, crudely speaking, a relational notion of the experience of death. In Heidegger's words, 'Death does indeed reveal itself as a loss, but a loss such as is experienced by those who remain. In suffering this loss . . . we have no way of access to the loss-of-Being as such which the dying man "suffers". The dying of Others is not something which we experience in a genuine sense; at most we are always just "there alongside".'[111] Heidegger objects that this latter process works by substitution; in this sense it also functions like a sign, and indeed Heidegger relates the whole issue to that of representation. Death as the 'possibility-of-Being', to use Heidegger's phrase, as non-relational and thus non-substitutable, attacks the very foundations of representation. Death must be an existential certainty for Heidegger. In other words, it must be apodictic.[112] This apodictic certainty is found in, or secured via, anxiety, where anxiety 'is the "ground" or "basic" state-of-mind [*Grundbefindlichkeit*] which in each case discloses that Dasein is grounded in death.'[113] For Heidegger, everyday Dasein is an inauthentic state, whereby death is consigned to 'inconspicuousness'.[114] Death is an endless deferral because it always occurs to someone else, outside the immediate frame of reference. News of an other person's death is inconvenient only insofar as it reminds one that other people die: its impact is purely alongside the self. Heidegger regards the recovery of genuine 'anxiety' as a rescuing of authentic individuality from the faceless masses; this is quite different from the recovery of the individual's death via the ethical community. Heidegger appears to be negating Kierkegaard's notion of death as an interruption, and Hegel's notion that death can have a reinscribed communal meaning. However, in the context of *The Phenomenology of Spirit* as a whole, death is neither an interruption or reinscribed meaning; it is also not an inconvenience, except in the sense in which it is theorized via various modes of false consciousness. Rather, death is simply effaced in favour of the destiny of the *Phenomenology*. This effacement is one of the starting points of Rosenzweig's *Star of Redemption*, where the terrorized cry of humanity cannot be passed over; it is a key textual moment for those looking for an alternative philosophy to that of Hegel's, and it is indirectly related to Baudrillard's more recent call for the irruption of the symbolic within the semiotic. In *The Star of Redemption* the recognition of the individual's fear of death relates to the notion that the system or code of postmodernity or poststructuralism fears first the symbolic, and second the efficacy of death as projected against the system or code. Rosenzweig inserts fear of death back into an otherwise unstoppable dialectic, whereas Baudrillard argues that a mechanism which is supposed to be devoid of emotion can be unbalanced by the fear of death.

Is death the crowning vision of the *Elective Affinities* essay? Compositionally, Benjamin's essay is triadic, where the central part of the essay is the attack upon the *Georgekreis* rather than the section on the fold, or death folded into life, the absolute folded into the finite. However, the detour on death, which brings the argument back to Rosenzweig, parallels this relocation or analogy foregrounded through the awareness of compositional factors in Benjamin's work. As Missac worries, however, in comparing the dialectical compositions of the *Elective Affinities* essay and *The Star of Redemption*: 'Whereas the part devoted to Revelation in *Star of Redemption* constitutes the highpoint of the book, its keystone or the dome that crowns it, in the essay on *Elective Affinities*, that place is occupied by the "polemical core" directed against Gundolf, a performance the author considered essential to his project but one that scarcely deserved to occupy such a place of honor.'[115] On reading Benjamin's essay via his own process of immanent critique, the attack or meditation upon institutions emerges as of far greater importance than Missac acknowledges; the 'polemic' is indeed war, or, a total risk, *a struggle to death*, with the meaning of the institutions themselves undergoing analysis.

Notes

1 Brodersen, *Walter Benjamin: A Biography*, p. 124.
2 Ulrich K. Goldsmith, *Stefan George*, London and New York: Columbia University Press, 1970, pp. 4–5.
3 I am indebted to Goldsmith for this reading; ibid., pp. 8–9.
4 Ibid., p. 10.
5 Ibid.
6 Ibid.
7 Ibid., p. 11.
8 Brodersen, *Walter Benjamin: A Biography*, p. 110.
9 Ibid.
10 Benjamin, 'The Task of the Translator', *Illuminations*, p. 80.
11 Brodersen, *Walter Benjamin: A Biography*, pp. 111–112.
12 Goldsmith, *Stefan George*, p. 11.
13 Ibid., p. 31.
14 Ibid.

15 Roland Barthes, 'The Struggle with the Angel: Textual Analysis of Genesis 32: 22–32', *Roland Barthes: Image, Music, Text*, trans. Stephen Heath, London: Fontana Press, 1977, pp. 125–141.
16 Ibid., p. 129, p. 131.
17 Genesis 32: 25.
18 Barthes, 'The Struggle with the Angel: Textual Analysis of Genesis 32: 22–32', *Roland Barthes: Image, Music, Text*, p. 135.
19 See Britt's discussion in chapter 3 of his *Walter Benjamin and the Bible*.
20 Benjamin, 'Goethe's Elective Affinities', *Selected Writings*, vol. i: *1913–1926*, p. 323.
21 Barthes, 'The Struggle with the Angel: Textual Analysis of Genesis 32: 22–32', *Roland Barthes: Image, Music, Text*, p. 140.
22 Benjamin, *The Arcades Project*, p. 470 [N7a,1].
23 Frank Kermode, *The Genesis of Secrecy: On the Interpretation of Narrative*, Cambridge, Massachusetts, and London, England: Harvard University Press, 1979, p. 65.
24 Genesis 32: 30.
25 Genesis 32: 32.
26 Barthes, 'The Struggle with the Angel: Textual Analysis of Genesis 32: 22–32', *Roland Barthes: Image, Music, Text*, p. 132.
27 Carlos Suarès, *The Cipher of Genesis: The Original Code of the Qabala as Applied to the Scriptures*, Boulder and London: Shambhala, 1978, p. 180.
28 Quoted in Clifford J. Green, *Bonhoeffer: A Theology of Sociality* (revised edition), Grand Rapids, Michigan, and Cambridge, UK: William B. Eerdmans, 1999, p. 117; italic removed.
29 Ibid.; italic removed.
30 Benjamin, 'Comments on Gundolf's *Goethe*', *Selected Writings*, vol. i: *1913–1926*, p. 99.
31 Ibid., p. 98.
32 Ibid.
33 Ibid.
34 Ibid.
35 Ibid., p. 99.
36 Benjamin, 'Against a Masterpiece', *Selected Writings*, vol. ii: *1927–1934*, pp. 378–385.
37 Ibid., p. 381.
38 Ibid., p. 379.
39 Ibid.
40 Ibid.
41 Ibid., p. 380.
42 Ibid.
43 Ibid.
44 Ibid.
45 Benjamin, *The Arcades Project*, p. 300 [J39a,4].
46 Benjamin to Gerhard Scholem, 8 November 1921, letter 107 in *The Correspondence of Walter Benjamin: 1910–1940*, pp. 193–194.
47 Benjamin, 'Goethe's Elective Affinities', *Selected Writings*, vol. i: *1913–1926*, p. 297.
48 Rochlitz, *The Disenchantment of Art: The Philosophy of Walter Benjamin*, p. 67.

49 Ibid., p. 70.
50 Benjamin, 'Goethe's Elective Affinities', *Selected Writings*, vol. i: *1913–1926*, p. 298.
51 Ibid.
52 Ibid., p. 299.
53 Ibid., pp. 299–300.
54 Witte, *Walter Benjamin: An Intellectual Biography*, p. 57.
55 But see Heidegger for a secular version of this 'beyond' in Martin Heidegger, 'The Origin of the Work of Art', in *Poetry, Language, Thought*, trans. Albert Hofstadter, New York: Harper and Row, 1971, pp. 17–87. See, also, David Farrell Krell's comments on this essay, and its connection with Heidegger's Nietzsche lectures, in Martin Heidegger, *Nietzsche: Volumes I and II (The Will to Power as Art and The Eternal Return of the Same)*, trans. David Farrell Krell, San Francisco: HarperSanFrancisco, 1991.
56 Benjamin, *The Arcades Project*, p. 470 [N7,6]; see Mark Wigley's discussion of Heidegger's use of the term 'kritischer Abbau' in Wigley, 'The Domestication of the House: Deconstruction after Architecture', in Peter Brunette and David Wills, eds., *Deconstruction and the Visual Arts: Art, Media, Architecture*, Cambridge: Cambridge University Press, 1994, pp. 203–227, at p. 206.
57 Gilloch, *Walter Benjamin: Critical Constellations*, p. 55.
58 Benjamin, 'Goethe's Elective Affinities', *Selected Writings*, vol. i: *1913–1926*, p. 302.
59 Ibid., p. 304.
60 Rochlitz, *The Disenchantment of Art: The Philosophy of Walter Benjamin*, p. 79.
61 Benjamin, 'Announcement of the Journal *Angelus novus*', *Selected Writings*, vol. i: *1913–1926*, p. 293.
62 Benjamin, 'Goethe's Elective Affinities', *Selected Writings*, vol. i: *1913–1926*, p. 320.
63 Ibid., p. 321.
64 Ibid.
65 Ibid.
66 See Foucault's discussion in his 'What is an Author?', in Michel Foucault, *Language, Counter-Memory, Practice: Selected Essays and Interviews*, ed. Donald F. Bouchard, trans. Donald F. Bouchard and Sherry Simon, Ithaca, New York: Cornell University Press, 1988, pp. 113–138; see, especially, p. 123.
67 Benjamin, 'Goethe's Elective Affinities', *Selected Writings*, vol. i: *1913–1926*, p. 322.
68 Ibid., p. 323.
69 Ibid.
70 Ibid.
71 Green, *Bonhoeffer: A Theology of Sociality*, p. 70.
72 Benjamin, 'Goethe's Elective Affinities', *Selected Writings*, vol. i: *1913–1926*, pp. 323–324.
73 Green, *Bonhoeffer: A Theology of Sociality*, p. 56.
74 Benjamin, 'Goethe's Elective Affinities', *Selected Writings*, vol. i: *1913–1926*, p. 324.
75 Ibid., p. 325.
76 See Sarah Kofman, 'Explosion I: Of Nietzsche's *Ecce homo*', *Diacritics*, 24:4 (winter 1994), 50–70, for just one of many poststructuralist accounts of the 'subject'.

77 Benjamin, 'On Ships, Mine Shafts, and Crucifixes in Bottles', *Selected Writings*, vol. ii: *1927–1934*, p. 554.

78 Ibid.

79 Bloch, *The Principle of Hope*, vol. iii, p. 1015 and p. 1017.

80 Benjamin, 'Goethe', *Selected Writings*, vol. ii: *1927–1934*, p. 174.

81 Ibid., p. 186.

82 For a compact reading, see John R. Williams, *The Life of Goethe*, Oxford: Blackwell, 2001, pp. 185–211.

83 Benjamin, 'Goethe's Elective Affinities', *Selected Writings*, vol. i: *1913–1926*, p. 317.

84 Gilles Deleuze, *The Fold: Leibniz and the Baroque*, trans. Tom Conley, London: Athlone, 2001, p. 30.

85 Ibid.

86 Ibid., p. 29.

87 Benjamin, 'On The Program of the Coming Philosophy', *Selected Writings*, vol. i: *1913–1926*, p. 102.

88 Ibid.

89 Caygill, *Walter Benjamin: The Colour of Experience*, p. 52; my emphasis.

90 Benjamin, *The Arcades Project*, p. 459 [N1a,3].

91 J. G. Fichte, *Science of Knowledge*, ed. and trans. Peter Heath and John Lachs, Cambridge: Cambridge University Press, 1982.

92 Ibid. [N1a,4]; my emphasis.

93 Ibid.

94 Caygill, *Walter Benjamin: The Colour of Experience*, p. 51.

95 Ibid., pp. 51–52.

96 Benjamin, 'Goethe's Elective Affinities', *Selected Writings*, vol. i: *1913–1926*, p. 334.

97 Caygill, *Walter Benjamin: The Colour of Experience*, p. 49.

98 Ibid., p. 51.

99 Jean Baudrillard, *Symbolic Exchange and Death*, trans. Iain Hamilton Grant, London: Sage, 1993, p. 126.

100 Ibid.

101 Manfred Frank, *What is Neostructuralism?*, trans. Sabine Wilke and Richard Gray, Minneapolis: University of Minnesota Press, 1989, p. 58.

102 Ibid., p. 61.

103 See, also, Jean Baudrillard, *The Spirit of Terrorism*, trans. Chris Turner, London and New York: Verso, 2002.

104 Baudrillard, *Symbolic Exchange and Death*, p. 36.

105 Ibid.

106 Simon Critchley, *Very Little . . . Almost Nothing: Death, Philosophy, Literature*, London and New York: Routledge, 1997, p. 26.

107 G. W. F. Hegel, *The Phenomenology of Spirit*, trans. A. V. Miller, Oxford: Oxford University Press, 1977, p. 270.

108 George Hunsinger, *Kierkegaard, Heidegger, and the Concept of Death*, Stanford Honors Essay in Humanities, no. XII, Stanford, California: Stanford University Press, 1969, p. 54.

109 Ibid., p. 55.

110 Heidegger, *Being and Time*, p. 282.

111 Ibid.

112 Where '*Apodictic* means "indisputable" or "clearly demonstrable" . . . from an
    ancient Greek word literally meaning "to show from".' Hunsinger,
    Kierkegaard, Heidegger, and the Concept of Death, p. 55.
113 Ibid.
114 Ibid., p. 58.
115 Pierre Missac, *Walter Benjamin's Passages*, trans. Shierry Weber Nicholsen,
    Cambridge, Massachusetts, and London, England: MIT Press, 1995, p. 129.

6

Kant's experience

Reduction and restriction

In his lectures on Nietzsche, Heidegger turns to the overcoming of Platonism. He quotes Nietzsche's *Twilight of the Idols* to summarize 'the form of Platonism that is achieved by the Kantian philosophy': 'The true world, unattainable, indemonstrable, unpromisable, but even as thought, a consolation, an obligation, an imperative.'[1] Heidegger glosses this extract from Nietzsche:

> *The supersensuous is now a postulate of practical reason*; even outside the scope of all experience and demonstration it is demanded as what is necessarily existent, in order to salvage adequate grounds for the lawfulness of reason. To be sure, the accessibility of the supersensuous by way of cognition is subjected to critical doubt, but only in order to make room for belief in the requisition of reason. Nothing of the substance and structure of the Christian view of the world changes by virtue of Kant; it is only that all the light of knowledge is cast on experience, that is, on the mathematical-scientific interpretation of the 'world'.[2]

This gloss of Heidegger on Nietzsche, and Nietzsche on Kant, expresses what for Benjamin is a major problem: the supersensuous as being regarded as outside of 'the scope of all experience and demonstration'. This is not the only issue with what Benjamin regards as the Kantian reduction and restriction of experience: in calling for an expansion, if not transformation, of the realm of valid experience within neo-Kantianism, Benjamin paves the way, even if inadvertently, for more contemporary philosophical concerns with, for example, non-western modes of thought, the thought of the so-called 'mentally ill', the anarchic, the subversive, the ludic and even the thought of the machine.

As previously noted, it is in Benjamin's 'On the Program of the Coming Philosophy' that we find the most sustained critique of Kant.[3] Benjamin was twenty-six years old when he wrote the essay while studying at the University of Berne, where he was finishing his doctorate. Apart from a number of courses in logic and philosophy at Berne, he also studied Freud and took a course on the 'Psychology of Suggestive, Hypnotic and Occult Phenomena' taught by Paul Häberlin.[4] Benjamin's unpublished essay compares with a number of highly reactive, protesting texts that were published at about this time (for example, in 1918, Ernst Bloch's *The Spirit of Utopia* and the first volume of Spengler's *The Decline of the West*; Karl Jaspers's *Psychology of Ideologies* was published in 1919, and Rosenzweig's *The Star of Redemption* eventually came out in 1921), texts protesting variously against the unfolding First World War (1914–18), against the bourgeoisie, and against the dominance in German philosophical circles of neo-Kantianism. In some respects, for Bloch, Benjamin and Rosenzweig, the promises of the entire Kantian project, dominating western thought since the eighteenth century and powerfully revived in Germany in the nineteenth century, are brought to a close by the catastrophic events of the First World War. They then had to produce a 'new thinking' either through synthesis, in Bloch's and Rosenzweig's case,[5] or through the trajectories of the critical constellation, historical materialism and the dialectical image, in Benjamin's case. But what precisely was the problem with neo-Kantianism? Safranski sketches out one major concern, with the disempowering relationship between neo-Kantianism and the scientific community:

> Wilhelm Windelband, Natorp, Rickert, and Hermann Cohen were called neo-Kantians because they advised the modern natural sciences to apply Kant's methodical reflection, and because on the question of the justification of ethical norms they also went back to Kant. They represented a massive philosophical current until World War I. Despite much acuity and polemical spirit in detail, the group as a whole was on the defensive against the superior strength of the scientific spirit of the day. It was a philosophy that hoped it would, after the end of philosophy, be able to live on in its 'children,' the sciences.[6]

For the new German-Judaic thinkers, a more serious concern was the fact that neo-Kantian philosophy insufficiently apprehended its relationship with the absolute; as Rosenzweig argued, neo-

Kantianism had 'found itself at a point where no further advance remained to it.'[7] It is important to recognize that this is also, in Rosezweig's opinion, a problem for theology, that is, one which is reduced by neo-Kantianism, and that Benjamin subsequently went back to the restricted concept of 'experience' as a way of grounding a new philosophical approach that could ultimately replace neo-Kantianism. Responding to Kant's anthropological approach, for example, Buber similarly argues that there is an evasion of the 'bigger' questions of subjectivity that haunt humanity: 'such as man's special place in the cosmos, his connexion with destiny, his relation to the world of things, his understanding of his fellowmen, his existence as a being that knows it must die, his attitude in all the ordinary and extraordinary encounters with the mystery with which his life is shot through, and so on.'[8] Buber argues that in Kantian anthropological philosophy 'not one of these problems is seriously touched upon'.[9] Ernst Bloch, in *The Spirit of Utopia*, launches into an even more scathing critique:

> Where his [Kant's] thought begins is restricted enough. He asks how the formula for gravity could be possible, in order to circumscribe the rational faculty with this possibility. One can justifiably doubt whether these boundaries and these theories of the spirit's transcendental composition, faithfully oriented to Newton and nothing else, really have any more significance within the greater phenomenological expanse of consciousness. For one can clearly just as well ask about the conditions of possibility for Javanese dance, Hindu mysticism, Chinese ancestor worship, or, if one wants to be Western European, and insofar as one can substitute scholasticism for Newton, scientific as well, how Christ's sacrificial death, the Apocalypse and certain other similar synthetic judgments are possible, in particular if one does not want to survey just a single nook – Eighteenth-century Europe – but rather the entire spirit apportioned to us human beings. That is why Kant's mockery of the world of the shades, of the aerial architects of speculation, signifies so little.[10]

To get an understanding of the origins of such a scathing critique, it is useful to sketch briefly the critical basis for Kant's notion of experience, one which was modified via neo-Kantianism. In *The Critique of Pure Reason*, Kant argues that the subject must have access to 'the raw materials for its own thought and experience'.[11] Kant also argues for the realms of outer and inner sense, where in relation to the outer realm 'objects of perception are real'[12] and 'immediately apprehended';[13] in comparison, as Collins expands in his *Possible Experience*, 'Inner realities are essentially temporal, transient, and private.'[14] Simply put, the inner realm apprehends or deals with the sense-data of the spatial outer realm. In other words, for Kant, inner intuition does not contribute directly towards knowledge of 'the real' or 'reality'; it merely works upon and/or with the 'representations' of outer sense. The inner realm or sense deals with the *representations of representations* of outer sense.[15] In relation to his expansion of this schema, Collins draws heavily on Henry Allison's reading of Kant: 'The concept of the mind affecting itself, however, is not exemplified by the production of representations *of the mind itself*. That is, when the mind affects itself, the mind does not become the object represented. Henry Allison, speaking of this passage [in Kant], says, "Quite simply, *this means that there are no sensible representations which we can recognize as representations of the soul, mind or self.*"'[16] Directly related to Benjamin's essay here is the dominance of the notion of sense-data experience, in other words, that Kant's *First Critique* is partly about the *fact* that the human subject has experience of 'an enduring world', and that Kant's entire schema depends upon this *as* fact.[17] Kant's resistance to scepticism also depends upon the factuality of experience or the ordinary sense-data of the everyday spatial world, although not in the sense of an empirical realm preceding that of intuition. As Kant says in his *Prolegomena to any Future Metaphysics that will be Able to Present itself as a Science* (1783): 'Hence pure mathematics as well as pure natural science can never bear on anything more than mere appearances, and can only represent either that which makes experience in general possible, or that which, as deduced from these principles, must always be capable of being represented in some possible experience.'[18] Obviously, Kantian philosophy is not somehow simply about factual objects, because fundamentally Kant analyses the grounds for exploring: 'the mode of our cognition of these objects, so far as this mode of cognition is possible *a priori*'.[19] Thus the opening moves of *The Critique of Pure Reason*, in the 'Transcendental Aesthetic', deal with pure intuition, and its principles of sensibility *a priori*.

Benjamin's critique, in his essay 'On the Program of the Coming Philosophy', while aiming at the broad reaches of Kant's entire philosophical oeuvre, and subsequent neo-Kantian developments, is also aimed quite specifically at the *Prolegomena*, where Kant replaces his initially ignored (by the educated public) 'synthetic' approach to metaphysics with that of an 'analytic' approach (one which is easier to understand, but not productive in the sense of moving philosophy forwards). In other words, Kant re-explains in clearer terms exactly what he wants to achieve – or has achieved – *with* his theory of transcendental *a priori* thought. Kant opens the *Prolegomena* with a suspension of current metaphysical activity because, he argues, such activity fails to ground itself on any scientific procedure whatsoever, and subsequently has in itself failed to develop or progress; the suspension is also a radical disregarding or active forgetting of what has gone before under the name of metaphysics, allowing Kant to ask 'whether such a thing as metaphysics is possible at all'.[20] Kant asks why, if metaphysics is not a science, it attempts to operate 'under the semblance of a science', subsequently keeping 'the human understanding in suspense with hopes that never fade and are never fulfilled'.[21] By setting up this immediate contrast with scientific thought, Kant can then argue that in comparison with scientific progress, metaphysics constantly revolves on the same spot; further, metaphysics has lost talented intellectual supporters who steer clear of such a low-reputation field of enquiry![22] While there is a natural progression in Kant's own argument here, setting a standard for metaphysics which metaphysics has already 'failed' to reach or measure up to, there is also a sense in which Kant is presenting demands not just for a progressive mode of thought, but for one which reaches the fulfilment of his demands. In other words, there is a tension between the infinite task of reason, and the need to show that the mapping of the processes of reason has already been achieved. The infinite task, however, is quite different from the notion of a being 'infinitely' beyond reason's boundaries or domain. The analytic account, it is made clear, is a mapping of a philosophical process that has already been completed: it is a text that constantly revolves around this completion, through a series of questions, answers and argumentative (but conclusive) supplements, all of which refer the reader to the absent book which precedes and follows the *Prolegomena*, Kant's *Critique of Pure Reason*. This is not the only absent book, however, because Kant refers to a book that should exist to reveal the apodictic propositions upon which a scientific metaphysics should have already been constructed, revealing in its pages 'knowledge of a highest being and of a future world', all proven from the principles of pure reason.[23] Kant names some potential alternative candidates as authors of this absent book, immediately undercutting them by suggesting that Wolff and Baumgarten have failed in their metaphysical tasks because they attempted to ground metaphysics from within, rather than from 'outside', that is, via pure laws; Locke and Hume are also potential authors of the absent book, but they have in turn failed for reasons elucidated throughout the *Prolegomena* (primarily through discussion of Hume). While Kant then compares this absent single book with Euclid (his *Elements*), there are further overtones in Kant's notion of a powerful, epoch-making 'single book' (that is, how he wanted the public to receive the *Critique of Pure Reason*), creating an allusive intertextual reference to a book that has been 'epoch-making', the Holy Bible. Ironically, the fulfilment or completion of the latter in itself involves a supplement, the New Testament, doubling, in some senses 'duplicating' but also surpassing, the original collection of texts; in Kant's case, *The Critique of Pure Reason* is also supplemented with another book, the *Prolegomena*, not to fulfil the first book (which is in itself complete or self-fulfilled), but rather to fulfil the reception that *The Critique of Pure Reason* should have received in the first place. The *Prolegomena* thus functions in ways analogous to Nietzsche's *Ecce homo: How One Becomes What One Is*, and it would not come as a surprise to the reader of the *Prolegomena* to come across chapters similarly titled 'Why I Am So Wise' or 'Why I Am So Clever'.

The direct attack upon speculative metaphysics is an essential component of the *Prolegomena*; Kant argues that what cannot be proven by scientific principles is not only unknowable, but should not even be guessed at, being 'beyond the bounds of all possible experience'.[24] Even the title 'metaphysician' comes under attack, with the suggestion that if what the latter does is not a science, then it is nothing whatsoever, a process that might as well not exist, whereas pure knowledge *a priori* is 'both real and grounded'.[25] The notion of something *a priori* being grounded is given further explanation: 'There is thus only one way in which it is possible for my intuition to precede the reality of the object and take place as knowledge *a priori, namely if it contains nothing else than the form of sensibility which in me as subject precedes all real impressions through which I am affected by objects.*'[26] In other words, there is an inextricable link between the realm of objects and *a priori* knowledge, where the realm of objects becomes the legitimate domain for knowledge production. Experience becomes the deciding factor or marker between the bounds of the known and the merely projected: 'appearance brings forth truth so long as it is used in experience, but as soon as it goes beyond the boundary of experience and becomes transcendent, brings forth nothing but illusion.'[27] Kant's intuitive grounds for his entire programme here, that is, the grounds of pure mathematics and pure natural science, function within and for the domain of possible experience only. At proposition 32, Kant steps up a gear to begin his major attack on the transcendent, repeating the essential requirement of objects of possible experience. Thus although Kant admits of the *noumena*, or 'special beings of the understanding', they are immediately quarantined:

> Thus beings of the understanding are admitted, but under inculcation of this rule which suffers no exception: that we know and can know nothing determinate whatever about these pure beings of the understanding, because both our pure concepts of the understanding and our pure intuitions bear on nothing but objects of possible experience, which are mere beings of the senses, and as soon as we depart from these not the slightest meaning is left to those concepts.[28]

Or, as Wittgenstein puts it in the closing proposition to the *Tractatus*: 'What we cannot speak about we must pass over in silence.'[29] Perhaps the deciding factor at this point in the *Prolegomena* is not so much the realm beyond 'possible experience' but the control over, interpretation of and definition of the word 'possible'. In fact Kant's next major question, 'how is nature itself possible?', leads once more to a boundary, and what Kant argues is the completion of transcendental philosophy. Once more, the necessity of possible experience is asserted in transcendental philosophy, whereas transcendent knowledge (that is, knowledge beyond 'possible experience') can, according to Kant, 'neither be given, as far as its *ideas* are concerned, in experience, nor its *propositions* ever be confirmed or refuted by experience'.[30] Kant examines the impossibility of proving the 'permanence of the soul' to make his point, where finitude, or death, is the limiting factor for otherwise possible experience.[31] However, that is not to say that transcendent ideas are completely useless as such: Kant argues that their utility consists of precisely revealing or showing the boundaries of the filled space of experience, and separating this region from the empty space of the *noumena*.[32] Furthermore, such boundaries are not to be perceived as negative, because the possible experience of reason is one that progresses to infinity, whereas supersensuous, empty space, provides 'as things in themselves' the completion and satisfaction that reason desires.[33] Here, Kant distinguishes between the limit and the boundary:

> We have indicated above (§§ 33, 34) limits of reason in respect of all knowledge of mere beings of thought; now, as the transcendental ideas still make the advance to them necessary for us, and have led us as it were only to the contact of filled space (experience) with empty space (of which we can know nothing, the noumena), we can also determine the boundaries of pure reason; for in all boundaries there is also something positive (e.g. surface is the boundary of bodily space, but is itself a space; line is a space which is the boundary of surface, point the boundary of line but still a place in space); whereas limits contain mere negations. The limits indicated in the above-mentioned paragraphs are not yet enough, since we have found that something lies beyond them (even though we shall never know it for what it is in itself). For the question now arises, how does our reason behave in this connecting of what we know with that which we do not know and shall never know? There is here a real connection of the known with a completely unknown (which will always remain so), and even if the unknown is not to become the least bit better known – which cannot in fact be hoped for – the concept of this connection must be capable of being determined and brought to clarity.[34]

Kant's system here removes hope from the subject's encounter with the absolute; in fact he removes hope as a possibility *per se*, transforming the potential plenitude of such an encounter with the hollowness and emptiness of unexperienceable space (whereas establishing 'the primacy of practical over theoretical reason'[35] may restore hope here). Literally, this means that the unproven encounter is one that, from a rational perspective, did not happen (that is, cannot be proven to have happened): in a general sense, *experience is the provable*.[36] However, Kant argues that the boundary experience is essentially positive, in part because it is indicative of the fact that the concepts of the understanding are not exhausted via experience; the boundary experience maps the movement beyond and suggests that there is a functional reason for this movement:

> the 'need' of reason to seek out the unconditioned defines reason's 'task' and holds out the prospect of certain 'satisfactions' for reason

to enjoy. What is . . . noteworthy is the fact that, in taking on these 'tasks' and seeking its own 'satisfaction,' reason leaves less and less for a transcendent agency to do, beginning with the very 'planning' of autonomy's vocation. Kant's own metaphors disclose the transfer of this task to the immanent domain of rationality itself.[37]

The despot of pure reason

Writing to Ernst Schoen in May 1918, Benjamin ponders what he calls 'revolutionary' thoughts, which:

> bear within themselves an urgent need to study their great adversaries very thoroughly so that it is possible to remain steadfastly objective when expounding them. The greatest adversary of these thoughts is always Kant. . . . it is unbelievable how necessary it is to track down this *despot*, to track down his mercilessly philosophizing spirit which *has philosophized* certain insights that are among the reprehensible ones to be found in ethics in particular. Especially in his later writings, he drives and senselessly whips his hobbyhorse, the logos.[38]

One of the best glosses of this fragment of correspondence, comprising also a summary of the essay 'On the Program of the Coming Philosophy', is found in Howard Caygill's *Walter Benjamin: The Colour of Experience*, where he argues that:

> Benjamin's speculative recasting of Kant's transcendental account of experience involves the introduction of the absolute or infinite into the structure of forms of intuition – space and time – and the linguistic categories (*logoi*) of the understanding. Benjamin sought to avoid both Kant's scission of experience and the absolute and what he regarded as Hegel's 'mysticism of brute force' which for him reduced the absolute by expressing it in terms of the categories of finite experience.[39]

It becomes clear that 'On the Program of the Coming Philosophy' is Benjamin's youthful attack, future project for studying *and* farewell to Kant. The Kantian system is still considered valid here in that Benjamin's essay is not an outright rejection of Kant; rather it is a desire radically to modify and develop (even if along contradictory lines) a future metaphysics.

'On the Program of the Coming Philosophy' opens with the 'central task' of future metaphysics, considered as a relation between current 'intimations', 'expectations' and the Kantian system.[40] Kant is put forward as virtually the only philosopher (Benjamin's exception being Plato) who argued most strongly for the scope, depth and, more importantly, justification of knowledge. However, this vague and preliminary praise for Kant is merely a short preface to an aggressive assault on Kant's notion of experience; Benjamin argues that what Kant takes to be experience is in fact a 'world view', that of the Enlightenment. Benjamin forcefully states that Kant's originary notion of experience was 'of the lowest order' and 'of the minimum of significance'.[41] This stripped-away or pared-down experience is also one whereby the notion of a higher authority is abandoned. In the *Prolegomena*, Kant argues that metaphysics is essentially the generation via intuition and concepts of *a priori* knowledge and *a priori* synthetic propositions.[42] The categories are also presented by Kant in the *Critique of Pure Reason* as the 'keys to possible experience'.[43] The importance of 'justification' supplied by these examples is undercut when the starting point is argued to be far too restrictive:

> the most important obstacle to linking a truly time- and eternity-conscious philosophy to Kant is the following: the reality with which, and with the knowledge of which, Kant wanted to base knowledge on certainty and truth is a reality of a low, perhaps the lowest, order. The problem faced by Kantian epistemology, as by every great epistemology, has two sides, and Kant managed to give a valid explanation for only one of them. First of all, there was the question of the certainty of knowledge that is lasting, and, second, there was the question of the integrity of an experience that is ephemeral. For universal philosophical interest is continually directed toward both the timeless validity of knowledge and the certainty of a temporal existence which is regarded as the immediate, if not the only, object of that knowledge.[44]

There are two intersecting demands here: that of universal knowledge, and that of the subject's ephemeral experience or existence; Benjamin wants a future metaphysics to develop a higher concept of experience via the 'discovery' or 'creation' of a concept of knowledge which entwines transcendent consciousness and experience 'exclusively'; the latter will reveal the logic of everyday *and* religious experience, an *a priori* that sets out the grounds for the possibility of experiencing God. Kant explicitly rejects such an approach, which in his system could lead dangerously to an immediate apprehension of the *summum bonum*, the highest good. As Žižek points out, in relation to the *Critique of Practical Reason*, Kant believes that there could be 'catastrophic consequences of our direct access to the noumenal sphere: if this were to happen, men would *lose* their moral freedom and/or transcendental spontaneity; they would turn into lifeless puppets.'[45] Žižek quotes a relevant passage from the *Critique of Practical Reason* that makes this point, but slightly further on in Kant's text, we read about the benefits of being *denied* direct access or experience to the supersensible world, leading to a share of, or sharing in, the *summum bonum*:

> when with all the effort of our reason we have only a very obscure and doubtful view into the future, when the Governor of the world allows us only to conjecture His existence and His majesty, not to behold them or prove them clearly; and, on the other hand, the moral law within us, without promising or threatening anything with certainty, demands of us disinterested respect; and only when this respect has become active and dominant does it allow us by means of it a prospect into the world of the supersensible, and then only with weak glances; all this being so, there is room for true moral disposition, immediately devoted to the law, and a rational creature can become worthy of sharing in the *summum bonum* that corresponds to the worth of his person and not merely to his actions.[46]

The subject has to become worthy before being rewarded not just with his or her share of what cannot be directly apprehended, but with a kind of defective or *weak* apprehension which 'awards' the subject an 'obscure and doubtful view' or system of hope (to be given sight with the blinkers firmly in place). In other words, as we have already seen Heidegger put it: 'The supersensuous is now a postulate of practical reason.'[47] Žižek thinks of this position in Kant's *Critique of Practical Reason* as an in-between state, precisely that which defines the Kantian subject.[48] Andrew Bowie elucidates the problem:

> If I am . . . subject to the division between the phenomenal and the noumenal, between how things appear to consciousness and how they are in themselves, my action can be subject to causality as phenomenon but free as something in itself. The will which determines the action is thus inaccessible to cognition in the same way as the thing in itself is inaccessible. We seem, therefore, to exist in two distinct realms: as sensuous beings in the realm of appearance we are

determined by the laws of nature, laws which are given to nature
by us. We are also, though, free agents.[49]

For Benjamin, the question of the subject's freedom begins to re-
work the base notion of experience: 'the concept of freedom stands
in a peculiar correlation to the mechanical concept of experience,
and was accordingly further developed in neo-Kantianism. But here,
too, it must be emphasized that the entire context of ethics can no
more be absorbed into the concept of morality held by Kant, the
Enlightenment, and the Kantians than the context of metaphysics
fits into that which they call experience.'[50] Benjamin is not arguing
merely for the experience of the absolute versus that of science or
mathematics; rather, he is opening a space for multiple, if discrete,
experiences, one of which includes a 'higher' experience. These
experiences, in turn (and in retrospect, so to speak), need to be
thought about in relation to Benjamin's entire critical constellation,
made up of elements such as the experience of Surrealist-based
profane illumination and the dialectical image.

In 'On the Program of the Coming Philosophy', Benjamin charts
the trajectory of a philosophy of the future, based upon salvaged
and/or radically revised Kantian elements. For example, he suggests
that Kant can be radically revised to create a typology that stands in
proleptically for a metaphysics of a 'higher experience'. In some
ways this is a reversal, if not parody, of Kant's *Prolegomena*. There is
a sense in which Benjamin is attempting to find what Husserl will
later call Kant's 'great discoveries', which are present only through
their partial, incomplete nature, that which Husserl calls their 'concealment'.[51] That is to say, Kant's *unquestionable* grounds in the
Critique of Pure Reason are reconfigured as *unquestioned* grounds that
'codetermine the meaning' of Kant's critical questions.[52] Klossowski,
of course, points out that the opposite may in fact be the case: that
if the 'concealment' related to Kant's own lived experience, the
system would never have been constructed in the first place.[53] Benjamin argues precisely for a revision of Kant because of the power
and autonomy expressed through reason's immanence; as Michalson puts it: 'Kant's account of reason in its specialized sense is both
instructive with respect to Kant's larger aims and illuminating as an
expression of his principle of immanence. We might say that the
element of personification involved in Kant's treatment of reason is
an indirect way of moving divine intentions off the philosophical

map'.[54] In other words, the *needs* of reason drive, in a self-sufficient way, cognitive processes. Benjamin switches gears at this point and argues that Kantian epistemology is inconsistent and 'weak'; whether this charge is justified or not, Benjamin attacks the subject–object relation and 'the relation of knowledge and experience to human empirical consciousness'.[55] Howard Caygill argues that the entire point of this attack on Kant is to open up philosophy so that it can 'move beyond classical philosophical problems and texts into [a] . . . critical reflection upon literature, art, and culture in the broadest sense.'[56] Furthermore, he argues that the problematic of the place of freedom in the coming philosophy is *not* worked out at this point, and observes that the program for the new philosophy 'ends with the demand that the philosophy of the future should "create on the basis of the Kantian system a concept of knowledge to which a concept of experience corresponds, of which knowledge is the doctrine."'[57] Caygill notes that at the end of the essay there are two incompatible options which meet the demand: 'The first is that philosophy be "designated" or "subordinated" to theology, and that the new "theory of orders" provide a universal and eternally valid framework for knowledge and experience. The second option . . . is that "Experience is the uniform and continuous multiplicity of knowledge."'[58] The first option is a Platonic move, whereby Kant's doctrine of the categories is simply replaced with 'a doctrine of eternal ideas', while the second move is in fact a radical 'anti-Platonism' whereby in a Nietzschean sense there is a 'dissolving of the categories' into a '"uniform and continuous" generation of a multiplicity of knowledges'.[59] With the first option, as Caygill makes clear, 'the categories are lifted out of time, producing an unspeculative formalism of abstracted and timeless ideas', whereas in the second option, 'they are submerged in time, threatening to disappear in a welter of diverse and continually changing patterns and orderings of experience.'[60] Caygill summarizes Benjamin's self-proposed task, and elegantly expands upon how exactly classical philosophical problems are opened up:

> Benjamin's elaboration of a non-Hegelian speculative philosophy of experience redefined the nature and limits of critique. The Kantian view that critique should confine itself to securing the legitimacy of judgements in terms of a categorial framework applicable only within the limits of spatio-temporal experience no longer sufficed. The extension of the bounds of experience brought with it the

demand for a new and extended notion of critique. Benjamin
responded to this demand by returning to the concept of criticism
developed by the Romantic, pre-Hegelian generation of Kant's
critics, above all Friedrich Schlegel and Novalis. [. . .]
   It is axiomatic for immanent critique that the criteria of critical
judgement be discovered or invented in the course of criticism. This
followed necessarily from the extension of the bounds of experience: if the absolute is immanent to experience, then the critical
judgement of experience must also be undertaken immanently.
There can be no externally given and secured criteria of critical
judgement . . .[61]

Benjamin had redefined the task of 'philosophy' as such in another
unpublished fragment, written the year before 'On the Program of
the Coming Philosophy', in a fragment called 'On Perception', in
which he offers a number of re-formulated definitions where
'Philosophy is absolute experience deduced in a systematic, symbolic
framework as language.'[62] Embedded in the word 'perception'
(*Wahrnehmung*) is the word 'truth' (*Wahr*): subsequently, for Benjamin, perception as a framework is an awareness of the true, which
is also the authentic (the real or the genuine). The typology retrieved
from Kant is articulated in Benjamin's formula 'Perception refers to
symbols.'[63] With the critical production of the essay form and immanent criticism, such symbols are merely retrieved from texts and presented in various juxtapositions, in the reading of the present or the
'now' via fragments of texts. Such a retrieval is also an overcoming
of Kantian judgment.[64] In his 'Truth and Truths', Benjamin again
rejects judgment, introducing into knowledge a notion of multiplicity and a totality of 'all' the acts of knowing: 'If the word "all" in this
definition is taken in its strict and absolute sense, if it extends to the
totality of knowledges in general and not just to all that is known
of a particular subject, then the concept of knowledge marks an illu-
sory point of intersection. Only in its multiplicity does the concept
of knowledge stand up. Its unity cannot lie in its own sphere; it
cannot be a summation, a judgment.'[65] The multiple surfaces of
experience are not enclosed and warped into hermetically sealed
spheres by finite acts of judgment: the totality is, paradoxically, final
and provisional in the sense that it is 'complete' up to the present,
but contains the necessary possibility of supplementarity, via change:
a Messianic upheaval in time, or the acknowledgment and even
random development of another (possibly secular) surface of ex-

perience. Benjamin's future metaphysics thus not only allows for the critical directions actually taken throughout his lifetime, such as the interest in developing a materialist or revolutionary aesthetic, but also explains the dialectical-theological structure of 'On the Concept of History'.

The opening pages of the 'Epistemo-Critical Prologue' also continues the redefinition of the task of the coming philosophy, and compares two main viable forms with which to proceed: doctrine and the esoteric essay. Benjamin speculates that in its 'finished form' philosophy will be entirely configured as 'doctrine', but 'mere thought' cannot 'confer such a form'.[66] This loosely veiled attack upon Kant's *Critique of Pure Reason* also widens into a rejection of any philosophy that has a scientific starting point as a way of clearing 'the problem of representation' as 'the sign of genuine knowledge'.[67] In fact, the treatise and the esoteric essay, in different ways, would focus on issues of representation as *essential* to the task, but these issues are approached via a historical organization: 'Philosophical doctrine is based on historical codification.'[68] In a letter to Scholem written prior to 'On the Program of the Coming Philosophy', we get a sense of Benjamin's early thoughts not only on specifically Kantian doctrine, but also on the intersection with historical studies:

> The most profound typology of conceiving doctrine has thus far always become clear to me in Kant's words and ideas. And no matter how great the number of Kantian minutiae that may have to fade away, his system's typology must last forever. To my knowledge, within the realm of philosophy this typology can only be compared with Plato's. Only in the spirit of Kant and Plato and, I believe, by means of the revisions and further development of Kant, can philosophy become doctrine, or, at least, be incorporated in it. [. . .]
> This winter I will begin to work on Kant and history. [. . .] I believe I recognize the ultimate reason that led me to this topic, as well as much that is apropos and interesting: the ultimate metaphysical dignity of a philosophical view that truly intends to be canonical will always manifest itself most clearly in its confrontation with history; in other words, the specific relationship of a philosophy with the true doctrine will appear most clearly in the philosophy of history; for this is where the subject of the historical evolution of knowledge for which doctrine is the catalyst will have to appear.[69]

In the 'Epistemo-Critical Prologue' the traces of Kant are still in the process of being obliterated, although the importance of 'doctrine' has increased immeasurably. Hanssen reads the importance of history in relation to Dilthey:

> Benjamin's notable insistence on the historical genesis of knowledge seemed to show affinities to Dilthey's enterprise of replacing Kant's ahistorical a priori with a critique of historical consciousness. This is borne out by 'On The Program of the Coming Philosophy,' which took on Kant's epistemology, criticizing it for its blindness to the transient or historically defined character of the mechanistic, indeed empirical, notion of experience upon which it rested.[70]

In the 'Epistemo-Critical Prologue', the relevance of metaphysical systems of thought resides primarily in the fact that they first and foremost reflect not immediately upon the empirical world, but upon the world of ideas. Thus Benjamin retrieves and recuperates Plato, Leibniz and Hegel in an attempt at 'an explanation of that simple and yet unpopular fact that even those philosophical systems whose cognitional element has long since lost any claim to scientific truth still possess contemporary relevance.'[71] This argument opposes Kant's *Prolegomena* and answers some of his scathing remarks and questions with which he suspends metaphysical activity; Benjamin argues that the 'fragile' metaphysical systems which appear to have been superseded are in fact highly relevant when examined in relation to the world of ideas, or the originary task of metaphysics: 'If it is the task of the philosopher to practise the kind of description of the world of ideas which automatically includes and absorbs the empirical world, then he occupies an elevated position between that of the scientist and the artist.'[72] Benjamin's triangle completes his rejection of Kant: metaphysics stands at the summit, bridging and superseding science and art. Yet it is no coincidence that a triangle can be turned or rotated, retaining its structural or immanent configuration, yet radically altering how we perceive the relationship between the points and their positioning at any particular moment. Benjamin examines in his triangular configuration or gestalt not just difference but also overlapping or shared identity: thus each type of activity overlaps with the others, even if in our everyday lives we focus in a hurried way only upon the extreme identity at the triangle's point (which would perhaps be a Kantian move):

The scientist arranges the world with a view to its dispersal in the realm of ideas, by dividing it from within into concepts. He shares the philosopher's interest in the elimination of the merely empirical; while the artist shares with the philosopher the task of representation. There has been a tendency to place the philosopher too close to the scientist, and frequently the lesser kind of scientist; as if representation had nothing to do with the task of the philosopher.[73]

Taking the global view of philosophical categories, and with indirect reference to Kant's three critiques, Benjamin argues not for the failure of the latter, or for a need to find a way to utilize the third critique as a functioning bridge between those of pure and practical reason; rather, the categories are 'monuments in the discontinuous structure of the world of ideas'.[74] In other words, Benjamin scraps the entire schemata of the Kantian system in favour of the link he has established between philosophy and representation, where the idea is perceived to be linguistic, or the 'element' of the 'symbolic' found in every word's 'essence'.[75] This terminology, so radically different and distant from contemporary modes of thought, is part of a project of recovery and restoration via the *logos*, whereby the idea is restored via its manifestation in philosophical contemplation. Sacred and profane exist here in parallel, developing via a chiasmus which Benjamin continually maintains.

The Kantian distance

While Benjamin was still working through and developing his critique of Kant in *The Origin of German Tragic Drama* (1928) – as noted above, critics have long been aware that in the 'Epistemo-Critical Prologue' he 'resumed the critique of Kant's predilection for mathematical formalization, whose shortcomings Benjamin had already taken up, along distinctly Hamannian lines, toward the end of his "Program . . ." '[76] – it is also the case that nearly a decade after writing *The Origin of German Tragic Drama* he considered the importance of investigating the way in which his concept of origin 'relates to Rosenzweig's concept of revelation'.[77] Hanssen argues that:

By qualifying the origin as a historical rather than a logical category, Benjamin envisaged the neo-Kantian attempt to ground philosophy in a logic of the origin, advanced by Hermann Cohen in his *Logik der reinen Erkenntnis* (Logic of Pure Knowledge; 1902). Cohen's theory of the origin was thus stripped of the positive validation it received in Franz Rosenzweig's *Star of Redemption*, which had considered Cohen's definition of the origin as 'determined nothingness' to be a decisive break with Hegel's foundation of logic in being. But the term must also be distinguished from the historicist, causal concept of genesis (*Entstehung*). Instead, Benjamin presented the origin as an eddy in the stream of becoming and defined the task of philosophical concept formation as 'to establish the becoming of phenomena in their being'.[78]

Benjamin also rejected the neo-Kantianism that aimed at a science of history, in particular the methodological separation of 'singularity and repetition.'[79] But it may appear strange in the context of the overall critique of Kant and neo-Kantianism – even given the specific comments on form in the 'Epistemo-Critical Prologue' – that Benjamin does not return to and broach Kant's writings that touch upon or cover theological notions, and instead muses on possible parallels with Rosenzweig. It is clear that Benjamin and Rosenzweig both critique Kant's impoverished notion of experience with its 'inattention to language and inattention to religion',[80] but still that does not explain this omission. One approach to comprehending the latter would be to look at the notion of an 'ethical commonwealth' in Kant that displaces and 'attenuates' the absolute: 'The already limited divine intervention that is associated with the realization of the highest good is now further diluted by corporate moral agency within the immanent sphere of history. In this new context, the theological question becomes the rather odd one concerning whether, or in what sense, Kant's God is a "member" of the ethical commonwealth.'[81] Michalson develops this avenue of investigation via the 'corporate recovery from radical evil', which occurs in stages. We can compare transcendent and immanent modes of gradualism in Kant briefly to follow this avenue: first, in the *Critique of Practical Reason*, where Kant argues that the 'moral destination of our nature' is both a supplement to speculative reasoning and an element solved via the 'postulate of *immortality*'.[82] In other words, Kant suggests that the impossible or endless gradualism of 'infinite progress' proves the immortality of the soul:

> The realization of the *summum bonum* in the world is the necessary object of a will determinable by the moral law. But in this will the *perfect accordance* of the mind with the moral law is the supreme condition of the *summum bonum*. This then must be possible, as well as

its object, since it is contained in the command to promote the latter. Now the perfect accordance of the will with the moral law is *holiness*, a perfection of which no rational being of the sensible world is capable at any moment of his existence. Since, nevertheless, it is required as practically necessary, it can only be found in a *progress in infinitum* towards that perfect accordance, and on the principles of pure practical reason it is necessary to assume such a practical progress as the real object of our will.[83]

In Kant's following sub-section of the *Critique of Practical Reason*, 'The Existence of God as a Postulate of Pure Practical Reason', God is thus shown to be the 'necessary condition of the possibility of the *summum bonum*'.[84] To turn to Kant's *Religion within the Limits of Reason Alone* (1793), the 'otherworldly' argument of the second *Critique* is replaced with the intersubjectivity and responsibility of the individual to the emerging community: 'The changed atmosphere signaled by the switch from revolutionary to evolutionary metaphors implies that the individual moral agent's destiny becomes inseparable from that of the entire moral community. Simultaneously, the shift in metaphorical usage marks the transfer of interest from a transcendent, noumenal context for moral perfection to the immanent arena of historical action.'[85] Michalson puts the point more succinctly in his preface: 'the inner momentum of his [Kant's] philosophy points beyond theism toward a fully emancipated theory of autonomous rationality. Roughly speaking, the part of Kant's thought that makes it "modern" effectively jettisons a traditional religious content, beginning with divine transcendence itself – notwithstanding Kant's own claim regarding the way morality leads inevitably to religion.'[86]

Contra Kant's distancing of human intersubjectivity from the divine, Benjamin's brief concern with the parallels between his concept of 'origin' and Rosenzweig's 'revelation' not only moves the entire philosophical-theological concern back into a language-centred realm, but also proffers another notion of 'experience' ('Erfahrung') from which to begin again and through which Kantian or neo-Kantian thinking 'remains accessible and intelligible' as 'problems for language thinking'.[87] Rosenzweig's 'experience' is also intersubjective, but in an entirely different sense from that of Kant: 'Experience is always of and within relations. (The word "and" is "the basic word of all experience.") And creation, revelation and redemption are the three relations to emerge out of the elementary facts of reality – God, human, and world.'[88] What is important about

Rosenzweig here is the way in which his recasting of 'experience' is taken to what Rubenstein calls 'an oxymoronic limit':

> he insists that the best name for his new thinking is 'absolute empiricism,' or as even more paradoxically phrased . . . 'speculative empiricism.' Rosenzweig implies that what is absolute about his empiricism is its refusal to claim to know of God and world anything more than experience teaches it. Experience marks an absolute limit. But it is no ordinary empiricism that can so coolly juxtapose God and world as comparable experiential categories; although it is no more extraordinary than a concept of experience that turns on the theological ideas of creation, revelation, and redemption.[89]

In the second part of *The Star of Redemption*, revelation is equated with experience, but because of the endless fractal-like reproduction of the macro-structure in every part of the book, there is a 'microcosmic' reproduction of the three categories of 'God, human, world' in revelation.[90] As Rubenstein notes: 'All revelation takes the form of relation. Creation is revelatory relation between God and world, redemption the relation between human and world, and revelation the one between God and human.'[91] Revelation, however, enters into dialogue with 'the summons by the proper name': 'With the proper name, the rigid wall of objectness has been breached.'[92] This 'breaching' is thus an historical event, one which is 'inward', to use Benjamin's term,[93] but which also exceeds categories and time by being 'its own' category and time: 'Wherever it is, there is a midpoint and wherever it opens its mouth, there is a beginning.'[94] Entering human history, Rosenzweig refers to Adamic naming, which is also Benjamin's covert reference point in his theory of 'origin', as he pointed out to Florens Christian Rang: 'Philosophy is meant to name the idea, as Adam named nature, in order to prevail over those that have returned to their natural state. I am adopting Leibnitz's concept of the monad for a definition of ideas.'[95] The 'origin' is thus explained via the tension generated and maintained by Benjamin between Platonism and a philosophy of sacred language.[96]

Notes

1 Quoted in Heidegger, *Nietzsche: Volumes I and II*, vol. i, p. 205. For an alternative translation of this key passage in Nietzsche, see Hollingdale's translation: 'The real world, unattainable, un-demonstrable, cannot be promised,

but even when merely thought of a consolation, a duty, an imperative.' Friedrich Nietzsche, *Twilight of the Idols and The Anti-Christ*, trans. R. J. Hollingdale, London: Penguin, 1990, p. 50.

2 Heidegger, *Nietzsche: Volumes I and II*, vol. i, p. 205; my emphases.

3 See, also, Walter Benjamin 'On Perception', *Selected Writings*, vol. i: *1913–1926*, pp. 93–96.

4 Brodersen, *Walter Benjamin: A Biography*, p. 101.

5 Rozenzweig *does* follow Cohen's theory of origin, however; see Hanssen, *Walter Benjamin's Other History*, p. 41; see, also, Franz Rosenzweig, 'Origins', *The Star of Redemption*, pp. 20–22, especially the comments re Cohen, Hegel and Kant.

6 Safranski, *Martin Heidegger: Between Good and Evil*, p. 36.

7 Rosenzweig, *The Star of Redemption*, London and New York: Routledge, 2002, p. 104.

8 Martin Buber, *Between Man and Man*, p. 142.

9 Ibid.

10 Bloch, *The Spirit of Utopia*, p. 174.

11 I closely follow Arthur Collins's reading of Kant in his *Possible Experience: Understanding Kant's Critique of Pure Reason*, Berkeley, Los Angeles, and London: University of California Press, 1999, p. 122.

12 Ibid., p. 23.

13 Ibid., p. 24.

14 Ibid.

15 Ibid., p. 109.

16 Ibid. (109; emphases Collins's and mine)

17 Ibid., p. 118.

18 Immanuel Kant, *Prolegomena to any Future Metaphysics that will be Able to Present itself as a Science*, trans. Peter G. Lucas, Manchester: Manchester University Press, 1966, p. 74.

19 Collins, *Possible Experience: Understanding Kant's Critique of Pure Reason*, p. 38.

20 Kant, *Prolegomena to any Future Metaphysics that will be Able to Present itself as a Science*, p. 3.

21 Ibid., and p. 4.

22 Ibid., p. 4.

23 Ibid., p. 27.

24 Ibid., p. 33.

25 Ibid., p. 34.

26 Ibid., p. 38.

27 Ibid., p. 50.

28 Ibid., p. 76.

29 Ludwig Wittgenstein, *Tractatus logico-philosophicus*, trans. D. F. Pears and B. F. McGuinness, London: Routledge, 1989, proposition 7, p. 74.

30 Kant, *Prolegomena to any Future Metaphysics that will be Able to Present itself as a Science*, p. 92.

31 Ibid., p. 99.

32 Ibid, p. 121.

33 Ibid.

34 Ibid.

35 Gordon E. Michalson, Jr, *Kant and the Problem of God*, Oxford: Blackwell, 1999, p. 87.

36 See the discussion concerning 'existence' and experience of a rule in H. L. A. Hart, *The Concept of Law*, Oxford: Oxford University Press, 1997, pp. 109–110.

37 Michalson, *Kant and the Problem of God*, p. 82.

38 Benjamin to Ernst Schoen, May 1918, letter 68 in *The Correspondence of Walter Benjamin: 1910–1940*, p. 125.

39 Caygill, *Walter Benjamin: The Colour of Experience*, p. 23.

40 Benjamin, 'On the Program of the Coming Philosophy', *Selected Writings*, vol. i: *1913–1926*, p. 100.

41 Ibid., p. 101.

42 Kant, *Prolegomena to any Future Metaphysics that will be Able to Present itself as a Science*, p. 24.

43 Kant, *Critique of Pure Reason*, p. 219.

44 Benjamin, 'On the Program of the Coming Philosophy', *Selected Writings*, vol. i: *1913–1926*, pp. 100–101.

45 Slavoj Žižek, *The Ticklish Subject: The Absent Centre of Political Ontology*, London and New York: Verso, 1999, p. 25.

46 Immanuel Kant, *Kant's Critique of Practical Reason and Other Works on the Theory of Ethics*, trans. Thomas Kingsmill Abbott, London: Longmans, 1959, p. 246.

47 Heidegger, *Nietzsche: Volumes I and II*, vol. i, p. 205.

48 Žižek, *The Ticklish Subject: The Absent Centre of Political Ontology*, p. 25.

49 Bowie, *Aesthetics and Subjectivity: From Kant to Nietzsche*, p. 17.

50 Benjamin, 'On the Program of the Coming Philosophy', *Selected Writings*, vol. i: *1913–1926*, p. 105.

51 Edmund Husserl, *The Crisis of European Sciences and Transcendental Phenomenology*, trans. David Carr, Evanston: Northwestern University Press, 1970, p. 103.

52 Ibid.

53 Pierre Klossowski, *Nietzsche and the Vicious Circle*, trans. Daniel W. Smith, London and Chicago: The University of Chicago Press, 1997, p. 4.

54 Michalson, *Kant and the Problem of God*, p. 91.

55 Benjamin, 'On the Program of the Coming Philosophy', *Selected Writings*, vol. i: *1913–1926*, p. 103.

56 Caygill, *Walter Benjamin: The Colour of Experience*, p. 23.

57 Ibid., p. 25.

58 Ibid.

59 Ibid., p. 26.

60 Ibid.

61 Ibid., p. 34.

62 Benjamin, 'On Perception', *Selected Writings*, vol. i: *1913–1926*, p. 92.

63 Benjamin, 'Perception is Reading', *Selected Writings*, vol. i: *1913–1926*, p. 92.

64 Benjamin, 'Theory of Knowledge', *Selected Writings*, vol. i: *1913–1926*, p. 276.

65 Benjamin, 'Truth and Truths / Knowledge and Elements of Knowledge', *Selected Writings*, vol. i: *1913–1926*, p. 278.

66 Benjamin, *The Origin of German Tragic Drama*, p. 27.

67 Ibid.

68 Ibid.

69 Benjamin to Gerhard Scholem, 22 October 1917, letter 55 in *The Correspondence of Walter Benjamin: 1910–1940*, pp. 97–98.

70 Hanssen, *Walter Benjamin's Other History: Of Stones, Animals, Human Beings, and Angels*, p. 28.
71 Benjamin, *The Origin of German Tragic Drama*, p. 32.
72 Ibid.
73 Ibid.
74 Ibid., p. 33.
75 Ibid., p. 36.
76 Hanssen, *Walter Benjamin's Other History: Of Stones, Animals, Human Beings, and Angels*, p. 39.
77 Benjamin, 'Notes (IV)', *Selected Writings*, vol. ii: *1927–1934*, p. 687: 'I ought to investigate the way in which my concept of origin, as it is developed in the work on *Trauerspiel* and in the Kraus essay, relates to Rosenzweig's concept of revelation.' See, also, the reference to Rosenzweig in 'Franz Kafka', ibid., p. 801.
78 Hanssen, *Walter Benjamin's Other History: Of Stones, Animals, Human Beings, and Angels*, p. 41.
79 Ibid., p. 43.
80 Britt, *Walter Benjamin and the Bible*, p. 58.
81 Michalson, *Kant and the Problem of God*, p. 101.
82 Kant, *Critique of Practical Reason and Other Works on the Theory of Ethics*, pp. 219–220.
83 Ibid., p. 218.
84 Ibid., p. 221.
85 Michalson, *Kant and the Problem of God*, p. 109.
86 Ibid., pp. viii–ix.
87 Rosenzweig, *Philosophical and Theological Writings*, p. 129.
88 Rubinstein, *An Episode of Jewish Romanticism: Franz Rosenweig's The Star of Redemption*, p. 47.
89 Ibid.
90 Ibid., pp. 47–48.
91 Ibid., p. 48.
92 Rosenzweig, *The Star of Redemption*, p. 186.
93 Benjamin, *The Origin of German Tragic Drama*, p. 47.
94 Rosenzweig, *The Star of Redemption*, p. 187.
95 Benjamin to Florens Christian Rang, 9 December 1923, letter 126 in *The Correspondence of Walter Benjamin: 1910–1940*, p. 224.
96 Rochlitz, *The Disenchantment of Art: The Philosophy of Walter Benjamin*, p. 33.

7

Casting the work of art

Aesthetic judgment

As the catastrophe of the twentieth century developed with the rise to power of the Third Reich, the arts became foregrounded as even more evidently a battleground: of revolution, totalitarianism and Fascism. The newer modernist approaches to art, such as photography and film, were also hotly contested sites of meaning: would photography continue to take over the role of painting? Was modernism to be considered degenerate[1] or was it still revolutionary? Was art in the age of technological reproducibility – art produced via radio, photography, film – potentially liberating or were these technologies profoundly powerful vehicles for state-sanctioned propaganda? Benjamin's well-known essay on photography and film intersects with these questions;[2] as Hansen notes in her introduction to Siegfried Kracauer's *Theory of Film*:

> The critique of the subject that Kracauer, Benjamin, and others sought to theorize through, in, and for the cinema . . . has to be understood in more specific terms than those by now familiar from poststructuralist recyclings of Nietzsche. The crisis of the subject that mandated such a critique was precipitated by a particular historical experience: *the experience of modernity as living on the brink of catastrophe* (rather than in the trajectory of progress, as which it had been touted for decades), a catastrophe that threatened the very bases of day-to-day existence.[3]

In the early history of photography there is manifest an immediate and compelling attraction that operated on the subject in parallel with all manner of anxiety – new technologies signify progress *and* painful, potentially disastrous change; Nadar (Félix Tournachon, 1820–1910) notes how he decided to use artificial lighting on his balcony overlooking the Boulevard des Capucines, attracting a great crowd to his photographic apparatus:

> The regular return, each evening, of this light (so little utilized at that time [1860–61]) arrested the crowd on the boulevard and, drawn like moths to the flame, a good many of the curious – both the friendly and the indifferent – came to climb up the stairs to our studio to find out what was going on there. These visitors (some well known or even famous) represented every social class; they were the more welcome insofar as they furnished us with a free supply of models, variously disposed toward the novel experience. It was thus that I managed to photograph, during these evening affairs, Niépce de Saint-Victor, . . . Gustave Doré, . . . the financiers E. Pereire, Mirès, Halphen, and many others.[4]

Nadar creates an artificial aura to bring the viewer to the work's technological apparatus; the viewer becomes transformed, wittingly or unwittingly, into the object of the artwork. The artificial aura is part of the 'art of machinery' creating 'the art of light and fire', which becomes a catalytic agent for the 'destructive power'[5] of photography or reproducible works. In *The Arcades Project*, Benjamin refers to the fact that the technological shift into photography is not a simple progression, owing to the retrograde nature of the technologies that immediately prefaced it: 'It is characteristic that the beginnings of the technologizing of the portrait, as instanced in this apparatus [the physionotrace], set back the art of the portrait qualitatively as much as photography later advanced it.'[6] Benjamin thinks of more advanced technologies as being 'latent' in earlier ones: 'Just as the illustrated newspaper virtually lay hidden within lithography, so the sound film was latent in photography.'[7] There is a temporal interpenetration at work here, just as there is a contextual interpenetration of technologies – the 'pace' referred to, as artistic tasks are placed under the command of the eye – pictorial reproduction, for example, is thus able to maintain pace with speech.[8] Benjamin's often-quoted passage on 'authenticity' in relation to technological change is directly about the authority of the authentic work in the face of mass-scale reproduction; the authentic work can maintain that authority within tradition and the second-order simulacrum of the hand-made copy (that is, the forgery), but not in the case of technological reproduction:

> The reason is twofold. First, technological reproduction is more independent of the original than is manual reproduction. For

example, in photography it can bring out aspects of the original that are accessible only to the lens . . . but not to the human eye; or it can use certain processes, such as enlargement or slow motion, to record images which escape natural optics altogether. This is the first reason. Second, technological reproduction can place the copy of the original in situations which the original itself cannot attain. Above all, it enables the original to meet the recipient halfway . . .'[9]

Technological reproduction exceeds the original, not just via multiplicity but via a technical pushing at, and transgression of, the boundaries of perception. This has important consequences for the subject, whose natural capacity for perception is supplemented by technological processes or machines, and, furthermore, whose judgments based upon perception are thus also supplemented (if not entirely surpassed). Snyder gives as an example an 'Olympic photograph' of a runner with both legs in the air: 'what we might have seen at the Olympics cannot serve as the standard of accurate representation for the photograph. Vision that is somehow not technically informed cannot come to terms with this kind of picture. It must reject the photograph.'[10] In other words, the issue of a 'standard' or 'principle' upon which judgments are based (or measured) is complicated *immeasurably* by this supplement.

Before investigating this example further, it is worth looking at Benjamin's second reason for the loss of authority in the authentic artwork: that the copy can function in multiple situations, unlike the original. In other words, the artwork is now refracted and mobile in a way completely different from its prior historical development (for example, in the case of a singular aesthetic object that is considered holy, and which has travelled across the centuries from church to church, given political change or religious upheaval within societies).[11] The work is consumed in different ways, but, in the newfound multiplicity of the copy, it is also consumed in parallel by myriad subjects at diverse locations: the work is disseminated, scattered, made virtual (or commutable). The 'here and now' of the work is devalued, according to Benjamin, which leads also to the loss of authority: 'The authenticity of a thing is the quintessence of all that is transmissible in it from its origin on, ranging from its physical duration to the historical testimony relating to it. Since the historical testimony is founded on the physical duration, the former, too, is jeopardized by reproduction, in which the physical duration plays no part.'[12] It is easy to read these words too quickly, to pass over what Benjamin is saying: that the truth of the work is lost as its historical witnessing is also degraded and abandoned; the work is no longer able to transmit the *essential* qualities that configure and create its value in the world. It is here that Benjamin adds his infamous comments concerning the work's aura: 'One might focus these aspects of the artwork in the concept of the aura, and go on to say: what withers in the age of the technological reproducibility of the work of art is the latter's aura. This process is symptomatic; its significance extends far beyond the realm of art.'[13] The aura is further defined – bearing in mind what it *gathers up* – as a 'strange tissue of space and time: the unique apparition of a distance, however near it may be.'[14] The interpenetration of space and time, the near and the far, is expressed literally as the 'einmalige Erscheinung', the unique or 'one-time appearance',[15] the gathering of the time of the work, and all of the contextual marking that the work bears witness to, through time and space. Now 'the masses' want to get closer to 'things', they want to 'overcome' the gathering process, which is both *now* and *cast across* history: they achieve these goals through 'assimilating' the work via its reproduction.[16] The gathering is reinterpreted as the same; the unique object is replaced via the commutable copy, in effect an arbitrary copy:

> The stripping of the veil from the object, the destruction of the aura, is the signature of a perception whose 'sense for sameness in the world' has so increased that, by means of reproduction, it extracts sameness even from what is unique. Thus is manifested in the field of perception what in the theoretical sphere is noticeable in the increasing significance of statistics. The alignment of reality with the masses and of the masses with reality is a process of immeasurable importance for both thinking and perception.[17]

The destruction of the aura is not just a removal of the almost imperceptible component of the authentic work, but it is an adjustment of perceptibility and a reconfiguration of reality: it leads (without the counteracting, actualizing and awakening force of the dialectical image[18]) to hyperreality. More radically, there is the notion that the standards by which judgments of the world have been made are not just altered, but *suspended*; as Snyder argues, 'Benjamin wants to show that perceptual standards are neither stable nor fixed for all time.'[19] Returning to the example of the Olympic photograph that cannot be verified by normal, everyday or natural modes of perception,[20] Snyder asks: 'what can it possibly mean to say that a picture that shows us something unseeable – something that can only be shown by means of a technical process – is, nonetheless, accurate?'[21] What the picture shows us is something that can be actively 'revealed' only through the technology of photographic imaging: it constructs a hyperreality that provides its own rules of performativity and perceptibility. Rodolphe Gasché, in an insightful essay on 'The Work of Art in the Age of its Technological Reproducibility', is at pains to stress that Benjamin celebrated the changes in perception via the loss of the auratic: 'let me emphasize that for Benjamin the loss of the aura in mechanically reproducible art is not something to be deplored as some of his Frankfurt School interpreters, in particular, have held. Nor is there a double response – positive in so far as it concerns the work of art, negative in the case of the human being – to be detected in "The Work of Art", or anywhere else for that matter, as Susan Buck-Morss, for instance, sees it.'[22] Gasché focuses on the cult value inherent in traditional works of art as an expression of power, before turning to the definition of the aura for closer analysis in relation to Kant's Third Critique:

> auratic objects are appearances, that is, manifestations according to the forms (or categories, as Benjamin incorrectly writes) of space and time (the reference to the pure forms of intuition is obvious), of a distance, of remoteness, of 'something' that is beyond, that transcends the phenomenal. All appearing (of the suprasensible, or the noumenal, supposing such a thing were possible) is necessarily a singularizing manifestation. Appearances in the Kantian sense are always singular (and merely give rise to a manifold). Auratic objects, for this reason, are *unique* singular appearances of the distance in question.[23]

With 'distance' as the substratum of uniqueness and singularity, Gasché contends that the latter two become functions of the 'phenomenal appearing' of 'something non-phenomenal, something distant that transcends the phenomenal.'[24] The gathering-up of the 'einmalige Erscheinung', the unique or 'one-time appearance', is an interpenetration of the phenomenal with the noumenal, in other words a making visible of what should remain hidden. The unique appearance – which Gasché implies is an impossibility (or as Thierry de Duve puts it, 'Kant's supersensible . . . never assumes a plastic form'[25]) – may thus be a mirage, 'just as mountains, seen from a great distance, appear to form part of the landscape lying before them.'[26] But if indeed the 'einmalige Erscheinung' is a mirage, induced via the ritual of cults, then the switch to a political and potentially revolutionary aesthetic is achieved by replacing the mirage with the hyperreal, the total image with that of the piecemeal image, its manifold parts constructed via *the most intensive interpenetration of reality with equipment*.[27]

Benjamin does give an example of the concept of the aura as 'a singularizing manifestation' in an earlier essay, 'Painting, or Signs and Marks' (1917). After distinguishing the realm of the sign (a mysterious spatial order) from that of the realm of the mark (a medium), which is bound in time, Benjamin gives an example of the convergence of sign and mark 'in the form of something lifeless' in Belshazzar's feast.[28] Belshazzar's destruction is brought about by his sacrilegious use of the stolen temple objects to worship false gods: sign and mark converge in the uncanny apparition of part of God's hand, which writes on the wall. Not until this text is interpreted by Daniel is Belshazzar brought to an end. The absolute mark is here 'a warning sign of guilt', and the interpretive completion of the sign appears to bring about divine retribution: 'Since the link between guilt and atonement is a temporal and magical one, this *temporal* magic appears in the mark in the sense that the resistance of the present between the past and the future is eliminated'.[29] The Messianic force sketched here is no different from that which is later detected by the historical materialist.[30] Marks do not just emerge on living beings: they also have architectonic presence, in the case of monuments or gravestones.[31] Here they form sculptural objects which are, for the masses, an 'involuntary memory of redeemed humanity', to use one of Benjamin's descriptions of the dialectical image.[32] In 'The Work of Art in the Age of its Technological Reproducibility', Benjamin turns near the close of the essay to the laws of architecture's reception, which he notes 'are highly instructive'.[33] The theory of distraction is revealed, through the eternal need for shelter and the subject's ongoing relationship with buildings, to be grounded upon habit-formation, in other words, upon the ability to perform repeatable tasks. This is distraction as productivity, which adds another possibility to Benjamin's formula 'Reproducibility – distraction – politicization'.[34] Benjamin utilizes the example of architecture to examine the two-fold reception of the subject: that is, use and perception, or the older model of tactile experience or labour versus the new optical mode of perception.[35] 'Attention' is

replaced by or subsumed under tactile habit and optical 'casual notic-
ing'.[36] Benjamin argues that 'this form of reception shaped by architecture acquires canonical value.'[37] It is at this point that he applies
such 'canonical value' or the 'aura of the habitual'[38] to the various
'historical turning points' of aesthetic-perceptual shifts: 'For the tasks
which face the human apparatus of perception at historical turning
points cannot be performed solely by optical means – that is, by way
of contemplation. They are mastered gradually – taking their cue
from tactile reception – through habit.'[39] The involuntary attainment
of new modes of apperception has been modelled by an 'eternal'
relationship with architectonic forms, and this may even include the
minted coins of the Greeks, or the Greeks' 'eternal art'.[40] At the point
in which total commutability appears to replace the 'einmalige
Erscheinung', architectonic forms continue to function in an adja-
cent metaphysical realm, one which touches upon the hyperreal at
points along an eternal continuum.[41] Marks, monuments and cast
coins continue to exist, and there may be a modern equivalent to
this connection of hyperreality and metaphysics: the casting and
sculptural production via destruction of everyday objects and/or otherwise unnoticed spaces.

'Space Under my Chair'

One method of conceiving of objects that function in ways equivalent to the theory of the photograph in the essay 'The Work of Art'
is via the collector's presentation of items, as such, 'in our space'.[42]
Benjamin calls the' latter the 'true method of making things present',
where the subject's being is not displaced into the object, but the
object steps 'into our life'.[43] Examples from the twentieth century
are Bruce Nauman's concrete sculpture *A Cast of the Space Under my
Chair* (1966–68) and the related works from 1966, *Shelf Sinking into
the Wall with Copper-Painted Plaster Casts of Spaces Underneath* (wood
and painted plaster) and *Platform Made up of the Space Between Two
Rectilinear Boxes on the Floor* (fibreglass). Nauman's manifestation of
spaces should not be thought of as occurring in isolation from his
well-known performative pieces; his sculptures can be categorized
as exploring four related conceptual approaches: 'works originating
from the idea of showing the backs of objects, or the play between
inside and outside; works having to do with hiddenness, or inaccessibility (physical and/or psychological); works based on molds of

"spaces between"; and participatory works.'[44] Nauman relates that *A Cast of the Space Under my Chair* functions 'outside of art'[45] because of the way in which, once given a conceptually understandable title, the casting process itself (not the artist) defines (and justifies) the space thereby represented. Rosalind Krauss calls *A Cast of the Space Under my Chair* 'the complete anti-Minimalist object'.[46] In part, this is because the sculpture is in itself not a dissemination of signification, but an 'implosion or congealing': 'and the thing to which it submits this stranglehold of immobility is not matter, but what vehiculates and subtends it: space itself.'[47] While Nauman theorizes his casts as being outside art because of the clarity of the work's captioning, Krauss strategically strips away the titles to present a more radical statement:

> Nauman's attack, far more deadly than anti-form – because it is about a cooling from which nothing will be able to extricate itself in the guise of whatever articulation – is an attack made in the very name of death or, to use another term, entropy. And for this reason, the ambiguity that grips these residues of Nauman's casts of interstitial space, the sense, that is, that they are object-like, but without the title attached to them like an absurd label, one has no idea of what they *are*, even of what general species of object they might belong to, seems particularly fitting. It is as though the congealing of space into this rigidly entropic condition also strips it of any means of being 'like' anything.[48]

While Krauss's point concerning the indeterminacy and entropic condition of an object that manifests something that is not visibly there in the first place is without doubt valid, the notion of stripping away titles is unclear, as this would be (ironically given her argument) a contextualization of the art-object into, or as, some other place: maybe the object is simply placed unlabelled and unnamed in a shopping mall, or on the street, something that in this instance at least is highly unlikely. Nauman's objects, in galleries or publications, are *not* unnameable. It is possible to see his sculptures not as ambiguous, and not in opposition to the residual mimesis of minimalism (that is, the object is still *like something* in the everyday world), but rather as a gathering of the entire art-making processes, including normally unseen stages and even mistakes; as van Bruggen argues, this way of conceiving the work relates to Nauman's interest in Wittgenstein:

Nauman found support for his method of reviewing the whole process of making an object (and if necessary, of backing up a step) in Ludwig Wittgenstein's *Philosophical Investigations* . . . which he read during the early 1960s: 'Wittgenstein would follow an idea until he could say either that it worked or that life doesn't work this way and we have to start over. He would not throw away the failed argument, but would include it in his book.'[49]

Another parallel with Wittgenstein's *Philosophical Investigations* is the way in which Nauman's casts of interstitial space initiate and facilitate the exploration of fundamental questions about the aesthetic object, just as the *Philosophical Investigations* functions in an initiatory sense with regard to philosophical reflection.[50] What we have in this set of analogies is the manifestation of otherwise virtually indeterminate space, a space which is fundamentally transient (is the space under my chair the same space when the chair has been moved to another room?), generating discussion about not just the singular object but the perception and perceptibility of art-objects in general.

A more recent, and sustained, production of such interstitial space can be seen in the works of Rachel Whiteread, a British artist who has been making casts of everyday objects since the 1980s,[51] casts usually made of plaster, resin, rubber and concrete of various objects (and the spaces around such objects), such as books, mattresses, sinks, closets, floors, tables, chairs, staircases, rooms and, most infamously, an entire house. Surface textures are a major part of the sculptures; earlier works had pieces of the original wooden furniture left embedded in them,[52] while later works, switching production materials, reveal various levels of imprinting: 'Whiteread seems to suggest that that the imprint of things on our memories is more important than the things themselves. The sculptures that emerge are also of course things, inverse repositories for our sensations.'[53] Krauss argues for the importance of the surface detail, especially in maintaining the 'grid of meaning' questioned by Nauman's work:

> Content to register the identity of the object that served as the mould for her casts, indeed to heighten this through a careful attention to surface detail, Whiteread's work self-evidently attaches itself (unlike Nauman's) to the whole array of indexically produced forms that extends from death masks to photographs, all of these extremely resonant with the sense that they have been cast (whether physically or optically) from 'life'. And like the death mask

and the photograph – at least the photograph as Barthes has wanted to consider it – this work is continually moving through a funerary terrain, a necropolis of abandoned mattresses, mortuary slabs, hospital accoutrements (basins, hot-water bottles), condemned houses.

Indeed Barthes has already written the outlines of a critical text on Whiteread's art, in his own consideration of photography as a kind of traumatic death mask which is paradoxically both 'structured' (thus constructed in terms of the paradigms or oppositions that undergird semiosis) and 'asymbolic'.[54]

The opposition between the structured and the asymbolic, Krauss argues, also places Whiteread somewhere between an articulation of meaning (at the level of a substrate upon which meaning can be developed) and a de-articulation as detail becomes amorphous as a result of the casting process (details are replaced by mass). The surface, in Whiteread's sculptures, is not always what it seems, however, because of the intricacies of casting. For example, an empty space, say a space under a chair, is artificially given surfaces, that produced by the materials used to bound or restrict the space to be filled by resin, rubber or concrete; in other words, the sculpture's surfaces, in this instance, are a composite imprint of the chair 'itself' and the artificially imposed boundary materials that were never there in the first place.

The series

It is generally agreed that Whiteread's sculptures have a complex relationship with time: via the series, the repeated thematic or cast object (or family resemblance with a series of objects), via remembrance (the foregrounding or manifestation of the functional space that has been lost through time or destroyed in the casting process), via recovery. Whiteread's work is not so much a remembrance of things past as a remembrance of things otherwise unnoticed. The asymbolic elements, to use Barthes's terminology via Krauss, are so outweighed by the symbolic reinvestment in the everyday object as to be of no real concern. Instead, the cast objects are overloaded with symbolic meaning, precisely where we would expect to find none. One way of approaching this overloading is via the theory of the found object, discovered as such, as the Surrealists put it, via 'objective chance': 'the object is also trapped in the network of objective chance – a movement in which it ultimately loses its 'aesthetic' character. It can be used to signify that which it is not, in appearance or at first glance.'[55] Whiteread's sculptures maintain a level of indeterminacy, but also a rapid oscillation between object and imprint, where the representation of the object continually breaks down and recovers itself in an ongoing chiasmus (the sculpture is not the object which is often instantly registered by a viewer, with the phrase, 'oh, that's an . . . X'; rather, it expresses a relationship with the object). The series of found objects (or sculptures produced via or as imprint of the found object) reveals, among many things, a repetition compulsion: 'In the compulsion operative in objective chance, the subject repeats a traumatic experience, whether actual or fantasmatic, exogenous or endogenous, that he does not recall. He repeats it because he cannot recall it: repetition occurs due to repression, in lieu of recollection. This is why each repetition in objective chance seems fortuitous yet foreordained.'[56] Hal Foster relates the repetition compulsion to Breton's 'portents', revealing a multi-temporality which is also aporetic and enigmatic: 'anxiety in Bretonian surrealism is a "signal" (*Angstsignal*), a repetition of a reaction to a past trauma triggered by a perception of a present danger. Repressed, the trauma is subsumed by the signal, just as in the uncanny the referent is subsumed by the sign. The enigma of the signal, then, attests not to a lack of signification to be filled in the future but to an overdetermination produced in the past.'[57] Whiteread's exploration of childhood claustrophobia[58] is merely the beginning of this overdetermination that begins to over-layer her work; bathroom fixtures, once cast and imprinted by Whiteread, become sacred vessels; libraries, involuted and imprinted, function to memorialize the Holocaust. As Foster also suggests, each repetition of the aporetic signal functions to shock the subject; in Whiteread's case, the shocks encountered are also analogous to those produced via photography. This multi-temporality of Surrealist objects and the photograph is of importance to Adorno and Benjamin: 'the link between photography and shock, with its moments both of violence and of instantaneousness (as we hear in the English "snapshot" and the German "Momentaufnahme"), is central not only to Adorno but also to Benjamin in the "Art work" essay. Further, Adorno interprets Surrealist shocks as having both prospective and retrospective import, as both awakening from the nineteenth century and anticipating the twentieth century.'[59] The transformed found object has a multi-temporality that has been interpreted along the twin-tracks of Adorno's and Benjamin's Surrealist shock interpretations, that is to say, via socio-historical (Adorno) and psychological (Benjamin) critique.[60] Adorno resists the latter precisely to reinscribe the Surrealist shock-image within a multi-temporality: the Surrealist shock-image looks 'both forward and backward in time'.[61] This debate between Adorno and Benjamin is also contextualized precisely by the transformation and shocks of the modern city via new technology and war:

> The Surrealist concern with the city looks forward to the explosive destruction of cities to come: "After the European catastrophe the Surrealist shocks lost their force. It is as though they had saved Paris by preparing it for fear: the destruction of the city was their center." At the same time, the Surrealist images, created through a montage technique, looked backward to reveal the libido encapsulated in the fetishized commodity objects of the late-nineteenth-century interior.[62]

The differences between Adorno and Benjamin, on the question of photography, converge once *The Arcades Project* is brought into the equation: Adorno's Surrealist shocks function to awaken or force the subject out of his or her uncritical unhistorical slumbers, just as awakening is the central force of *The Arcades Project* (Benjamin called the book 'an experiment in the technique of awakening').[63] The centrality of awakening leads to the dialectical turn of 'remembrance' in *The Arcades Project*; this dialectical turn is one way of describing the notion of the image constellation: 'wherein what has been comes together in a flash with the now to form a constellation. In other words: image is dialectics at a standstill.'[64] Benjamin's montage process here brings together and transmutes the temporality of dialectics via image: 'the relation of what-has-been to the now is dialectical: not temporal in nature but figural [*bildlich*]'.[65]

Whiteread transmutes the ordinary object in the casting process via a subtle shifting of the form, character and substance of the object; in her work, we have a concrete example of construction via destruction. Two main examples (cast everyday objects and *House*) are explored here and then related to the new authority developed in her sculptures, a new authority that invests the works with auratic potentiality derived in part from an intersection of the mass-produced and the singular. Perhaps the closest Surrealist object to the processes developed by Whiteread is the bronze glove in Breton's *Nadja*. Breton had been visited at the Centrale Surréaliste by a woman wearing blue gloves; she had refused to remove these gloves for Breton, and eventually returned and left instead a bronze glove:

> The eerie appeal of the object is not difficult to decode, for it not only casts a human form in a deathly mold, but also captures a fetishistic response to castration, which Breton can both recognize (in the displaced form of a "severed" hand) and disavow (although empty, the hardened glove remains on, as it were, to cover any absence). It is thus a doubly uncanny reminder of both the primordial condition of inanimation and the infantile fantasy of castration.[66]

Salvador Dali's definition given in Breton's 'Surrealist Situation of the Object' (1935) is 'an object which lends itself to a minimum of mechanical functions and is based on phantoms and representations liable to be provoked by the realization of unconscious acts'.[67] The bronze glove, completely functionless, although still pointing towards its everyday use, is one more in a series of fetishistic objects, in Foster's reading 'a fetishistic substitute for a lost object',[68] returning via the uncanny throughout Breton's text. However, the anonymous photograph of the bronze glove in *Nadja* (1928) reveals not a glove being used as such, with a foreign substance substituting for the hand and wrist that would otherwise fill the glove, but a bronze version of an unused glove, even an abandoned or lost glove that has been cast. This is less a displaced or castrated human form, and more a reminder of the everyday object itself, cut off not from its human wearer but from its missing opposite. In fact it may be essential that the glove is in the singular – because of the implications of the referent of the cast brought back into the equation, the deictic statement that displaces the cast and recovers the object, or the misrecognition of the cast and recognition of the absent object that it refers to – and not one of a present pair, since the latter leads inevitably to the question of restitution.[69] The blue gloves, so desired and feared by Breton, may have in fact been phantoms, impossible manifestations of the gloves that might have once belonged to Van Gogh: 'Here the blue gloves, *joined like two hands* ... in a waiting passive mood, *are paired in diagonal symmetry* with a branch of cypress, a gesticulating tree that was deeply poetic to Van Gogh ... the gloves and the branches *belong together*'.[70] Derrida's 'Restitutions' is an elaborate critique and play on the desire to restore (or claim) ownership of the represented object, and the desire to claim the authority and knowledge even to make the critical connections between represented object and owner in the first place. More than a simple question of interpretation, the process of restitution operates both at the level of specific analysis (creating a narrative of ownership upon which and through which concepts are developed, as in Foster's reading above) and as a component of an elaborate metaphysics of presence. Van Gogh, in this instance, infamously appears in Heidegger's 'The Origin of the Work of Art', but Derrida, questioning the location and destination of 'the' painting referred to, reveals the ghosting effect that is also the beginning of a series of objects and owners: 'the identification, among many other identifications, of Heidegger with the peasant and Schapiro with the city dweller, of the former with the rooted and the sedentary, the latter with the uprooted emigrant. . . . in this restitution trial, it's also a question of the shoes, or even the clogs, and . . . of the feet of two illustrious Western professors, neither more nor less.'[71] Thus Derrida's 'Restitutions' is also a text that is concerned with the pull of the earth, the soil, the rural encounters so beloved of Heidegger, versus the restoration of a sceptical, urban perspective, and the ways in which each perspective builds an ideology of truth, the truth of the art-object, the truth of locating the art-object, and of the ownership that the art-object concerns itself with. In other words, the text deconstructs the philosophical claims made concerning the represented object, and reveals how this leads to radically different notions of the work.

The artwork is the site of a struggle and a claiming that disturbs the grounds upon which aesthetic categories are constructed in ways as radical, in Derrida's reading, as that of Duchamp's *Fountain*, or signed found object: a urinal (signed with a fake name).[72] The deconstruction of Heidegger's claiming of the work is also expressed by Levinas's notion of Heidegger's 'suspicion of outsiders':

> Levinas's fundamental argument against Heidegger is that his distinction between Being and beings, and the alleged priority of the former to the latter, is a manifestation of the most vicious of all tyrannies, that of the "same" over the "other." In Levinas's view, Heidegger's thought had its origins in a primal peasant mentality, a mentality suspicious of all outsiders and determined, through a pre-technological power of possession, to make everything its own.[73]

The artwork must be claimed, by Heidegger, for this primal mental-
ity, just as Heidegger's authority once re-appropriated is similarly
problematic. Breton's narrative of the blue gloves, and its substitution by the single bronze glove, is also a deconstruction of ownership: the pair of gloves in the Van Gogh (my interjection in Breton's
and Foster's narratives) are first appropriated by being worn by an
anonymous woman and then replaced by the object, now accessible
via an anonymous photograph (the photograph of the bronze glove
in *Nadja*). The blue gloves are transmuted first via form, from the
pair to the singular, which is also to shift the distinctive characteristic of the humanly worn gloves, and then transmuted via substance,
from blue to bronze, from paint and text to bronze and the photograph. The bronze glove is part of a complex critical constellation
that can be read as triggered (or given explosive energy) via phantoms and the realization of unconscious acts, or, in the case above
(reclaiming the Van Gogh, at the same time as inserting his painting
in an arbitrary manner into the interpretive narratives), triggered via
the conceptuality embedded in the word 'anonymous', countering
the restitutional claims made within the constellation with further,
deeply problematic, restitutional claims.

Whiteread's cast everyday objects also make restitutional claims:
they belong to an absent, unspecified number of people, being mass-
produced objects that were once claimed, owned and eventually
abandoned. Photographs of these originary objects (the word 'originary' being replete with irony) show them after being unceremo-
niously dumped in public places: a poorly constructed wardrobe
being held together with plastic tape, leaning precariously against
some railings; an ugly lounge suite and a radiator stacked together
(the sofa flipped over, sitting on top of the chairs), similarly dumped
by some railings; a mattress abandoned but also neatly bent, as it
leans against a car parked in a street; a smashed pile of a flat's contents thrown from a height (the flat probably being public housing)
onto the ground, a mattress neatly perched on top of the pile
(whether the pile will be collected or not, is unclear).[74] The photographs neatly embody the practice of 'fly tipping' in London,
where objects of little value are illegally abandoned rather than the
owner incurring the cost of depositing them at official rubbish
dumps. But these objects have another side in the pathos that they
generate, being visibly shoddy and cheaply constructed items that
are likely to have belonged to the urban poor, who cannot afford or

be bothered to throw them away. The destruction and disposal of the objects have been delayed, deferred and redirected (or claimed) via the casting process: the objects are photographed and negatives are printed, or the objects are removed and brought into the artist's workshop or studio, to be destroyed in the casting process whereby they enter another order of existence as sculpture or work. The casting process is a consummation of the objects, that is, not a supplementary completion (an endless task), but an unexpected direction, in Heidegger's sense: '"consummation" does not mean a last addition of the still missing part, nor the final repletion of a gap hitherto neglected. [. . .] It is the unconditioned and complete installation, for the first time and in advance, of what is unexpected and never to be expected. Compared with what has been up to now, the consummation is novel.'[75] Held together in Heidegger's definition is the ludic, the playful (the open) and the closed, the completion (as in the end, close or completion of metaphysics in Nietzsche, or completion of history in a Messianic sense). The unexpected in Whiteread's work is that the everyday mass-produced object should find completion in its destruction and afterlife as sculpture: in this case, a destruction that parallels the usual processes of landfill, combustion and recycling. Whiteread's *House*, the most hyped and visible manifestation in Britain of Whiteread's consummation of everyday objects, underwent, however, a further stage: that of its demolition. *House*, an Artangel project in London's East End, was, and involved, an elaborate cast, as object and of characters:

> *House* was completed on October 25 1993. There had deliberately been almost no press until one day before. Slowly at first and then more quickly, interest and comment began to grow . . . Newspaper leaders and letters, columns and cartoons appeared and multiplied. Visitors grew day by day. On November 23 two decisions were made simultaneously in different parts of London. A group of jurors at the Tate Gallery decided that Whiteread had won the 1993 Turner Prize, and a gathering of Bow Neighbourhood Councillors voted that *House* should be demolished with immediate effect. It was an incendiary combination.[76]

The destruction of the object's afterlife took Whiteread's *House* to another level: that of the 'incendiary' and explosive work situated firmly within an urban environment where, however, art-objects are not to be ignored or securely accommodated in galleries and archives. While Benjamin asserts that 'the art of the present is geared toward becoming worn out',[77] the spectacular destruction of *House* re-interjects the work into the Surrealist discourse of the 'fixed-explosive'.[78] The auratic potentiality derived in part from an intersection of the mass-produced and the singular is modified here with the repeated attempt at destroying the object: the work's singularity is constantly recovered, transformed and lost again, via material processes. The work, in the process, becomes highly charged, to the point of being explosive. Working backwards, from *House* to the entire range of earlier cast objects, and forwards, to Whiteread's *Holocaust Memorial*, the taking-over of the essentially modernist phrase 'fixed-explosive' needs to be investigated, especially in relation to the explosive potentiality of Benjamin's dialectical image.

Fixed-explosive

The Surrealist category of 'the marvellous' parallels the processes of profane illumination and approaches, conceptually, dialectics at a standstill, where 'In order to combat the continuum of historical progress, the dialectical image fixes attention on the contradictions of history without resolving them in a Hegelian *Aufhebung*'.[79] Hal Foster elucidates the critical constellation of the marvellous:

> the primary purpose of the surrealist marvelous is clear: the 'negation' of the real, or at least of its philosophical equation with the rational. If 'reality,' Aragon writes in 1924, 'is the apparent absence of contradiction,' a construct that effaces conflict, then 'the marvelous is the eruption of contradiction in the real,' an eruption that exposes this construct as such. [. . .] . . . the marvelous is a 'dialectical urgency' in which one 'bourgeois' reality is subverted, and another revolutionary world advanced. Here the marvelous appears responsive to historical contradiction, which, Aragon implies, might be invoked through aesthetic 'displacement.'[80]

The eruption of an unresolved or non-sublated contradiction in the real can be related to a process theorized by Heidegger as 'rift-design'; Heidegger argues that 'Truth establishes itself as a strife within a being that is to be brought forth only in such as way that the conflict opens up in this being, that is, this being is itself brought into the rift-design.'[81] The rift-design is the 'basic design', 'outline sketch' or schemata that holds in tension the essential (from Heidegger's perspective) conflicts of being without resolving them, bringing into clear outline originary components of subjectivity. Notions of the subject's 'strife', 'striving' and 'testing' are also brought into the open by this schemata. The rift-design is closer to Aragon's definitions of the marvellous than Breton's, but nonetheless both examine production via the marvellous of 'convulsive beauty' as modified by Foster in the following formula: 'Beauty will be not only convulsive or will not be, but also compulsive or will not be. Convulsive in its physical effect, compulsive in its psychological dynamic . . . it partakes of the uncanny.'[82] The further Surrealist definitions of convulsive beauty include the 'veiled-erotic', the 'fixed-explosive' and the 'magical-circumstantial'.[83] The fixed-explosive relates intimately to photographic shock, which Foster reads in psychoanalytic terms where 'the shot that arrests one is an uncanny fore-image of death.'[84] The fixed-explosive is 'reality convulsed in shock'.[85] In other words, reality undergoes a process of folding, convolution and involution: the uncanny is now placed in the foreground and comes abruptly to the surfaces of experience; contradictions are revealed and held in tension as rift-design. Via the fixed-explosive the otherwise smooth and homogenous surfaces of the real are broken down into ruins, which is also a temporal intervention: as with dialectics at a standstill, which 'blasts the epoch out of the reified "continuity of history" . . . [and] explodes the homogeneity of the epoch, interspersing it with ruins – that is, with the present.'[86] For Benjamin, rift-design processes are multivalent, that is to say, the tensions in the valences increase and decrease according to structural repositioning:

> To thinking belongs the movement as well as the arrest of thoughts. Where thinking comes to a standstill in a constellation saturated with tensions – there the dialectical image appears. It is the caesura in the movement of thought. Its position is naturally not an arbitrary one. It is to be found, in a word, where the tension between dialectical opposites is greatest. Hence, the object constructed in the materialist presentation of history is itself the dialectical image. The latter is identical with the historical object; it justifies its violent expulsion from the continuum of historical process.[87]

The caesura is potentially a shock moment in the 'gap' between thoughts; it is also the explosive potential as the dialectical opposites increase in tension, yet are still held in place. Without the spacing of the caesura, thought itself would not exist; but similarly, without the opening created by the caesura, the dialectical opposites would far too rapidly proceed onwards via sublation.

Sublation can be thought as a sequential reprocessing, or can be thought in an instant or moment, because Absolute Spirit drives the dialectic from the start. That is to say, while Absolute Spirit from one perspective drives sublation towards the terminus, from another perspective it has always already arrived; the sequential processing takes place in time, but the short-circuit of having always already arrived is in this regard other to or outside such a definition of time. Heidegger calls this Hegelian treatment 'nothing less than leaving time behind on the road to spirit, which is eternal'.[88] He expands upon the question of 'otherness' and time:

> At the beginning of its history, absolute knowledge must be different from what is at the end. Certainly. But this otherness does not mean that knowledge is at the beginning *not yet and in no way* absolute knowledge. On the contrary, this knowledge *is* right at the beginning already absolute knowledge, but has not yet come to itself, not yet *become* other. Rather, it is simply other. The absolute is other and so is *not absolute*, but relative. The not-absolute *is* not yet absolute. But this 'not-yet' is the not-yet *of the absolute*. In other words, the not-absolute is absolute, not in spite of, but precisely because of its being not-absolute. The 'not' on the basis of which the absolute can be relative pertains to the absolute itself. It is not *different* from the absolute. It is not finished and *lying* dead *next to* the absolute. [It] . . . expresses a mode of the absolute.[89]

Dialectics at a standstill is a necessary *intervention*, replacing the 'instant', whereby dialectics is both inside and outside time. The crude division between inside and outside here concerns a primarily human history, and the alternative Messianic event that signals the end of or completion of such a history. From Benjamin's perspective, this 'outside' is an end which humanity is *not* responsible for, regardless of the technologies of destruction being developed, and the subsequent cancelling out of knowledge, progress and the 'burial' of the subject.[90] This end is not the culminating event of European nihilism, but one where the struggle is survival beyond this point.[91] For Britt, Messianic time (or more accurately the interpenetration of human time with 'chips' or splinters of Messianic time) is approached via the dialectical image, where the latter is defined as 'the historiographic archive of pure language, merging opposites in a dense representation that yields fleeting insight'.[92] This merging or conflation of opposites, following the interpretation of a non-sublatory rift-design, would have to happen *after* the caesura or event of the rift-design (which holds opposites apart); in other words, it would be the next move after the caesura, instead of, or as an alternative to, the move of sublation. Britt argues for a union of 'theology and politics' because Benjamin is arguing for a history which 'represents both the "Messianic cessation of happening" and "a revolutionary chance in the fight for the oppressed past." These two functions coincide in the critical retrieval of memory.'[93] The latter is the process of seizing hold of memory 'as it flashes up at a moment of danger'.[94] The task here is to think through this caesura-seizure in relation to the aesthetics of Whiteread's casting process, the 'incendiary combination' of casting and destruction, or production and destruction, in the same work.

Benjamin calls his process of dialectics at a standstill 'materialist historiography', where the objects chosen are not arbitrary: materialist historiography 'does not fasten on them but rather springs them loose from the order of succession.'[95] The object of Whiteread's *House*, a house that once existed in London's East End, can be thought of as an object loosened from the 'progressive' policies of Bow Council, which involved knocking down perfectly sound properties to make way for parkland, at a time when Londoners desperately needed housing more than open spaces (the parkland in question runs alongside a relatively disused canal which connects Victoria Park with the Thames). The caesura-seizure in question involves transforming a process and discourse of private and public housing into a death-mask that memorialized, however briefly, the tensions and disputes in relation to the uses of urban spaces. The dialectical image can be thought of not just as freezing time, but as holding two competing potential movements in tension: progressive time, and a revolutionary alternative (be it sacred or profane); similarly, the cast object can contain or freeze 'two histories': 'its own past and the past of the object it replicates'.[96] For Richard Shone, the perfect example of such a dual process, one that has in itself a vast historical range, is the death-mask: 'It captures all the physical accretions of the human face soon after that face has completed its living existence and before rigor mortis accelerates it towards disintegration. It remains in the world to remind us of the dead, as both portrait and memorial, a replica and an object in its own right.'[97] The fact, as Shone points out, that a house had to be demolished before Whiteread's work 'could come into being' relates it intimately to the death-mask;[98] furthermore, the cast brings the contradictions of the aesthetic and socio-political urban space to the fore, and it is these contradictions, rather than the work itself, that may have contributed to the need to destroy it (again): a repetition compulsion of dismantling and regeneration, or an eternal recurrence of the same. The death-mask and the death drive come together in the technologies of photography: as Foster suggests, 'Photography points to the logic of the death drive in two ways: in its shock . . . and in its tense (the future anterior of the photograph: this will have been).'[99] The repetition compulsion is 'keyed not only to primordial death but also to personal trauma . . . the basis of its third category, the marvelous as magic-circumstantial.'[100] It is at this point in Foster's own analysis of Surrealism that he brings in the notion of the sublime:

> In/animate and im/mobile, the veiled-erotic and the fixed-explosive are figures of the uncanny. Breton recodes the 'morbid anxiety' provoked by this uncanniness into an aesthetic of beauty. And yet finally this aesthetic has to do less with the beautiful than with the sublime. For convulsive beauty not only stresses the formless and evokes the unrepresentable, as with the sublime, but it also mixes delight and dread, attraction and repulsion: it too involves 'a momentary check to the vital forces,' 'a negative pleasure.' In surrealism as in Kant, this negative pleasure is figured through feminine attributes: it is an intuition of the death drive received by the patriarchal subject as both the promise of its ecstasy and the threat of its extinction.[101]

The holding in tension, or holding apart, of the rift-design, signalled in Foster's phrases 'In/animate' and 'im/mobile', reveals also the caesura-seizure operative in the sublime cast object; that is to say, there is a 'negative pleasure' associated with the experience of the cast object or work, a tension that gathers together the pleasure and pain involved in recovering memories of the originary (dispersed, mass-produced) object and the pleasure and pain involved in the concomitant feelings of loss.

As with the sublime, the viewer both is detached from the cast and the processes that go into its construction and is the protagonist in the scene of the cast, or the scene(s) invoked by the cast. In the case of *House*, this is the scene of domesticity, and regardless of the scale or lack of luxury involved in the historical object in London's East End, it invokes a shared experience, regardless (also) of whether there is an affirmation or interrogation of domesticity under way: 'Potentially at least it exposes the complexity of meaning of "home".

House emphasizes – indeed it throws in our faces – the fact that its meaning always has to be interpreted; that there was never any simple "authenticity"; that the meaning(s) of home are always open to contestation.'[102] The juxtaposition in the phrase 'home/*House*' deliberately reveals the jarring involved in describing and naming the cast object not as someone's home, but as a historical location that sequentially is called 'house' with layered meanings or accretions (*House* names not 'my' experience of domesticity, but a palimpsest of socio-economic changing conditions and existences), for example, in terms of the ways in which the building was interpreted by visitors to the site after it had been re-configured and transformed by Whiteread. Some visitors sneered at the apparent meanness and poverty of a terrace house, some decried its loss as a valuable housing space compared with the brutalist modernist public housing estates that scar the neighbourhood (and much of Britain's cities), some realized that the house had features that made it a cut above a lower-class terrace house, and so on. The debates about the destruction of the original house would, bizarrely, be paralleled by the debates about the destruction of Whiteread's original work *House*; after its destruction, the sublime event of *House* revealed its narrative and momentary 'incendiary' status, as it was violently 'expulsed' 'from the continuum of historical process'.[103]

Memorial aesthetics

The demolition of *House* appears to contradict the saying *Vita brevis, ars longa*, 'Life is short, art is long'. As caesura-seizure, or dialectical image, the work in question removes the contradiction: *House* functioned, in part, as a memorial, that is, an act of remembrance, and as a utopian hope for the future (be it in the realm of aesthetics or politics). The phrase 'memorial aesthetics' has been used elsewhere, notably by J. M. Bernstein in *The Fate of Art*, where he argues that the Kantian complex of pleasure and pain in the beautiful is also a memorial, that is to say 'a remembering that is also a mourning'.[104] Bernstein asks what is mourned in the *Critique of Judgment* as a whole, and summarizes by saying that it is the separation of beauty, truth and goodness: 'Of course, the architectonic goal of the third *Critique* is, through reference to the supersensible, to engineer a reconciliation or unity of nature and morality, understanding and reason, truth and goodness, through judgement and beauty. Kant's argument in this regard has convinced no one since the German Romantics.'[105] In place of this failure to convince, Bernstein explores the post-aesthetic philosophies of art that 'employ art in order to challenge truth-only cognition'.[106] In other words, in Bernstein's text, the work of Adorno, Derrida and Heidegger, read as continuing the radical possibilities of Kant's *Critique of Judgment*. The memorial aesthetics of the dialectical image, however, functions as a critical constellation that does not abandon the absolute, even while it mourns the subjects lost with the termination or culmination of reason's self-certainty and power, in other words, with the Shoah. The absolute is reinscribed in memorial aesthetics via the traces of utopian thought that are immanent to mourning, where hope is defined as having 'its positive correlate' as Bloch puts it, 'the still unclosed determinateness of existence, superior to any res finita [finite thing]'.[107] Thus, utopian thought is not a subjective, arbitrary dream-state, but a determinate component of thinking: 'what is designated by this concept [the utopian] lies in the horizon of the consciousness that is becoming adequate of any given thing, in the risen horizon that is rising even higher. Expectation, hope, intention towards possibility that has still not become: this is not only a basic feature of human consciousness, but, concretely corrected and grasped, a basic determination within objective reality as a whole.'[108] The utopian element of memorial aesthetics is directed towards what Benjamin calls 'the perfected state of the world' with 'the now of knowability' or manifest visibility, 'das Jetzt der Erkennbarkeit'.[109] Knowledge and image come together in this phrase, translated in relation to the dialectical image as 'the now of recognizability'. In 'das Jetzt der Erkennbarkeit', Benjamin argues that there is a binding between the inauthentic and the authentic, between the imperfect and the perfect; this binding can be reconstructed via memorial aesthetics, where the failure of an event and its utopian possibilities (or transformations) are simultaneously symbolized (literally, 'thrown together'). In his 'Theory of Knowledge' Benjamin moves towards the interpenetration of the binding or nexus, the overcoming of the false disjunction between subject and object, and the 'appearance of the knowing man', but then he withdraws, steps back from the 'perfected state of the world' which would also seem to exclude the binding or nexus, the thrown together.[110] The repetition compulsion which leads to the creation and destruction cycles in the cast as memorialization also approaches and withdraws from 'das Jetzt der Erkennbarkeit' in this sense of knowledge and 'total' recoverability.

There are obviously cultural differences in the time of this approaching and withdrawal as memorialization, as Bartomeu Marí reminds us: 'The tradition of the memorial is specific to the Jewish culture in which it is practised very frequently. The Christian tradition confines the commemoration of the dead or tragic events to anniversaries. The Jewish culture extends this to more everyday manifestations of remembrance.'[111] Building a Holocaust memorial which incorporates cultural and temporal differences became one element of the task that resulted in Whiteread's cast of a library, situated in Judenplatz, Vienna. Adorno's infamous question about post-Holocaust literary production is answered not with the fine points of philosophical or theoretical argumentation, but by an imprint of an object that contains the library of knowledge, regardless of the category of text: philosophy *and* fiction, theology *and* science. The library also symbolizes the moral law (and its rejection or transgression by the Nazis): the ultimate object of Kant's sublime event or scene, where reason surpasses all else. The memorial points not just towards a singular event, however, but towards the realm of knowledge that encodes, and potentially decodes, the ongoing event as multiple or plural catastrophes: 'The *truth* of a given circumstance is a function of the constellation of the true *being* of all other circumstances.'[112] The memorial brings together or binds the plurality with the library: a simultaneously closed and exposed structure, the latter in the sense of a structure radically open to interpretation.[113] The cast of the moral law is also a cast of the history of the catastrophe, one manifest in the object and the repetition compulsion, this time, of the desire to halt the destruction of the object, the book and its library housing. Whiteread's cast or imprint of books is exposed to damage, decay, defacement from passing subjects: the books are no longer sheltered; they are themselves out in the open. This clearing reveals a hidden, but repeated, event: the event of the systematic murder and effacement of a people, the function at the centre of the National Socialist project.

Notes

1 So-called 'degenerate art' became a powerful commodity with a skewed exchange value owing to the Nazi quest for 'Aryan' art. See Hector Feli-

ciano, *The Lost Museum: The Nazi Conspiracy to Steal the World's Greatest Works of Art*, New York: BasicBooks, 1997.

2 See Shierry Weber Nicholsen's discussion of the Adorno–Benjamin debate concerning this key essay, in chapter 5 of her *Exact Imagination, Late Work: On Adorno's Aesthetics*, Cambridge, Massachusetts, and London, England: MIT Press, 1997.

3 Miriam Bratu Hansen, 'Introduction', in Sigfried Kracauer, *Theory of Film: The Redemption of Physical Reality*, Princeton, New Jersey: Princeton University Press, 1997, p. xi; my emphases.

4 Benjamin, *The Arcades Project*, p. 674 [Y2,3].

5 Ibid., p. 672 [Y1a,2].

6 Ibid., p. 676 [Y3a,1].

7 Benjamin, 'The Work of Art in the Age of its Technological Reproducibility', 'Second Version', *Selected Writings*, vol. iii: *1935–1938*, p. 102.

8 Ibid.

9 Ibid., p. 103.

10 Joel Snyder, 'Benjamin on Reproducibility and Aura: A Reading of "The Work of Art in the Age of its Technical Reproducibility"', in Smith, ed., *Benjamin: Philosophy, Aesthetics, History*, pp. 158–174, at p. 160.

11 Richard J. Lane, *Jean Baudrillard*, London and New York: Routledge, 2000, pp. 66–67.

12 Benjamin, 'The Work of Art in the Age of its Technological Reproducibility', 'Second Version', *Selected Writings*, vol. iii: *1935–1938*, p. 103.

13 Ibid., pp. 103–104.

14 Ibid., pp. 104–105.

15 Ibid., p. 123, translator's note 5.

16 Ibid., p. 105.

17 Ibid.

18 Benjamin, *The Arcades Project*, 'Materials for the Exposé of 1935', p. 917 [No. 24].

19 Snyder, 'Benjamin on Reproducibility and Aura: A Reading of "The Work of Art in the Age of its Technical Reproducibility"', p. 161.

20 See Henri Lefebvre's analysis of perception and judgment concerning the real/unreal in relation to everyday life, in his *Critique of Everyday Life*, trans. John Moore, London and New York: Verso, 1991 (first published 1947).

21 Snyder, 'Benjamin on Reproducibility and Aura: A Reading of "The Work of Art in the Age of its Technical Reproducibility"', p. 161.

22 Rodolphe Gasché, 'Objective Diversions: On some Kantian Themes in Benjamin's "The Work of Art in the Age of Mechanical Reproduction"', in A. Benjamin and Osborne, eds., *Walter Benjamin's Philosophy: Destruction and Experience*, pp. 180–201, at p. 181.

23 Ibid., p. 184.

24 Ibid., pp. 184–185.

25 Thierry de Duve, *Kant after Duchamp*, Cambridge, Massachusetts, and London, England: MIT Press, 1996, p. 315.

26 Benjamin, *The Arcades Project*, 'Materials for the Exposé of 1935', p. 912, No. 15.

27 Benjamin, 'The Work of Art in the Age of its Technological Reproducibility', 'Third Version', *Selected Writings*, vol. iv: *1938–1940*, p. 264.

28 Benjamin, 'Painting, or Signs and Marks', *Selected Writings*, vol. i: *1913–1926*, p. 84.

29 Ibid.

30 Benjamin, 'Paralipomena to "On the Concept of History"', *Selected Writings*, vol. iv: *1938–1940*, p. 402.

31 Benjamin, 'Painting, or Signs and Marks', *Selected Writings*, vol. i: *1913–1926*, p. 86.

32 Benjamin, 'Paralipomena to "On the Concept of History"', *Selected Writings*, vol. iv: *1938–1940*, p. 403.

33 Benjamin, 'The Work of Art in the Age of its Technological Reproducibility', 'Third Version', *Selected Writings*, vol. iv: *1938–1940*, p. 268.

34 Benjamin, 'Theory of Distraction', *Selected Writings*, vol. iii: *1935–1938*, p. 142.

35 Benjamin, 'The Work of Art in the Age of Its Technological Reproducibility', 'Third Version', *Selected Writings*, vol. iv: *1938–1940*, p. 268.

36 Ibid.

37 Ibid.

38 Benjamin, *The Arcades Project*, p. 461 [N2a,1].

39 Benjamin, 'The Work of Art in the Age of its Technological Reproducibility', 'Third Version', *Selected Writings*, vol. iv: *1938–1940*, p. 268.

40 Benjamin, 'Theory of Distraction', *Selected Writings*, vol. iii: *1935–1938*, p. 142.

41 Marcel Duchamp gives instructions for a painting or sculpture wound up as 'a reel of cine-film'; this bizarre hybrid form turns each exposed painting or sculpture into a 'take' interlinked in a sequence, although he stresses that such sequential continuity 'may have nothing in common with cinematographic film [. . .] nor resemble it'. *À l'infinitif/In the Infinitive*, a typotranslation by Richard Hamilton and Ecke Bonk of Marcel Duchamp's *White Box*, Over Wallop, UK: The Typosophic Society, 1999, p. 12.

42 Benjamin, *The Arcades Project*, p. 206 [H2,3].

43 Ibid.

44 Jane Livingston, 'Bruce Nauman', in Jane Livingston and Marcia Tucker, *Bruce Nauman: Work from 1965 to 1972*, Los Angeles: Los Angeles County Museum of Art, 1972, pp. 9–29, at p. 11.

45 Ibid., p. 12.

46 Rosalind Krauss, 'X Marks the Spot', in Fiona Bradley, ed., *Rachel Whiteread: Shedding Life*, London and Liverpool: Tate Gallery Liverpool, 1996–97, pp. 74–81, at p. 74.

47 Ibid., pp. 74–75.

48 Ibid., p. 75.

49 Coosje van Bruggen, *Bruce Nauman*, New York: Rizzoli, 1988, p. 9.

50 Robert J. Fogelin, *Wittgenstein* (second edition), London and New York: Routledge, 1995, p. 110.

51 'Rachel Whiteread', in *Doubletake: Collective Memory and Current Art*, London: The South Bank Centre and Parkett, 1992, p. 240.

52 Ibid.

53 Ibid.

54 Krauss, 'X Marks the Spot', p. 76.

55 Chénieux-Gendron, *Surrealism*, p. 162.

56 Foster, *Compulsive Beauty*, p. 30.

57 Ibid., p. 31.

58 'Rachel Whiteread', in *Doubletake: Collective Memory and Current Art*, p. 240.

59 Nicholsen, *Exact Imagination, Late Work: On Adorno's Aesthetics*, p. 197.

60 Ibid., p. 198.

61 Ibid., p. 67.

62 Ibid., pp. 197–198.

63 Benjamin, *The Arcades Project*, 'First Sketches, Paris Arcades I', p. 838 ⟨F°,7⟩; Nicholsen, *Exact Imagination, Late Work: On Adorno's Aesthetics*, pp. 198–199.

64 Benjamin, *The Arcades Project*, p. 463 [N3,1].

65 Ibid.

66 Foster, *Compulsive Beauty*, p. 33.

67 André Breton, 'Surrealist Situation of the Object', in *Manifestoes of Surrealism*, trans. Richard Seaver and Helen R. Lane, Ann Arbor: University of Michigan, 1972, pp. 255–278; p. 276.

68 Foster, *Compulsive Beauty*, p. 33.

69 Jacques Derrida, 'Restitutions', *The Truth in Painting*, trans. Geoff Bennington and Ian McLeod, Chicago and London: The University of Chicago Press, 1978, pp. 255–382.

70 Meyer Schapiro, *Van Gogh*, quoted in Jacques Derrida, 'Restitutions', *The Truth in Painting*, p. 270; emphases in the quotation in italics are by Derrida.

71 Ibid., p. 260.

72 See de Duve, *Kant after Duchamp*.

73 Allan Megill, *Prophets of Extremity: Nietzsche, Heidegger, Foucault, Derrida*, Berkeley, Los Angeles, and London, England: University of California Press, 1985, p. 307.

74 Bradley, ed., *Rachel Whiteread: Shedding Life*, p. 21.

75 Martin Heidegger, *Nietzsche*: Volumes III and IV (*The will to Power as Knowledge and as Metaphysics* and *Nihilism*), trans. David Farrell Krell, San Francisco: HarperSanFrancisco, 1991, vol. iii, p. 7; for a discussion of Heidegger's destruction/de-construction in comparison with Derrida, see Richard J. Lane, *Functions of the Derrida Archive: Philosophical Receptions*, Budapest: Akadémiai Kiadó, 2003, pp. 58–73.

76 James Lingwood, 'Introduction' to James Lingwood, ed., *Rachel Whiteread: House*, London: Phaidon, 2000, p. 7.

77 Benjamin, 'Theory of Distraction', *Selected Writings*, vol. iii: *1935–1938*, p. 142.

78 Foster, *Compulsive Beauty*, p. 23.

79 Britt, *Walter Benjamin and the Bible*, p. 124.

80 Foster, *Compulsive Beauty*, p. 20.

81 Heidegger, *Nietzsche: Volumes I and II*, vol. i, p. 63.

82 Foster, *Compulsive Beauty*, p. 23.

83 Ibid.

84 Ibid., p. 28.

85 Ibid.

86 Benjamin, *The Arcades Project*, p. 474 [N9a,6].

87 Ibid., p. 475 [N10a,3].

88 Heidegger, *Hegel's Phenomenology of Spirit*, p. 147.

89 Ibid., p. 33.

90 Heidegger, *Being and Time*, p. 452; this passage is highlighted by Karl Löwith, *Martin Heidegger and European Nihilism*, trans. Gary Steiner, Chichester and New York: Columbia University Press, 1995, p. 224: 'I recall his [Heidegger's] letter of 1920, in which it was said that his work is independent of

the peripheral consideration whether that work will give rise to a "culture"
or to an "acceleration of decline"!' (ibid.).

91 Pieper, The End of Time: A Meditation on the Philosophy of History, p. 66.
92 Britt, Walter Benjamin and the Bible, p. 128.
93 Ibid., pp. 128–129.
94 Benjamin, 'Theses on the Philosophy of History', Illuminations, p. 247;
   quoted in Britt, Walter Benjamin and the Bible, p. 129.
95 Benjamin, The Arcades Project, p. 475 [N10a,1].
96 Richard Shone, 'A Cast in Time', in Lingwood, ed., Rachel Whiteread: House,
   pp. 50–61, at p. 52.
97 Ibid.
98 Ibid.
99 Foster, Compulsive Beauty, p. 28.
100 Ibid.
101 Ibid.
102 Doreen Massey, 'Space-Time and the Politics of Location', in Lingwood, ed.,
    Rachel Whiteread: House, pp. 34–49, at p. 42.
103 Benjamin, The Arcades Project, p. 475 [N10a,3].
104 J. M. Bernstein, The Fate of Art: Aesthetic Alienation from Kant to Derrida and
    Adorno, Cambridge: Polity, 1993, p. 17.
105 Ibid.
106 Ibid., p. 4.
107 Bloch, The Principle of Hope, vol. i, p. 6.
108 Ibid., 7.
109 Benjamin, 'Theory of Knowledge', Selected Writings, vol. i: 1913–1926, p. 276.
110 Ibid., pp. 276–277.
111 Bartomeu Marí, 'The Art of the Intangible', in Bradley, ed., Rachel Whiteread:
    Shedding Life, pp. 61–73, at p. 68.
112 Benjamin, 'Theory of Knowledge', Selected Writings, vol. i: 1913–1926, p. 276.
113 See Jean-François Lyotard's discussion in his The Differend: Phrases in Dispute,
    trans. Georges Van Den Abbeele, Manchester: Manchester University Press,
    1988: 'silence imposed on knowledge does not impose the silence of for-
    getting, it imposes a feeling . . . the common person has a complex feeling,
    the one aroused by the negative presentation of the indeterminate' (p. 56).

8

Disrupting textual order

Shuffle, or order and de-formation

A reading of Benjamin always runs the risk of imposing unity where there is disunity, solidity and uniformity where there is a heap of broken images, and order where there are myriad warnings of disorder and ongoing catastrophe. Questions of narrative order and processes of de-formation ('Entstaltung')[1] are central concerns of the modernist aesthetics that Benjamin had long explored to produce not only an unsettling critical practice, comparable to the practices of an entire range of twentieth-century experimental authors and artists, but also one which elucidates and implicates the role of the reader, consumer or collector of a text. The focus in this chapter is on B. S. Johnson's *The Unfortunates* and Benjamin's *The Arcades Project*, theorized as acts of 'Entstaltung' which both create a related 'principle of textual openness'[2] or radically new approaches to a text's binding. Binding is a way of creating a repeatable experience, a memorialization of the text: it is also a childhood act that conjoins modern technological processes and 'accomplishments' to 'the old worlds of symbol'.[3] As Benjamin says in convolute N of *The Arcades Project*: 'There is nothing in the realm of nature that from the outset would be exempt from such a bond. Only, it takes form not in the aura of novelty but in the aura of the habitual. In memory, childhood, and dream.'[4] Benjamin and Johnson worked on the book's binding until it let in more light: they created texts that function like shop windows, revealing the goods inside.[5] The binding can be thought, via catachresis, as a theological concept (which may also bind Benjamin and Kierkegaard)[6], or it is analogous to the Duchampian transparent 'bindings' or boxes: Duchamp's showcases 'with sliding glass panes'.[7] Benjamin also thought of his boxed book

The Arcades Project as a strong-box, a safekeeping of materials, where transparency is achieved via 'concrete dialectical analysis' rather than being that of the display kiosk which now needs protecting from bombs.[8] The shop window or the kiosk, in a time of emergency or crisis, may be too public, too open to catastrophic destruction, but the display case is usually put together for more intimate perusal, in either a museum or a private collection.

In 'Unpacking My Library', Benjamin argues that 'there is in the life of a collector a dialectical tension between the poles of disorder and order.'[9] Collectors and readers have different relationships with texts, readers more often than not unconsciously effacing the materiality of the text in favour of the content – the fictional, critical, philosophical narratives that the reader is 'drawn into'. In contrast, the collector is confronted with the materiality or physicality of the text, and the conditions of its collection (its provenance): a collectible book may have uncut, unreadable pages, and it becomes more valuable, not less so; a collectible book may be tracked down across many cities, many borders, many nation states – when it is finally acquired, it has gained layer upon layer of significance via experience and memory. There is a way in which collecting also neutralizes the materiality of the text, effacing its *thingness*, its being in the world, with almost as much force as the average content-reader. As Jean Baudrillard argues in *The System of Objects*, the collected object is abstracted from its function: 'objects in this sense have another aspect which is intimately bound up with the subject: no longer simply material bodies offering a certain resistance, they become mental precincts over which I hold sway, they become things of which I am the meaning, they become my property and my passion.'[10] The object is not only abstracted, but transformed by infinite substitution: 'what is possessed is always an object *abstracted from its function and thus brought into relationship with the subject*. In this context all owned objects partake of the same *abstractness*'.[11] The collector of rare books, special editions and so on may just as well be collecting smooth pieces of coloured glass from a beach: the relationship between subject and object is essentially the same. In the process of collecting, the materiality of the text can be, ironically, negated, just as use-value is superseded by exchange-value in another related process of abstraction; in other words, not only does the collected object have minimal, if not zero use-value, but its 'value' always derives from elsewhere. The issue here is one of the materiality or *thingness* of the text *per se*: how do content readers or collectors account for the sheer *physicality* which B. S. Johnson's box-book *The Unfortunates* or Benjamin's *The Arcades Project* so powerfully foregrounds? As Henry Sussman argues: 'If anything in the world of literature, of text, may be richly characterized as a *Thing*, it is surely Walter Benjamin's *Arcades Project*.' Sussman continues:

> Not a history, not a treatise; not even strictly speaking a sourcebook, for it also delivers Benjamin's comments, not a work of criticism, in its utter disjointedness, not even, properly, a work. *The Arcades Project* may well be described as a Thing that confronts us in its arbitrariness, its *Geworfenheit*, its Thrownness, its irreducible and irrefutable materiality. Its aggressive repudiation of any prior known or recognized genre qualifies it to be the literary counterpart of an exile.[12]

Still we have a *thing-as-text*, which 'solicits us to explore the dimensionality of literary space' and utilizes 'literary montage' to create competing narratives of nineteenth-century Paris.[13]

B. S. Johnson was a British experimental writer who lived from 1933 to 1973; his work became effaced and forgotten and is now undergoing a process of recovery and recuperation,[14] just as *The Arcades Project* is being manoeuvred centre-stage in Benjamin scholarship.[15] Jonathan Coe writes that:

> *The Unfortunates* stands at the centre of Johnson's output: it was the fourth of his seven novels. The first, *Travelling People*, was described by Anthony Burgess as 'original in the way that *Tristram Shandy* and *Ulysses* are original', and by the time of his sixth, *Christie Malry's Own Double Entry*, he was picking up endorsements from Samuel Beckett . . . Johnson was, at the time, one of Britain's best-known – if not best-selling – writers, famous for his uncompromising, bluntly expressed views on the conservatism of most modern fiction, and for the eye-catching devices which tended to characterize his books, such as holes cut in the pages and . . . unbound sections published together in a box.[16]

In *The Unfortunates* there are twenty-seven sections, with the first and last sections marked as such; all the others can be shuffled into any order. It is a book that is both open and ordered, permutational yet structured, alive to the random playfulness of the reader yet still packaged, coffin-like. Why compare this text with Walter Benjamin's? *The Arcades Project* can be seen as a large notebook, a prepatory work or as a fabulous and insightful work of modernist montage. The translators note that 'it has become customary to regard the text . . . as at best a "torso," a monumental fragment or ruin, and at worst a mere notebook, which the author supposedly intended to mine for extended discursive applications . . . Certainly, the project as a whole is unfinished; Benjamin abandoned work on it in the spring of 1940 . . . Did he leave behind anything more than a large-scale plan or prospectus?'[17] This perspective on *The Arcades Project* generates more questions than answers:

> Why revise for a notebook? The fact that Benjamin also transferred masses of quotations from actual notebooks to the manuscript of the convolutes, and the elaborate organization of these cited materials in that manuscript . . . might likewise bespeak a compositional principle at work in the project, and not just an advanced stage of research. In fact, the montage form – with its philosophic play of distances, transitions and intersections, its perpetually shifting contexts and ironic juxtapositions – had become a favorite device in Benjamin's later investigations . . .[18]

The work is complete, like the Lloyds Insurance building in the City of London: it reveals and revels in its exposed architectonics, and the hidden framework is transformed into a visible exoskeleton, creating new significations with the play of revealed incongruous material.

Johnson's *The Unfortunates* and Benjamin's *The Arcades Project* problematize notions of textual order and affirm the playful nature of signification divided as such between content and form – as these components impact upon the reader; both texts also abandon the liberal humanist notion of the self-present controlling subject (the disruptive nature of subjectivity and textuality being prioritized over an originary, commanding point). Johnson operates critically on the interplay of text and memory, beginning *The Unfortunates* with 'But I know this city!' and ending with 'the loss to me, to us', with no full stop. In between, the ludic shuffling of memories recreates the problematic of 'recreation': a mimetic doubling which forces the reader to occupy the narrator's ontological space. Benjamin 'knows' a city in a way that works via complex spacing (fragmentation and rearrangement) and temporality (reconfiguring the historical), the multi-perspectival experiences and interpretations of this place being reproduced via text: 'the convolutes of *The Arcades Project* both encompass and codify a certain history, and perform the demolition, in the progression toward fascism and anomie, of the utopianism that that history promised.'[19] The architectural blueprint that Benjamin constructs does not deal as such with 'orders' of simulation, but rather with 'registers', where according to subtle differences in perspective or angle of vision, new worlds that were always already present come into sight.[20] Benjamin's architectural blueprint is reconstructed via each individual reading of *The Arcades Project* as with the re-shuffling or ordering of *The Unfortunates*. Benjamin notes that: 'To write history means giving dates their physiognomy'[21] – this allusion to Spengler's *Decline of the West* also points towards Wittgenstein's methodology in the *Philosophical Investigations* and the application of a conceptual configuration in the three-dimensional space of the engineering blueprint.

From the note on the inside box-cover of B. S. Johnson's *The Unfortunates*:

This novel has
twenty-seven sections,
temporarily held together by a
removable wrapper.

Apart from the first
and last sections
(which are marked as such)
the other
twenty-five sections
are intended to be read
in random order.

If readers prefer not
to accept the random order in
which they receive the novel,
then they may
re-arrange the sections into any
other random order before
reading.

The problem of order and its deformation is an essential one for *The Unfortunates* and *The Arcades Project*; the former is framed by first and last sections, stable points which rule out total permutational anarchy, whereas with *The Arcades Project* it is more a question of the macro- and micro-organization of the convolutes. In the act of placing side by side to create a new reading – shuffling the box-book, the montage effects of the convolutes – certain affinities are generated; in the history of modernism, the Surrealists prefigure this approach, but Benjamin was wary of too close an identification with any particular movement. In a letter to Scholem, Benjamin says:

> An all too ostentatious proximity to the surrealist movement might become fatal to the project, as understandable and as well-founded as this proximity might be. In order to extricate it from this situation, I have had to expand the ideas of the project more and more. I have thus had to make it so universal within its most particular and minute framework that it will take possession of the *inheritance* of surrealism in purely temporal terms and, indeed, with all the authority of a philosophical Fortinbras.[22]

The most directly inherited process is that of montage – the juxtaposing of quotations and commentary within *The Arcades Project*, in turn held together globally by bundles, 'of manuscripts or printed materials that belong together'[23] (in the German meaning of the word *Konvolut*), exhibiting a certain arbitrariness, strangeness, even magical quality. As the translators say in the use of the English term: '"Convolute" is strange, at least on first acquaintance, but so is Benjamin's project and its principle of sectioning.'[24] The notion of too much order is as problematic as that of too little: the project is one of creating juxtapositions that exceed the pattern of their positioning, tearing new meaning from old. The convolutes, like Johnson's shuffleable chapters, are in a state of permanent flux, although they can be bound in one set order (as with the unread text? The unopened box-book?). As Buck-Morss argues: 'With the relentless tenacity of the collector . . . Benjamin refused to let go of any of his concerns that had the power to charge the material. Instead he superimposed them, with the result that the project's fragments are bewilderingly overdetermined. Moreover, the conceptions double back on each other, so that chronological divisions in no way correspond to thematic ones.'[25] The convolution of the project, the folding into bundles or chapters, moves at the moment of fission into a state of convulsion, both a contraction and a loss of control. In this state of convulsion, the order of the convolutes can simply be rejected, its programmatic status torn up (the plastic wrapper from a pack of cards is removed; the cards can be shuffled and they maintain their physical occupation of a certain amount of space, regardless of order – the cards can explosively fan out, or burst into space in all directions as the entire pack is thrown into disarray).[26] The actual process of moving from convolutions to convulsions is both internal to the structuring of *The Unfortunates* and *The Arcades Project*, and external, in that different temporality and spatiality are necessary possibilities of reading. Such inherent uncertainty or simultaneity thus maintains the undecidable event or state of the marvellous: 'Advanced by Breton, the marvelous has two cognates: convulsive beauty and objective chance, the first announced in *Nadja* (1928), the second developed in *Les Vases communicants* (1932) and both refined in *L'Amour fou* (1937). [. . .] it is not clear whether it [the marvellous] is an external or internal event, of otherworldly, secular, or psychic agency.'[27] Hal Foster suggests that there are two 'types' of the marvellous put forward by Aragon and Breton: Aragon was interested in the irruption of contradiction with the marvellous, whereas Breton ironed out contradiction as his marvellous functions to disorient and dislocate the subject.[28] For Aragon the objectivity of the political slides into the subjectivity of the personal, but that does not mean that either position is uncontaminated by the other; Foster argues that the marvellous is in effect the uncanny, but 'projected, at least in part, away from the unconscious and repressed material toward the world and future revelation'.[29] One of the main aims of *The Arcades Project* is to awaken the collective from their slumbers; at the same time, the dream-like state or trance of the *flâneur* has revolutionary potential. The seemingly contradictory status of such assertions may in part derive from the issue of the structuring of constellations, where the subjectivity of the reader's response (the 'shock') comes into contact with the objectivity of sequencing, positioning, cataloguing and so on. Foster indicates that there is some confusion in the Surrealist camp by asking: 'Is the marvellous a subjective experience? Is chance an objective event?'[30] The psychology of the contamination, the shock of the constellations or marvellous, is in need of investigation:

> first the marvellous as convulsive beauty will be seen as an uncanny confusion between animate and inanimate states; then the marvellous as objective chance – as manifest in the sudden encounter and the found object – will be revealed as an uncanny reminder of the compulsion to repeat. Both these terms, convulsive beauty and objective chance, connote shock, which suggests that the marvellous also involves traumatic experience . . .[31]

Approaching and plunging into either *The Unfortunates* or *The Arcades Project* for the first time is a traumatic experience. But why? Is it purely the shock effect of the new meanings generated by new juxtapositions? Or is it more to do with the traumatic retrieval of repressed memory, a memorial aesthetics that is constantly at work? *The Unfortunates* creates a pulsation of memories pushing their way backwards and forwards into consciousness; Benjamin's project was brought into existence alongside his translation of Proust's *Remembrance of Things Past*, which he was writing with Franz Hessel. The translators of *The Arcades Project* note that the essay from 1927, 'the only completed text we have from the earliest period of work on *The Arcades Project* . . . may have been written by Benjamin and Hessel together.'[32] But there are differences between notions of memory and recovery with this Benjamin–Johnson–Proust constellation, differences that are marked by narrative. Benjamin and Johnson contain and restrain through cutting, splicing and the rearrangement of narrative commentary or segments, while Proust, admittedly through chance initiators of memory, uses chance to generate vast, intricately woven narratives. While translating Proust, Benjamin called the experience unproductive: 'Unproductive involvement with a writer who so splendidly pursues goals that are similar to my own, at least former goals, occasionally induces something like symptoms of internal poisoning in me.'[33] Yet the Benjamin–Hessel collaboration was generally deemed, overall, a great success. In Friedrich Burschell's gushing letter of praise to the editors of the *Literarische Welt*, he identifies a kind of division of labour between the two translators, suggesting that Benjamin 'represents the subtle, exact, unremittingly probing, critically transcending side which is never satisfied with a single solution, and that corresponds with the other aspect of Proust's talent: the passionate compulsion not to leave anything untouched and to retain in the depths of memory and knowledge all that has been experienced.'[34] Compulsion works here in myriad ways: as the compulsion to constantly dis-order and re-order, always to seek one more reading, one more solution to memory, 'closer' to consciousness, or more distant depending upon one's mood; as the compulsion to reveal all the dusty detritus of the arcades, of history, tearing the veil of contemporary indifference aside; and as the compulsion to repeat, embedded in the workings of the marvellous. Compulsive repetition functions in Proust at the level of narrative, analysed in exemplary fashion by Gérard Genette, the latter asserting that the apparent chronological progression of *Remembrance of Things Past* is counterbalanced by the actual temporal disruptions and disjunctions, for example: 'the narrator had the clearest of reasons for grouping together, in defiance of all chronology, events connected by spatial proximity, by climatic identity (the walks to Méséglise always take place in bad weather, those to Guermantes in good weather), or by thematic kinship'.[35] Such anachronic groupings, in this example, are called by Genette 'syllepses', and are of special interest to him when it comes to the analysis of narrative frequency and *iterative* narrative (narrating one time, or at one time, what happened n times, or the 'pseudo-mathematical formula' $1N/nS$). It could be argued that the earliest draft of *The Arcades Project* moves from sylleptic formulation based upon iterative narrative to *repeating narrative* (narrating n times what happened once, or $nN/1S$). In other words, the earliest draft 'condenses' iteration while the later drafts expand upon singular concepts or themes. But what of the convolutes themselves? These exist in an uneasy tension between the second variation of the singulative, and the repeating and sylleptic modes where the singulative equals narrating once what happened once ($1N/1S$) *and* narrating n times what happened n times (nN/nS), because, as Genette argues, 'from the point of view . . . [of] relations of frequency between narrative and story, this anaphoric type is still in fact singulative and thus reduces to the previous type, since the repetitions of the narrative simply correspond . . . to the repetitions of the story. The singulative is therefore defined not by the number of occurrences on both sides but by the quality of this number'[36].

Is this relationship between narrative and story, derived from distributional analysis of Proust, transferable to *The Arcades Project*? Certainly Benjamin had long been blurring the boundaries between orthodox ways of 'doing' philosophy and other literary-critical approaches, and in part this is a function of his initial interest in early Romanticism, which in itself prefigures much structuralist and post-structuralist theory.[37] Further, the overdetermined 'Work of Art' essay relies heavily not just on apperception, optics, technology and technique, but also on the importance of film *narrative*; rather than the 'Work of Art' essay marking a break with Benjamin's earlier theological theory of language, the essay can be regarded as creating a montage effect, whereby the theory of divine language or 'signs' is now placed side by side with the theory of the copy. Marcel Duchamp, in his box-book *À l'infinitif/In the Infinitive*, theorizes: 'a kind of writing. which no longer has an alphabet or words but signs (films) already emancipated ~~from all the important grammatical rules~~ from the ". . . baby talk . . ." of all ordinary languages.'[38] Crossing out his statement concerning the emancipation of this new language 'from all the important grammatical rules' is also to place under erasure a serious 'linguistic' discourse, immediately replaced by the notion of rule-bound languages as 'baby talk'; of interest here, however, is the formula 'signs (films)', which expresses the Benjaminian concept of language after the essays 'On Language as Such' and 'The Work of Art' are juxtaposed and interpenetrated. This formula can also be applied to the montage effects of *The Unfortunates*. One way of thinking through the commanding structuralist analysis of the story/plot binary opposition is to assign the exposés of *The Arcades Project* to abstracted stories and the convolutes to the actual narrative (that is to say, the narrative order in which they are actually placed). Of course this is complicated by the versioning that occurred throughout the different phases of the project. There is some point to utilizing this opposition in such a way: the desire for a 'completed' text can now be seen as leading to one more abstracted story as such. In other words, the relationships between the convolutes and the exposés may simply have been misunderstood, where more 'refined' versions of the exposés simply leave the convolutes untouched (and what of the sense, held by some, that the early drafts are somehow more effective than the later ones?). The Benjamin–Johnson–Proust constellation of 'signs (films)' thus reveals that temporal frequency is one of the keys to *The Arcades Project*, where there is a complex relationship between drafts and convolutes, and the pseudo-mathematical formulae $1N/1S$-nN/nS, $nN/1S$ and $1N/nS$. But how does Johnson's *The Unfortunates* come into more detailed play in relation to this narratalogical analysis?

The problem of memory becomes, also, one of quotation; locating the past is highly problematic for Johnson's narrator, overdetermined instances being countered by extreme uncertainty of time and location: did I come here before? Am I conflating several locations into one? When did I first visit this place? Did multiple events happen in this one place? Or am I condensing multiple events, at multiple locations, into a falsely unified location? Such overdetermination is transferred to the reader, for example: 'all memories are curious, for that matter, the mind as a think of an image Two days I was ill . . .' Where does this quotation, with its fascinating use of spacing, occur? It could be located, first, as page 5, in which case,

it is one of all the page 5s in all the shuffleable chapters; more precisely, it could be argued that it is in the chapter with a certain
individual symbol assigned to it: ✪. But where does this chapter,
chapter ✪, come in the book? A foolish question, perhaps, but one
that is deemed logical, under the conditions of reading of both book
and archive (the latter, a form of institutional or private memory,
depends upon issues such as provenance, or the dominant organiz-
ing principles of the archive, that is, generation or storage). If a
momentary, random shuffling of the box-book equals x (. . . symbol
. . . symbol . . . etc.), then the chapter can only be located in the
sequence of x, or at the very least the surrounding chapters, giving
something like: x = (. . . , ✳, ✪, ✛ . . .). There is a further indeterminacy, or subjective reordering, that must be taken into account: the
possibility that someone else may shuffle the book in between individual readings, for example, if the book is a library copy that has
been returned and then taken out again. In the latter case, x = (. . . ,
✳, ✪, ✛ . . .) becomes an even more ephemeral sequence. To preserve
the sequence for the time of this reading, here are the juxtaposed
sentences:

> The area had to be this large in order to try to kill all the explosive,
> runaway, zealous, monstrous cells of the tumour: if one single cell
> escaped to another part of the body, by insinuating itself into the
> bloodstream, then it would grow and multiply there too. (✳, p. 8)

> The estate.   That enormous flat. It seems enormous to me, now.
> But I was very ill there.   I must have arrived at about
> four in the afternoon. Tony was there in the downstairs hall, on the
> phone. (✪, p. 1)

> I cannot place this, though, it will not fall into place. But it was cer-
> tainly on that visit, that June was angry at my laziness, weariness,
> as we all three came in tired, Tony and I sat and talked, she had to
> prepare a meal on her own, for us. (✪, p. 8)

> Then he was doing research, enjoying not having the tie of lectures
> to attend, he said, or wrote, and they had moved from the Park, or
> the Estate, whatever it was called, and were living in one of the
> towns on the outskirts of this city, contiguous with it, really, at least
> connected by ribbon development, if it is not a suburb, it has its
> own name, something beginning with B, how soon I forget the
> simple things . . . (✛, p. 1)

The sequence disintegrates, no matter how many times it is reconstituted (there is, after all, nothing to stop someone actually placing the chapters in a certain order). Disintegration also happens materially, as the chapters yellow and fall apart: what is left is an even looser 'manuscript' format, with fragile leaves of paper that disrupt further the symbol-based system of location and citation, a manuscript that works through subtraction as well as ludic iteration.

There is a sense in which the box-book cannot let go – even though the narrator is struggling with memory, with the act of remembrance; shuffling and re-reading the book is as compulsive as the narrator's attempt to weave a coherent pattern out of life's ludicrous arbitrariness. The narrator deals in fragments, but their interweaving constructs a totality, a 'Total object, complete with missing parts'.[39] As with the above observation on translation from Friedrich Burschell, there is a 'passionate compulsion' in *The Unfortunates*, one which aims to account for all that has been experienced in relation to Tony. This passionate compulsion is that of the chronicler:

> the 'historian' of the 'Theses on the Philosophy of History' inherited certain qualities from the chronicler: A chronicler who recites events without distinguishing between major and minor ones acts in accordance with the following truth: nothing that has ever happened should be regarded as lost for history. To be sure, only a redeemed mankind receives the fullness of its past – which is to say, only for a redeemed mankind has its past become citable in all its moments. Each moment it has lived becomes a *citation a l'ordre du jour* – and that is Judgement Day.[40]

The reconstitution of the memories that are called 'Tony' may be a fragile, ephemeral, even subtractive affair, but nonetheless, in the compulsion to bring him back, all of his past becomes viable grist for the historical mill. It is no coincidence that Tony's subjectivity as such is tied in with the experience of revisiting a city – 'But I know this city!' – just as it is no coincidence that *The Arcades Project* is fundamentally a city-space (both cities in question offer a refractive vision which is problematic *and* liberating or productive). Howard Caygill argues that the 'understanding of urban experience through the use of spatio-temporal contrasts and counterfactuals is not only an epistemological device for gaining knowledge of urban experience, but itself a feature of modern urban experience.'[41] This includes the haunting of the city, the ghosts and the projected desires or fantasies of the city inhabitants.

Just gaming: Benjamin, Johnson and Wittgenstein

Are these texts – *The Arcades Project* and *The Unfortunates* – examples of performative meaning? That is to say, do these texts function by generating meanings that are tied in to a particular configuration in the present play that we call their reading? Put another way, can we say that plot and story are performed by the reader as such, and that the reader does not have to rely on abstracted systems of thought to make sense of the texts in question, because each reconfiguration is the meaning of the text? In this case any particular interpretive guide to the text(s) would be redundant. This appears too ludic by far, too postmodern, too relativistic, as if the texts could say anything and mean anything. There are definite, related processes at work in both texts, which means that they have a family resemblance, where the latter is defined not as a shared, single property but as a bundle of traits or 'a whole series of overlapping similarities'.[42] As Wittgenstein puts it in the *Philosophical Investigations*: 'we see [in family resemblance] a complicated network of similarities overlapping and criss-crossing: sometimes overall similarities, sometimes similarities of detail.'[43] To map out the family resemblance is to trace not the shared architectural framework upon which both texts hang, but instead the structures and processes which make these texts compulsive reading, structures and processes that make the reading of these texts both a painful and a pleasurable experience. They are both, potentially, fetishized objects, collectibles, collectors' items, lavishly packaged in an age of cheap and tacky mass production. Both texts play with 'reproduction', strategically inserting themselves into the market economies that they also resist. In some ways *The Arcades Project* now looks like a particularly big airport crime-thriller or pornographic novel, with the cut-out hole to peep in at Benjamin himself, who may actually be peeping out. Removing the loose cover sleeve reveals large, garish lettering on the spine: perhaps it will wear off in time? The 1999 edition of *The Unfortunates* seems to strive to look as disappointingly normal as possible,[44] although there is something essentially 'retro' about the title itself, with its mock 'Dymo Tape' appearance, as if it had been hand-made and simply stuck on to the box. Both texts play with appearances, suggesting by their covers or containers strikingly different books from the ones found inside. From this first point of material contact, the texts are subtly (or not so subtly) manipulating the reader. Fogelin has noted a related quality in Wittgenstein's *Philosophical Investigations*, where the intention is not simply to put across a different systematic viewpoint, but to engage the reader in an act of persuasion: 'This work is not primarily an attack upon particular solutions to philosophical problems, but an inquiry into the moves that initiate philosophical reflection; for the most part it is not a criticism of the results of philosophizing, but an interrogation of its source.'[45] Wittgenstein's circuitous methodology – annoying, confusing at times, irritating at others – is designed to engage the reader in working out problems for himself or herself; it also forces the reader back to the text, over and over again.

Introductory accounts of the *Philosophical Investigations* take a necessarily considerable amount of time looking at the text's methodology, just as with *The Arcades Project* and *The Unfortunates*; all three texts are written with an acute awareness of the reader's engagement with form, and all three distinctly disrupt normative reading processes. In a Russian Formalist sense, these texts 'make strange' normative reading processes, foregrounding the ways in which 'normative' can actually be more accurately described as 'normalizing' (an active self-negation of the text's architectonics). In the texts under discussion, however, 'making strange' is also intricately tied in with 'persuasion': the embedded notion that the reader has been conned or duped elsewhere by normalizing narratives. For Benjamin, it is the narratives of capitalism that need disruption; for Johnson, it is narratives of determinate remembrance and/or memorialization. Benjamin and Johnson both break processes of perception and representation down into component parts: in the process of this fragmentation we learn not only how they work, but how they might work differently. This latter can lead to a rejection not just of the text itself, but also of the methods of its author: Johnson's experimentalism, for example, can be dismissed as mere inconsequential playfulness, or an empty obsession with form; Benjamin's project can be dismissed as incomplete, lacking the master's final configuration of the dialectical images, a kind of condemnatory compliment, whereby the suggestion is that the text would have ultimately worked, but it just does not quite work now. Such disgruntled rejection fails to take into account the ephemeral nature of these texts, their multiple successes and failures that occur with each reading: this ephemeral nature is one of their key family resemblances. Of course saying that texts share certain key features is not to argue that they are identical; Fogelin illuminates precisely this point with the following diagram:[46]

O_1	O_2	O_3	O_4	O_5	O_6
A	B	C	D	E	F
B	C	D	E	F	A
C	D	E	F	A	B
D	E	F	A	B	C

The key element here is the fact that there is a common thread of three shared features with two other groups (where On equals a group) 'but there is no single feature that runs through the lot.'[47] A similar table can be produced where Johnson's and Benjamin's texts stand as 'groups', with the following list of features: A = performativity; B = shuffleable chapters; C = dialectical images; D = fixed constellations; E = variable constellations; F = autobiographical; G = historical analysis; H = subject or memory analysis; I = 'makes strange' the reading process . . . etc. The table could be constructed thus:

The Arcades Project		*The Unfortunates*
A	I	A
C	I	B
D	I	E
E	I	F
G	I	H
I	I	I
. . .	I	. . .
. . .	I	. . . [etc.]

It is clear that the texts are not identical, but they have significant shared features; not to labour the point, this turn to family resemblance is necessary to move away from an overly critically 'fixed' product. This was precisely one of the objectives of Wittgenstein's methodological shift, where family resemblance 'helps dispel the commitment to definiteness of sense by exhibiting a set of concepts that violate this standard but are still perfectly serviceable . . . [in] the *Tractatus* . . . this demand for definiteness of sense was a driving force that led away from everyday language as it actually appears to the postulation of a sublime structure that underlies it.'[48] Crudely put in literary-critical terms, readings of texts often move from text to system, abstracting the text via appreciative, intuitive or more obviously theory-driven strategies of reading (I include 'appreciative' and 'intuitive' as being in themselves theories of reading), whereas what is important in *The Arcades Project* and *The Unfortunates* is the engagement with the text as a re-occurring process and the temporary interpretive framework(s) brought to bear. For example, what if I decide to shuffle *The Unfortunates every* time I read it? What if I decide to re-shuffle the book *as* I read it, rather than shuffling and reading the entire text sequentially? This constant re-shuffling is closer to my actual experience of *The Unfortunates* and the way in which I dip in and out of Benjamin's convolutes.

Here is an example of what happens during a constantly re-shuffled reading of *The Unfortunates*, using chapter ❋ as the starting point of a small three-chapter sequence (that is, starting from this chapter each time I come across it after having re-shuffled the book), placed into a 'family resemblance' chart (n = reading; number (for example N1) equals the number of times the box-book has been re-shuffled, where a 'shuffle' equals a random sequence of interleaving):

N1	N2	N3	N4
❋	❋	❋	❋
✪	✳	❋	✛
✛	◎	◎	✪

How does this compare with my dipping in and out of the convolutes? While I do read the convolutes themselves in different sequences, there is also the issue of dipping in and out of a single convolute. Does this mean that *The Arcades Project* functions like a doubled version of *The Unfortunates* (where a convolute has re-shuffleable entries, and the convolutes themselves can be re-shuffled)? I tend to read through an entire convolute, or sections of a convolute, in a fairly linear fashion, once my attention has been caught, even given any re-ordering; these readings could be described as macro- and micro-re-ordering, for example: 'macro-shuffling' for summer of 2001: $n + 1$ = convolute D + K + N; $n + 2$ = convolutes D + K + N + Early Drafts + Addenda; micro-shuffling for reading on 20 August 2001: n + 1 = convolute V1,3, V1,4, V1,5; n + 2 = V4,3, V4,1, V4,2 . . . and so on. What do these differences in ordering mean? How do we account for them beyond simple tables and charts, even given the point concerning family resemblance? Sequential re-shufflings can be compared, to see if any major differences in the narrative's meanings or effects are generated. If we are dealing with texts whose material changes and interactivity with the reader are dynamic, temporarily arranged, modified and ludic, while also being structured along modernist lines, then I would suggest that a theory of dynamic modernist narrative is needed.[49] Postmodern narrative theory deals with, among many other things, issues such as indeterminacy and self-reflexivity; here, with Benjamin's and Johnson's texts, we are still in the realm of high modernism as such: there are controlling structures and an even more radical intervention on the part of the reader than is found in many a postmodern text. A theory of dynamic modernist narrative which examines material changes in the text would do well to start with Genette's work on plot and narration, but then show how all the categories he works with are dependent upon *chance* and *change* when it comes to the texts in question. The architectonics of interactivity will fundamentally transform Genette's anachronisms.

Aphorism

Benjamin had long worked with theoretical and textual forms resistant to immediate or hasty interpretation: the fragment and the aphorism are not only major components of his critical armoury, but they also problematize any attempted segregation of apparently literary or narrative works from philosophical concerns. Probably the most famous such text prior to the publication of *The Arcades Project* was Benjamin's 'Einbahnstrasse' or 'One-Way Street' (1928), where the physiognomy of the city provides the headings for a sequence of aphoristic passages that are in many ways radically disjunctive (especially if the headings are simplistically read as descriptions of the 'content' that follows). Rochlitz argues that Nietzsche is one of Benjamin's 'models' here:

> The philosophy of *Einbahnstrasse* is situated halfway between that of Nietzsche, who is assuredly one of Benjamin's models, and that of Adorno's *Minima moralia*. It is an approach that exploits both the

resources of a unique experience and a singular intelligence in order
to counter the intellectual conformity of the environment, and that
associates a sort of historical mission with this subversive status of
subjectivity. The dream and personal experience are instrumental-
ized in the name of a cause of general interest and are invested with
historical significance.[50]

Fairly early on in 'One-Way Street' – in the sequence or section
'Chinese Curios' – Benjamin theorizes two types of relationship with
the text: that of the reader versus that of the copier. There is a
tension between the text's interpretive control, that is, the text's own
textual *affects*, and reading as adjacency whereby the text is virtually
ignored by the reader (although it may create the grounds for
reading as the 'free flight' of dreaming):

> The power of a country road when one is walking along it is dif-
> ferent from the power it has when one is flying over it by airplane.
> In the same way, the power of a text when it is read is different
> from the power it has when it is copied out. [. . .] Only the copied
> text thus commands the soul of him who is occupied with it,
> whereas the mere reader never discovers the new aspects of his
> inner self that are opened by the text, that road cut through the
> interior jungle forever closing behind it: because the reader follows
> the movement of his mind in the free flight of daydreaming,
> whereas the copier submits it to command.[51]

The command of the text arises from immersion and mimesis: the
copying and reproduction of text, or the reader as scribe; without
naming the outmoded subject, the secular or theological scribe is
compared with a rambler wandering down a country road, whereas
the reader as dreamer is analogous to the perspective of flight. The
aphorism is about the scribbler as someone who travels (or works
through, *travails*) a text, submitting to the command. But what
precisely is the command, or the experience of the command?
Benjamin appears to be arguing that the perspective of the rambler
(copier) is superior to that of the flyer (reader) because the latter
perceives the external laws of the terrain's or text's organization,
whereas the former 'learns of the power it commands' which is
expanded thus: 'from the very scenery that for the flier is only the
unfurled plain, it calls forth distances, belvederes, clearings,
prospects at each of its turns like a commander deploying soldiers at
a front.'[52] The shifting, multiple perspectives of the rambler or copier

opens up a multitude of further perspectives. But why the military discourse of strategic deployment? The passage also narrates the existential experience of passing through a landscape or text: the aerial view is that of 'armchair' generals or strategists examining a distant view or simulacrum of the battlefield, whereas the rambler or commander is immersed in multiple perspectival unfolding experiences. It would appear that the position of greatest freedom offers a perspective so detached that it misses altogether the experiences themselves (it becomes an experience of self-obsession).

Commanding and the call of the command are linked to freedom and perspectivism, which announces another intertextual field beyond the notion of the scribe: the open, perspectival texts of Nietzsche. Reading Nietzsche, Heidegger also ponders the 'commanding nature of knowledge'[53] where he argues that 'the word *command* does not mean merely *making* a demand *known* and requiring its fulfillment':

> True commanding is obedience to what is taken on in free responsibility, perhaps even first created. Essential commanding first posits the whither and wherefore. *Commanding* as making known a demand already directed, and *commanding* as founding this demand and taking on the decision contained in it, are fundamentally different. Original commanding and being able to command always arise only from *freedom* and are themselves fundamental forms of true being free. Freedom – in the simple and profound sense that Kant understood its essence – is in itself *poetizing*: the groundless grounding of a ground, in such a way that it grants itself the law of its essence. But commanding means nothing other than this.[54]

The lesson learnt via 'command' is that the text has its own necessity; furthermore, as Heidegger argues, necessity, or 'the *must* of commanding and poetizing', actually 'arises from freedom'.[55] Benjamin's aphorism is a warning: do not think that the emphasis upon dream and surreality in 'One-Way Street' means that the text is merely a free-play of (purely relativistic) meaning, but, also, do follow the text closely, even as far as to reproduce it, to experience the text's command. Heidegger's division between two types of command reveals a fundamental or grounding difference; in fact in the extract quoted, commanding is a faithfulness to what Derrida calls 'différance' ('the nonunitary synthesis of all these very different types of difference and, as such, the matrix from which they draw their existence'[56]). The contradictory-sounding non-originary origin is thus another way of thinking Heidegger's poetizing, or 'the ground-less grounding of a ground'.[57] Can Derrida's 'différance' find its way back to itself, however, as Heidegger's question appears to demand as an essential component or force of the command?[58] Benjamin's command is also a strategic deployment that opens up perspectives; the command determines the placing of the subject in relation to the perspectives, but does not compose the perspectives themselves (and within the perspectives are new landscapes that contain buildings used for the gaining of a view, for example, the belvedere). This is deliberately to utilize or put on the mask of Frank's analysis of 'différance':

> If the meaning-producing movement of *différance* . . . determines the places of possible positivities, it is not also a positivity itself: it should be considered neither as a subject nor as a substance nor as something present nor even as a something at all. In this sense it can be called 'autonomous' like Hegel's negation. This, to be sure, has an implication Derrida does not express *in this way*, one that we, however, need to supply here: *différance* makes relations possible, and it cannot exist without an open field of relations between givens; yet it itself does not participate in the play of these relations (otherwise it would be *something*, and not the condition of possibility), and in this sense it has to be taken to be absolutely singular and relationless, like Hegel's negation. In other words, *différance*, although it is the condition of possibility for the play of differentiations, is itself, however, still distinguished from this play: it does not exist *without* this play, but it is not the play itself; and it does not exist *due* to this play . . .[59]

How far from Benjamin's 'Epistemo-Critical Prologue' have we travelled with the non-originary grounding or command of the aphorism in his 'One-Way Street', where the scribe comes to discover 'new aspects of his inner self'?[60] The aphorism form in Benjamin functions as an incredibly condensed version of the esoteric essay, while traces of doctrine are deeply buried, but are nonetheless maintained; the aphorism's force is one which powers or produces multiple conceptual possibilities, and it is still a mode of maintenance.[61]

The aphorism has been thoroughly explored elsewhere in relation to the form of Nietzsche's philosophy, although this can also be read as an evasion of the full force of Nietzsche's radically different styles.[62] Nehamas notes how Nietzsche's aphorisms are often hyperbolic, simultaneously working via form to 'disarm' hyperbole through a process of quarantine and isolation: 'The aphorism has bracketed the hyperbole [in Nehamas's example from *The Gay Science*]; it prevents it from functioning as part of a continuous narrative or, more important, as a premise in an argument. The spaces that separate aphorisms from one another also act as frames that magnify the power of exaggeration within them but don't allow it to penetrate beyond their confines.'[63] Benjamin's command aphorism both is quarantined and interpenetrates the entire sequence of *Einbahnstrasse*; the notion of an enclosed aphorism, a kind of monadology of aphorisms, is replaced with the aphorism as generating a non-originary origin or groundless ground, whether read in the Derridean or the Heideggerian sense. The former would assert that each aphorism is a 'bundle' or convolute of traces ('Every trace is the trace of a trace'[64]), whereas the latter would assert that command is one Nietzschean category of life, the others being poetizing, the perspectival and the horizonal.[65] Benjamin's aphorisms are monadological and differential: they 'replicate' via the matrix and are folded in the Deleuzian sense. In 'Imperial Panorama' ('A Tour through the German Inflation'), the perspectival view of the individual, divorced from a sense of society or community, is problematized:

> A blind determination to save the prestige of personal existence – rather than, through an impartial disdain for its impotence and entanglement, at least to detach it from the background of universal delusion – is triumphing almost everywhere. That is why the air is so thick with life theories and world views, and why in this country they cut so presumptuous a figure, for almost always they finally serve to sanction some utterly trivial private situation. For just the same reason the air is teeming with phantoms, mirages of a glorious cultural future breaking upon us overnight in spite of all, for everyone is committed to the optical illusions of his isolated standpoint.[66]

How do we distinguish the positive multiple and perspectival unfolding of experiences from the 'optical illusions' of the 'isolated standpoint'? One approach is to become immersed in the 'recurrent themes' of the aphorism sequence: 'an ethnography of cities, reflections on love, childhood memories, transcriptions of dreams, and remarks on the revolutionary crisis of humanity'.[67] Benjamin's aphorisms attack the boundaries between competing 'spheres of reality': 'Metaphorically or literally, he effaces the opposition between public life and private life, exterior and interior (furnishings and the soul living among them), the human and the animal, conscious thought and the dream; in his view, these separations are characteristic of "bourgeois" thought, which is responsible for all abstraction.'[68] The decomposition of bourgeois boundaries utilizing the tropes of narrative and aphorism is an early example and after-effect of what Benjamin will call 'spectrum analysis'.[69] That is to say, the decomposition is not an arbitrary critical act, but one designed to discover the origin or source of society's ills. While this is clearly a shift into 'materialist' analysis, it is not an abandonment of the concept of the Messianic: 'Just as a physicist determines the presence of ultraviolet light in the solar spectrum, so the historical materialist determines the presence of a messianic force in history.'[70] But Benjamin does add that the attempt to know the parameters of a redeemed society involves posing questions to which there are no straightforward answers. The aphorism as spectrum analysis involves a dialectic of observation and critical decomposition: ultimately, the aphorism, in Benjamin's hands, turns upon itself (aphorism as boundary-setting form versus aphorism as deconstructive form).

As boundary-setting form, the aphorism in 'One-Way Street' is always already contaminated by narrative, by the expansionist tendencies of prose, regardless of its opposing intra-deconstructive force; such a contamination leads to the thoughts on 'good prose' and the three steps: 'a musical stage when it is composed, an architectonic one when it is built, and a textile one when it is woven'.[71] Prose should not be thought of in opposition to spectrum analysis; rather, it forms a constellation that Benjamin develops via Leskov where the different types of 'artistic' prose embody the entire spectrum of historical types.[72] 'One-Way Street' is written in 'liberated prose', that is to say, it belongs to the realm of technical reproduction. The aphorism as sequence of observations has an elective affinity with that of the output of the chronicler; the aphorism as intra-deconstructive force gives it the analytical and interpretive power of the historian:

> it will take no effort to gauge the difference between one who writes history (the historian) and one who narrates it (the chronicler). The historian's task is to *explain* in one way or another the happenings with which he deals; under no circumstances can he content himself with simply displaying them as models of the course of the world. But this is precisely what the chronicler does, especially in his classical avatars . . . By basing their historical tales on a divine – and

inscrutable – plan of salvation, at the very outset they have lifted the burden of demonstrable explanation from their own shoulders. Its place is taken by interpretation, which is concerned not with an accurate concatenation of definite events, but with the way these are embedded in the great inscrutable course of the world.

Whether this course is determined by salvation history or by natural history makes no difference. In the storyteller the chronicler is preserved in changed form – secularized, as it were.[73]

But where is the sequence of aphorisms, and their dialectics of revealing and interpreting, to be published? As a book? Is such a framing device still acceptable to Benjamin? The traditional form of the book, Benjamin argues, is nearing its end.[74] The book, that is to say the Lutheran Bible, belonged essentially to the people (a similar argument could be made for Tyndale's English Bible, and then the Authorized, or King James); the contemporary book is interpenetrated, ruthlessly introverted or ripped inside out and appropriated by the visual methods of capitalism, primarily via advertising: 'Script . . . is pitilessly dragged out into the street by advertisements and subjected to the brutal heteronomies of economic chaos. This is the hard schooling of its new form.'[75] Benjamin traces modernist texts that experiment with typographic excess, mentioning Mallarmé and the Dadaists, but his real interest lies in the new technologies that are replacing the book itself, such as the 'card index' and statistical and technical diagrams.[76] In parentheses, Benjamin adds that the contemporary book is 'an outdated mediation between two different filing systems. For everything that matters is to be found in the card box of the researcher who wrote it, and the scholar studying it assimilates it into his own card index.'[77] The outmoded book, if not blasted apart by the typographic excesses of modernism and capitalism, is raided and sampled by the scholar, for his or her card index. We can think of The Arcades Project as precisely this type of archiving technology, with its concomitant apparatus of information categorization and retrieval. The opposing antiquated 'Fat Book' is parodied in the aphorism 'Teaching Aid': its bloated repetitious nature is ridiculed and offers a foil for the apparently equally 'bloated' text of The Arcades Project: given a computational approach, the permutations of the latter are not regarded as excessive, merely indicative of the devices needed to maintain vast modern databases ('keep your notebook as strictly as the authorities keep their register of aliens'[78]).

'One-Way Street' appears to narrate the demise, also, of the philosophical book, especially as 'One-Way Street' is a cityscape, an erotics of an urban space or dreamscape and the images and people that inhabit it. The aphorism 'Interior Decoration' reminds us of what can remain hidden behind the blank façade:

> The tractatus is an Arabic form. Its exterior is undifferentiated and unobtrusive, like the façades of Arabian buildings, whose articulation of begins only in the courtyard. So, too, the articulated structure of the tractatus is invisible from the outside, revealing itself only from within. If it is formed by chapters, they have not verbal headings but numbers. The surface of its deliberations is not enlivened with pictures, but covered with unbroken, proliferating arabesques. In the ornamental density of this presentation, the distinction between thematic and excursive expositions is abolished.[79]

The boundaries between the centrifugal (excursive) and centripetal (thematic) forces of the tractatus are dissolved by the proliferating patterns of propositions; Benjamin visualizes propositions as a presentation of 'ornamental density'. He is also reminding us that the architectonics of the cityscape are not always what they at first seem; blank walls may hide dense and convoluted interiors. By penetrating these interiors with glass arcades, connecting previously separate streets and people, a transformative glimpse is directly or immediately obtained.

Notes

1 Benjamin, 'Imagination', *Selected Writings*, vol. i: *1913–1926*, p. 280.
2 Henry Sussman, 'Between the Registers: The Allegory of Space in Walter Benjamin's *Arcades Project*', *boundary 2*, 30: 1 (Spring 2003), special issue: *Benjamin Now: Critical Encounters with 'The Arcades Project'*, ed. Kevin McLaughlin and Philip Rosen, 169–190, at 171.
3 Benjamin, *The Arcades Project*, p. 461 [N2a,1].
4 Ibid.
5 Duchamp, *À l'infinitif/In the Infinitive*, p. 5.
6 Sussman, 'Between the Registers: The Allegory of Space in Walter Benjamin's *Arcades Project*', p. 175 and footnote 10.
7 Duchamp, *À l'infinitif/In the Infinitive*, p. 7.
8 Benjamin to Max Horkheimer, 31 January 1937; letter 285, in *The Correspondence of Walter Benjamin, 1910–1940*, p. 537.
9 Benjamin, 'Unpacking My Library: A Talk about Book Collecting', *Illuminations*, p. 62.
10 Jean Baudrillard, *The System of Objects*, trans. James Benedict, London: Verso, 1996, p. 85.

11 Ibid., p. 86.
12 Sussman, 'Between the Registers: The Allegory of Space in Walter Benjamin's *Arcades Project*', p. 169.
13 Ibid., p. 172.
14 See Philip Tew's groundbreaking critique in his *B. S. Johnson: A Critical Reading*, Manchester and New York: Manchester University Press, 2001.
15 See, for example, *boundary 2*, special issue: *Benjamin Now: Critical Encounters with 'The Arcades Project'*; see also Esther Leslie, 'Elemental: Walter Benjamin's *Arcades Project*', in A. Benjamin and Osborne, eds., *Walter Benjamin's Philosophy: Destruction and Experience*, pp. 304–308, appendix 2.
16 Jonathan Coe, 'Introduction' to B. S. Johnson, *The Unfortunates*, London: Picador, 1999, p. v.
17 Benjamin, *The Arcades Project*, pp. x–xi.
18 Ibid., p. xi.
19 Sussman, 'Between the Registers: The Allegory of Space in Walter Benjamin's *Arcades Project*', p. 180.
20 See Sussman (ibid.), and see also Rex Butler's discussion of Borges in *Jean Baudrillard: The Defence of the Real*, London: Sage, 1999, pp. 41–42.
21 Benjamin, *The Arcades Project*, p. 476 [N11,2].
22 Benjamin to Gerhard Scholem, 30 October 1928, letter 181 in *The Correspondence of Walter Benjamin, 1910–1940*, p. 342.
23 Benjamin, *The Arcades Project*, p. xiv.
24 Ibid.
25 Buck-Morss, *The Dialectics of Seeing: Walter Benjamin and The Arcades Project*, p. 53.
26 Playing with these texts may be closer to gambling than reading as we conventionally know it, where the most important critical moves are made rapidly and '. . . at the last possible moment' (Benjamin, 'Notes on a Theory of Gambling', *Selected Writings*, vol. ii: *1927–1934*, p. 297). Furthermore, compression and acceleration of time through the reader's intervention (and this is different from jumping ahead a few chapters: the reader literally compresses events) is one of the defining features of gambling, of play, as Anatole France argues: 'what is play . . . but the art of producing in a second the changes that Destiny ordinarily effects only in the course of many hours or even many years, the art of collecting into a single instant the emotions dispersed throughout the slow-moving existence of ordinary men, the secret of living a whole lifetime in a few minutes . . . ?' (*The Garden of Epicurus*, trans. Alfred Allinson, London: Bodley Head, 1926, p. 23). Finally, then, a theory of dynamic modernist narrative must take into account the 'hand-to-hand encounter with Fate' (ibid.) that is the experience of reading Benjamin's and Johnson's texts.
27 Foster, *Compulsive Beauty*, p. 19.
28 Ibid., p. 20.
29 Ibid.
30 Ibid., p. 21.
31 Ibid.
32 Benjamin, *The Arcades Project*, p. 871.
33 Quoted in Brodersen, *Walter Benjamin: A Biography*, p. 166.
34 Ibid., p. 169.
35 Gérard Genette, *Narrative Discourse*, Oxford: Basil Blackwell, 1986, p. 85.

36 Ibid., p. 115.

37 Bowie, *Aesthetics and Subjectivity: From Kant to Nietzsche*, p. 43.

38 Duchamp, *À l'infinitif/In the Infinitive*, p. 20; crossed out by hand in the original.

39 Samuel Beckett, *Proust and Three Dialogues with Georges Duthuit*, London: John Calder, 1999, p. 101.

40 Rochlitz, *The Disenchantment of Art: The Philosophy of Walter Benjamin*, pp. 228–229; Benjamin, 'Theses', *Illuminations*, p. 246.

41 Caygill, *Walter Benjamin: The Colour of Experience*, p. 119.

42 Fogelin, *Wittgenstein*, p. 133.

43 Ludwig Wittgenstein, *Philosophical Investigations*, trans. G. E. M. Anscombe, Oxford: Basil Blackwell, 1991, proposition 66, p. 32.

44 Especially compared with the vibrant and striking packaging of the first edition.

45 Fogelin, *Wittgenstein*, p. 110.

46 Ibid., p. 133.

47 Ibid.

48 Ibid., p. 138.

49 This would also be a narrative theory that can deal with meta-temporal issues; see Richard J. Lane, 'Beckett and Nietzsche: The Eternal Headache', in Richard J. Lane, ed., *Beckett and Philosophy*, Basingstoke: Palgrave, 2002, pp. 166–176.

50 Rochlitz, *The Disenchantment of Art: The Philosophy of Walter Benjamin*, p. 120.

51 Walter Benjamin, 'One-Way Street', *Selected Writings*, vol. i: *1913–1926*, pp. 447–448.

52 Ibid.

53 Heidegger, *Nietzsche: Volumes III and IV*, vol. iii, p. 118.

54 Ibid., p. 118, p. 119.

55 Ibid., p. 121.

56 Rodolphe Gasché, *The Tain of The Mirror: Derrida and the Philosophy of Reflection*, Cambridge, Massachusetts, and London, England: Harvard University Press, 1986, p. 205.

57 Heidegger, *Nietzsche: Volumes III and IV*, vol. iii, p. 119.

58 See Frank, *What is Neostructuralism?*, p. 270.

59 Ibid., p. 270.

60 Benjamin, 'One-Way Street', *Selected Writings*, vol. i: *1913–1926*, p. 448; my emphasis.

61 Geoffrey Bennington with Jacques Derrida, *Jacques Derrida*, trans. Geoffrey Bennington, Chicago and London: The University of Chicago Press, 1993, p. 71.

62 See Alexander Nehamas, *Nietzsche: Life as Literature*, Cambridge, Massachusetts, and London, England: Harvard University Press, 1985, p. 22.

63 Ibid., p. 23.

64 Bennington, *Jacques Derrida*, p. 75.

65 Heidegger, *Nietzsche: Volumes III and IV*, vol. iii, p. 122.

66 Benjamin, 'One-Way Street', *Selected Writings*, vol. i: *1913–1926*, p. 453.

67 Rochlitz, *The Disenchantment of Art: The Philosophy of Walter Benjamin*, p. 120.

68 Ibid.

69 Benjamin, 'Paralipomena to "On the Concept of History"', *Selected Writings*, vol. iv: *1938–1940*, p. 402.

70 Ibid.
71 Benjamin, 'One-Way Street', *Selected Writings*, vol. i: *1913–1926*, p. 455.
72 Benjamin, 'Paralipomena to "On the Concept of History"', *Selected Writings*, vol. iv: *1938–1940*, p. 404.
73 Benjamin, 'The Storyteller: Observations on the Works of Nikolai Leskov', *Selected Writings*, vol. iii: *1935–1938*, pp. 152–153.
74 Benjamin, 'One-Way Street', *Selected Writings*, vol. i: *1913–1926*, p. 456.
75 Ibid.
76 Ibid., pp. 456–457.
77 Ibid., p. 456.
78 Ibid., p. 458.
79 Ibid., p. 462.

9

Conclusion: exile and the time of crisis

Reconfiguring repetition

Repetition in Surrealist objective chance reveals not just a fore-life (the repressed event, that which fails to be recollected[1]) but also an after-life of the experience (portents, prophetic signs, a warning *and* miraculous event); in other words, the time of Surrealist repetition is 'differential'.[2] In what sense, then, can repetition be said to have actually taken place? In the casting of the work of art, Whiteread constructs an object (the after-life) from another object (the fore-life) that is destroyed or was not 'present' in the first place (the space under a chair, and so on). In the shuffling of Johnson's *The Unfortunates*, memorialization is produced precisely through the disruption, the deformation and the reconfiguration of narrative and/or textual order; memorialization is not re-call, but construction or affirmation through destruction. In both cases (Whiteread and Johnson), the resulting product is a memorial aesthetics that functions by citing without quotation marks.[3] Andrew Benjamin notes that:

> Apart from introducing the continuity of convention, the use of quotation marks works, conventionally, to mark the act of recitation and hence of what could be described as a re-situation. What the convention brings with it, in addition to itself, is a form of continuity. The quotation marks indicate that what is cited (and re-sited) is not new but is the reiteration of what has already been; an intended repetition of the Same in which the singularity of the past's content is itself maintained.[4]

Both Whiteread and Johnson work against continuity, that is, repetition as a maintenance and reiteration (contributing also to a smooth art-historical progression); repetition, as Benjamin shows, can be radically reconfigured.

In *The Arcades Project*, there appears a 'twofold exclusion of repetition', an 'extrusion of repetition' in convolute N[5]:

> For the materialist historian, every epoch with which he occupies himself is only prehistory for the epoch he himself must live in. And so, for him, there can be no appearance of repetition in history, since precisely those moments in the course of history which matter most to him, by virtue of their index as 'fore-history,' become moments of the present day and change their specific character according to the catastrophic or triumphant nature of that day.[6]

Andrew Benjamin notes that the interpenetration of 'now and then' in the dialectal image would appear to obviate repetition, along with the obvious demands of continuity, but this does not account for the category of 'after-history' or 'after-life' which '. . . is itself unthinkable except as a form of repetition'.[7] Thus:

> Given this possibility, what will then have to be argued is that what is involved in the distinction is a reworked concept of repetition. What this will entail is a repetition that has been subjected to the process marked out by the distinction between 'fore-history' and 'after-history'. It is only the interpolation of such a construal of repetition that will allow further insight into . . . why Benjamin's introduction of 'a form of memoration' (*eine Form des Eingedenkens*) checks the dialectical presentation of history via the introduction of memory, but in so doing maintains the dialectical image as the ground of the historical itself.[8]

Andrew Benjamin explores reconfigured repetition via Benjamin's debt to Leibniz's *Monadology* – as Kierkegaard notes, Leibniz being the only modern thinker with a true grasp of what is at stake.[9] Of interest here is the way in which montage is not just a spatial form, but one which constitutes the 'epochal present' through interpenetration or co-presence of time.[10] For Andrew Benjamin, repetition (citation without quotation marks) plays 'a redemptive role'[11]; we can think here of the analogous tension or contradiction in Kierkegaard's *Repetition* between the denial of repetition and the possibility that repetition is atonement. The methodology in Benjamin is once again that of destruction:

> The possibility of 'quoting without quotation marks' is another formulation of Benjaminian destruction. A movement that . . . involves blasting 'the historical object . . . out of the historical process' (N10,3). Here, in opposition to either Cartesian destruction,

which is the attempt to differentiate the present from itself in an absolute and all-encompassing manner, or Heideggerian sacrifice, in which the present ('metaphysics') is given away for a specific end (the thinking of being), Benjamin's 'destruction' will necessitate the centrality of relation and with it of repetition. Both the dialectical image and 'now-time' are relations. And yet they are more than mere simple relations. In part, the departure from simplicity pertains to time and, in part, to repetition. It goes without saying that these two parts are related. Opting for the distinction within quotation – the absence and presence of marks as always signifying more than that which is given by the either/or of absence/presence – will capture these two interrelated parts. What has to be taken up, therefore, is quotation, to be understood as a form of repetition.[12]

Repetition as contributing to narrative order (the narrative of progression) is disrupted by repetition as citation without quotation marks; the shuffling of Johnson's *The Unfortunates* is a constant re-insertion of a fore-life or fore-history into the text, as such a disruptive citation, one which constantly undermines a sense of progressive development or of memorialization as harmonization. Continuity is literally blasted apart[13]: 'Historical materialism must renounce the epic element in history. It blasts the epoch out of the reified "continuity of history." But it also explodes the homogeneity of the epoch, interspersing it with ruins – that is, with the present.'[14]

Weapons of mass destruction

Benjamin's position within the network of German-Jewish 'new thinkers' is one which resists being neatly explained by or slotted into any number of coherent narratives that otherwise account for the emergence of new modes of Messianism. As Mendes-Flohr argues: 'The relation of Judentum and Deutschtum must cease to be that of a choice – an "or." It must be a relation founded in an authentically compelling "and." '[15] Similarly, Michael Löwy argues that Benjamin represents not some particular category of 'new thinking' but instead is situated 'At the heart of this network, at the intersection of all the threads of this cultural fabric, embodying opposite poles'.[16] And what does Benjamin find 'at the heart of this network'? Technological change that is about to revolutionize the entire field in which the 'new thinking' operates, and its entire existential framework of production – although the unpredictability of this transformation is also central to openness which is concomitant to the 'authentically compelling "and" '.[17] The notion developed in 'The Work of Art in the Age of its Technological Reproducibility' – that the mass-produced contemporary art-work meets the viewer halfway – distracts from the re-formulation of this process from its opposing perspective: the withdrawal of the human subject from the art-work in the perceptual shift brought about by technology. This process of withdrawal leads away from the 'maximum possible use of human beings' to a minimal immersion of the human in a particular situation: 'The achievements of the first technology might be said to culminate in human sacrifice; those of the second, in the remote-controlled aircraft which needs no human crew.'[18] Benjamin regards modern technology as essentially ludic: experiments are not just produced for verification; they endlessly unfold. Initially, this appears to be the point at which human beings not only distance themselves from nature but also, in the Kantian sense, attempt to manipulate and master nature; however, Benjamin argues that it is actually the case that the pre-technological age attempted to master nature whereas the technological age 'aims rather at an *interplay* between nature and humanity'.[19] One of the main mechanisms for developing and comprehending this interplay is war. In a review essay, primarily a discussion of Ernst Jünger's edited collection *War and Warriors*, Benjamin ponders the futural as predicated upon 'total mobilization' or the 'landscape of the front', which he combines into a nightmarish 'landscape of total mobilization':

> The pioneers of peace . . . were evacuated from these landscapes, and as far as anyone could see over the edge of the trench, the surroundings had become the terrain of German Idealism; every shell crater had become a problem, every wire entanglement an antimony, every barb a definition, every explosion a thesis; by day the sky was the cosmic interior of the steel helmet, and at night the moral law above. Etching the landscape with flaming banners and trenches, technology wanted to recreate the heroic features of German Idealism. It went astray. What it considered heroic were the features of Hippocrates, the features of death. Deeply imbued with its own depravity, technology gave shape to the apocalyptic face of nature and reduced nature to silence – even though this technology had the power to give nature its voice. War, in the metaphysical abstraction in which the new nationalism believes, is

nothing other than the attempt to redeem, mystically and without mediation, the secret of nature, understood idealistically, through technology.[20]

The essays under review in Benjamin's text do not uniformly support the new technologies of mechanized warfare: heroism can easily lead to 'boredom' under the bureaucratic conditions of mass-produced murder. What worries Benjamin more than this issue (in itself of great concern) is the expectations of the transformation of government and state via 'the magical forces that the state itself must mobilize in the event of war'.[21] The 'war engineers of the ruling class' are seen as the complement to 'managerial functionaries':

> God knows their designs on leadership should be taken seriously; their threat is not ludicrous. In the person of the pilot of a single airplane full of gas bombs, such leadership embodies all the absolute power which, in peacetime, is distributed among thousands of office managers – power to cut off a citizen's light, air, and life. The simple bomber-pilot in his lofty solitude, alone with himself and his God, has power-of-attorney for his seriously stricken superior, the state; and wherever he puts his signature, the grass will cease to grow – and this is the 'imperial' leader the authors have in mind.[22]

The modern management of death is passed over to the single moment, be it that of the remote-controlled or piloted bomber; this new moment whereupon the manipulator of the bomb has 'power-of-attorney' contrasts with an entire sequence of 'moments' theorized up to this point: 'from Ernst Bloch's "darkness of the lived moment" to Carl Schmitt's "moment of decision," from Ernst Jünger's "sudden fright" to Paul Tillich's *Kairos* – all refer, as does Heidegger, to the "moment," which began its career with Kierkegaard.'[23] Three discursive formations come together here in relation to Benjamin: that of Judeo-Christian thought, that of (the rejection of) Decisionism (Schmitt and Heidegger) and that of a new theory of materialist dialectical images. Safranski elucidates the Kierkegaardian roots of the moment:

> Kierkegaard's 'moment' is the one when God bursts into life and the individual feels summoned to make the decision to risk his leap into faith. At such a moment the historical time that separates the individual from Christ loses its significance. Anyone addressed by Christ's message and work of salvation exists 'simultaneously' with Christ. The entire cultural tradition, in which religion is dragged

along as a cultural possession and conventional morality, is burned
to nothing at that existentially heated moment. [. . .]

The moment thus understood promises a relation with the
'entirely Other,' it means a different experience of time and the
experience of a different time. It promises sudden turns and transformations, perhaps even arrival and redemption, but at any rate it
enforces decision.[24]

The moment of the bomber about to unleash his weapons of mass
destruction (and the recognition of this transposition of power
usually held by modern 'civil' society or the state) is one of crisis
(the German word *Krise*, derived from the Latin *decision*, and the
Greek *krisis* and *krinein*, to decide). The individual has been given
juridical power to commit mass-murder on behalf of the state; but
the state is already a manager or manipulator of 'mass' life and
death. For Benjamin, contemporary philosophical research reveals
that the basic unresolved questions are 'closely bound up with the
current social crisis'.[25] Writing on the failure of the SPD (Social
Democratic Party of Germany), Benjamin re-introduces Messianic,
redemptive thought into Marxism as a last or final hope to counter
the 'final solution' of such a state.[26] But it must be made clear that
the moment of the bomber, of technological consummation, is not
simply 'in time' or in 'the present time'; as the moment of mass
destruction, it is also the effacement of an entire culture (the Shoah)
and the projection and production of a new entity, be it at the level
of 'man', 'race' or 'state'. Reading Nietzsche's *Zarathustra*, Heidegger
thinks of the moment as a gateway and a riddle: 'The gateway
"Moment," with its avenues stretching infinitely onward and
counter to one another, is the image of time running forward and
backward into eternity.'[27] The bundling together or folding of multi-
directional temporality is called by Benjamin a 'constellation': 'Artic-
ulating the past historically means recognizing those elements of the
past which come together in the constellation of a single moment.
[. . .] But knowledge within the historical moment is always knowledge of a moment.'[28] In an important section of the 'First Sketches'
of *The Arcades Project*, Benjamin theorizes this constellation contra
Hegel:

> On the dialectical image. In it lies time. Already with Hegel, time
> enters into dialectic. But the Hegelian dialectic knows time solely as
> the properly historical, if not psychological, time of thinking. The
> time differential [*Zeitdifferential*] in which alone the dialectical image

is real is still unknown to him. [. . .] Real time enters the dialectical image not in natural magnitude – let alone psychologically – but
in the smallest gestalt. [See N1,2.] All in all, the temporal momentum [*das Zeitmoment*] in the dialectical image can be determined only
through confrontation with another concept. This concept is the
'now of recognizability' [*Jetzt der Erkennbarkeit*].[29]

The 'smallest gestalt' or configuration allows the entry of 'real time',
imaged as *Kugelblitz* or ball lightning; the moment of the bomber is
that of the *Blitzkrieg*, involved in the lightning strike of total war. The
Blitzkrieg is an act of doing away with the past (people, culture, architecture), whereas the *Kugelblitz* reveals the way in which the dialectical image lights up the entire horizon of 'the past'.[30]

In *The Arcades Project*, Benjamin writes that 'knowledge only
comes in lightning flashes', which leads him to question whether the
Marxist understanding of history (which appears, following this
question, to negate the 'perceptibility of history') can be conjoined
with 'a heightened graphicness' ('Anschaulichkeit',[31] combining the
vividness of ball lightning with the concreteness or materiality of the
dialectical image). Buck-Morss calls the 'illumination' of the dialectical image 'a mediated experience', one which is 'ignited within the
force field of antithetical time registers, empirical history, and Messianic history'.[32] Can the bomber plane be reconfigured as a historical object here? Buck-Morss quotes Pierre-Maxime Schuhl, from
The Arcades Project: 'The bombers remind us of what Leonardo da
Vinci expected of man in flight: that he was to ascend to the skies
"in order to seek snow on the mountaintops and bring it back to the
city to spread on the sweltering streets in summer." '[33] The utopian
vision of Leonardo da Vinci is negated by the use of the bomber plane
in modern warfare: the 'double focus' of the interpenetrated image
– originary image and present form[34] – reveals the utopian potential
of the technological object and its radical transformation in the
present day. Both visions of technology are present in a space which
resists the co-presence of contradiction; in other words, the space
does not 'resolve' the contradictions, or make a decision as such, or
reveal a crisis in the co-present image. The space is explosive precisely because it is bursting with the impossible co-presence, and
partly because it is contextually and temporally disruptive. As
Andrew Benjamin puts it: 'The revelation in another setting, a revelation constructed by that setting, is the explosive "now-time", the
instantiation of the present by montage; by the movement of the

montage (a montage effect whose determinations are yet to be fixed).'[35] He raises some serious issues concerning the production of the dialectical image: is it an energy that can be deliberately brought into being, or, is it an arbitrary process? In the latter case, is there the possibility that rather than getting the *Kugelblitz*, all that is produced is 'no more than a weak imagistic flutter'?[36]

Disrupting singularity

The fugitive rejects the decision of Nazi Germany, one which has already been brought into existence, but which is periodically punctuated by a call to bring one's self to accord, which is an act of submission. As Heidegger put it in 1933 in relation to Hitler's withdrawal from the League of Nations, and the ensuing 'supplementary election':

> The German people has been called to a vote by the Führer. But the Führer asks nothing of the people. On the contrary, he is giving the people the most immediate possibility of the highest free decision: whether it – the whole people – wills its own Dasein, or, whether it does not will this. This election is absolutely incomparable with all previous elections. What is unique about this election is the simple greatness of the decision which is to be made in it. [. . .] The ultimate decision extends to the furthest limit of the Dasein of our people. And what is this limit? It consists in the primordial demand of all Dasein, namely that it receive and save its own essence.[37]

The decision, which is unique, but also a return to the primordial, is an 'alignment' between the German people and Hitler: 'in order to make it known abroad that Germany and Hitler were the same'.[38] The decision 'extends to' but also creates a boundary (and a shared boundary experience), that of a people receiving and saving their own essence, and that of a limit 'between what can be demanded of a people and what cannot'.[39] By using the phrase essence of 'the Dasein' of the people, Heidegger wipes out domestic and foreign politics: 'There is only the one will to the full Dasein of the state. The Führer has brought this will to full awakening and welded it into one single decision in the whole people. No one can stay away on the day on which this will is manifested!'[40]

One of Benjamin's responses to Hitler took the form of an essay written in 1934 (which remained unpublished during his lifetime) called 'Hitler's Diminished Masculinity'. By comparing Hitler with

Charlie Chaplin, Benjamin punctures the mass-media manipulations of the National Socialists, stripping away the aura of the decision. Chaplin is 'the plowshare that cuts through the masses', loosening them up with laughter, whereas the opposing image created by Benjamin is that of the ground (the people) under the Third Reich, 'stamped down hard and firm . . . no more grass grows there'.[41] Benjamin compares the ban on puppets in Italy with the ban on Chaplin's films in the Third Reich: 'every puppet can put on Mussolini's chin, and every inch of Chaplin can become the Führer.'[42] Chaplin's mimetic parody of Hitler is an attack upon the latter's 'singularity':

> Chaplin's docility is apparent to all eyes; Hitler's, only to those of his bosses
>
> Chaplin shows up the comedy of Hitler's gravity; when he acts the well-bred man, then we know how things stand with the Führer
>
> Chaplin has become the greatest comic because he has incorporated into himself the deepest fears of his contemporaries[43]

All signs point towards instability and uncertainty; even Chaplin's wobbling, loose bowler hat 'betrays the fact that the rule of the bourgeoisie is tottering'.[44] Chaplin's films are banned not just because of his parody, but also because in their entertainment value they are a potential distraction ('Zerstreuung'). How far has apperception been transformed by new technologies here? Is the gaze of the viewer distracted negatively or positively by the moving image? Examples might include the image of 'Hitler's plane flying divinely through the clouds in [Leni] Riefenstahl's film "Triumph of the Will"',[45] or any scene from a Charlie Chaplin movie, perhaps the 1940 release of *The Great Dictator*. A formula from Benjamin's 'Theory of Distraction' links the new technologies with politics: 'Reproducibility—distraction—politicization'.[46] The technological apparatus not only re-trains but can also subsume the individual (negative distraction): 'The experience is one of being mastered by the apparatus – Benjamin may also be thinking, in this regard, of the fascist mass rallies of his own day – instead of mastering it for the good of humanity.'[47] Positive distraction means mastering the energies and intensities of modernity, the intoxication, rapture or *Rausch* which charges the subject. But does this mastery counteract the Nazi propaganda machine? Once again, there is the importance of singularity, a singularity constructed via repetition and a manifestation of the act: '"That happens only once, and never comes again." Hitler did not accept the title of the president of the Reich; his aim was to impress upon the people the singularity of his appearance. This singularity works in favor of his magically transposed prestige.'[48] The mass-produced repetition of the Nazi propaganda machine is a repetition of the same: an eternal return to the singularity that is the Führer. The boundary experience of this eternal return is more than just to do with the subject being mastered by the machine; the subject has been legislated in advance as being fit or unfit for the decision. For Benjamin, in 1934, this meant that 'the fashion keynote' for Hitler would not be the image of the military subject, but instead 'that of the gentleman in easy circumstances'.[49] In other words, the German people, who were to pass through the decision of indivisibility from Hitler, necessarily needed to decontaminate the ideal subject of the gentlemen. The singularity is countered by 'Zerstreuung', people not just being overcome but also scattered and driven away from the fearful inviolable image. This process also occurs at a more funda-mental level, whereby the ontological scatter is matched by an apperception that has learnt to function via mimesis: 'The ontolog-ical scatter that is accessible to an intensively scattered perception bespeaks a crisis of the object, a crisis of meaning. . . . the technolo-gization and commodification of things (involving, as it does, the unmooring of metaphysical substance) can be seen as a manifesta-tion of this crisis.'[50] The crisis (or decision) is a moment of great danger for the fugitives who have been, and are being, expelled from the boundary experience; the state of emergency in which the fugi-tives permanently live must be revealed to be the norm: 'Then we will clearly see that it is our task to bring about a *real* state of emer-gency, and this will improve our position in the struggle against fascism.'[51] Final hope, again, in the face of the onslaught.

Postscript on crisis time

Writing to Adorno on 2 August 1940, Benjamin sketches a feeling of 'complete uncertainty' concerning the immediate future: 'about what the next day and even the next hour will bring'.[52] This uncer-tainty 'has dominated my existence for many weeks. I am con-demned to read every newspaper (they now come out on a single sheet of paper) like a summons that has been served on me and to detect in every radio broadcast the voice of the messenger of bad tidings.'[53] Benjamin, the intellectual who had never been allowed to teach in the university system, was fleeing from a Germany where the philosophers were rapidly joining the Nazi party.[54] Bad tidings are traced by him in every daily paper, their exponential shrinking a *reductio ad absurdum* of the form which had appeared to offer an alternative space to that of the academy. The single-sheet newspaper is transmogrified into a summons, a personally addressed order or call supplemented by the broadcast voice. This single sentence by Benjamin evokes a nightmare world, a heightening of the sense of crisis: the summons brings with it a charge, for there is no evidence required of this man; he is simply to answer for his 'crime' of being Jewish. Benjamin had no intention of answering the summons: he was travelling in an alternative direction while still remaining within European territory. For Husserl, such a geographical mobility, fleeing or wandering, was not enough to define the subject's belonging to the 'spiritual shape of Europe'.[55] Pondering this issue in 1935 in his Vienna lecture – originally titled 'Philosophy and the Crisis of European Humanity' – Husserl argued that 'In the spiritual sense the English Dominions, the United States, etc., clearly belong to Europe, whereas the Eskimos or Indians presented as curiosities at fairs, or the Gypsies who constantly wander about Europe do not.'[56] The wandering subject, for Husserl, cannot partake of the unity of European spiritual life, or its 'purposeful activity, institutions, organizations'.[57] Husserl gives an evasive, morphological definition of this life:

> [We must] exhibit the philosophical idea which is immanent in the history of Europe (spiritual Europe) or, what is the same, the teleology which is immanent in it, which makes itself known, from the standpoint of universal mankind as such, as the breakthrough and the developmental beginning of a new human epoch – the epoch of mankind which now seeks to live, and can only live, in the free shaping of its existence, its historical life, through ideas of reason, through infinite tasks.[58]

The shape of Europe's spirit is that which shapes itself, but also that which exhibits the immanent 'entelechy' – that which encourages others to 'Europeanize' themselves while a European would have no desire to take up any other identity.[59] Husserl wrote at a time of recognized crisis, precisely a time of the breakdown of 'ideas of reason' and a loss of faith in the 'infinite tasks' or the recognizing and attaining of the infinite in Europe's midst. The *Existenzphilosophie* of Jaspers and Heidegger was for Husserl symptomatic of this crisis, and it gave expression to 'something real', in other words 'a deeply felt lack of direction for man's existence as a whole, a sense of the emptiness of Europe's cultural values'.[60] Husserl's response to his errant students was to recast and reintroduce phenomenology via the thought of crisis. Derrida sketches this recasting as 'the Husserlian form of the "crisis of European sciences" or the "crisis of European humanity": the teleology that guides the analysis of history and the very history of this crisis, of the recovery of the transcendental theme in and since Descartes, [which] is guided by the idea of a transcendental community, the subjectivity of a "we" for which Europe would be at once the name and the exemplary figure.'[61]

Infinite tasks and transcendental communities do not work for the people who live in the present, who live the crisis each day or register crisis as the meaning of everyday life, particularly those who are fugitives from Europe's entelechy.[62] The critical constellation of 'crisis, nation or race, leadership, and order'[63] constitutes the parameters of reality in Nazi Europe, including the time of the real. But while crisis as such is recognized, the moment of absolute crisis (the height of crisis?) is only known, according to Sluga, retrospectively, thus making it a 'conjectural' mode.[64] This is what Sluga calls the 'paradox of historical crisis':

> The idea of a great and unique crisis could play its symbolic role in the Nazi system, of course, only because the Germans were ready to accept the idea as a symbol of their condition; they were predisposed to experience their time as a decisive moment. The existence of that experience is not in question. Yet there is something paradoxical about it, and to understand the sources and the power of that experience, to understand its philosophical origin and character, means to face, first of all, the paradox.
>
> The notion of crisis . . . is epistemically peculiar insofar as one can have only retrospective evidence that such-and-such a moment was a real crisis and that it was of such-and-such magnitude. It is only after the event that we can recognize a particular moment as the point at which the process of destabilization reached its climax and had to give way to something else. It is only afterward that we can properly say what decision was reached and of what significance it proved to be.[65]

But what if the lived experience of crisis was that of the possibility of every moment being radically transformative? In other words, not an 'anticipation' of crisis or a retrospective summary or accounting for what has happened (and changed), but an immediate knowledge of crisis: an ownmost knowledge of crisis as 'now-time'. This would make of crisis not something that occurs in the moment, but, via the active decision, something that defines or structures the moment. Or, to put this another way, crisis is fully grasped by the subject as it occurs.

Jaspers argues that being 'is gained in time, by our own decisions.'[66] Objective knowledge of crisis is precisely an effacement of the experience of crisis when being 'is realized in choices made in temporal historicity' (which is not to say that objective knowledge is irrelevant – the opposite is the case).[67] As Jaspers continues: 'Thus, despite its objective disappearance, Existenz [or being] achieves reality as fulfilled time. Eternity is neither timelessness nor duration for all time; it is the depth of time as the historic appearance of Existenz.'[68] Sluga's argument concerning the paradox of historical crisis maintains that the question of magnitude is retrospective: 'For historical turning points are not necessarily announced with trumpet blasts; they come just as often on cat's paws, quietly in the night.'[69] The question of measurement here intersects with the time of the crisis having 'peaked' where the magnitude of the crisis is one 'that is equal only to itself'.[70] Yet measurement works via comparison, and even with Spengler's insistence on the singular crisis of the modern age, he 'proves' this via a comparative approach. How can that crisis which is equal only to itself be compared? Because this is what is happening with the retrospective knowledge of crisis: it is being compared with the current situation and all that has gone before. Kant, in his *Critique of Judgment*, addresses these issues in relation to the sublime, where he theorizes estimation of magnitude via numerical and aesthetic processes.[71] The latter provides a clue as to how a conception of crisis can be immediate and allow for present knowledge (the knowledge of now-time); Kant is discussing intuitive estimation of magnitude via the imagination and its immanent two-fold 'acts':

> *apprehension (apprehensio)* and *comprehension (comprehensio aesthetica)*. Apprehension involves no problem, for it may progress to infinity. But comprehension becomes more and more difficult the farther apprehension progresses, and it soon reaches its maximum, namely, the aesthetically largest basic measure for an estimation of magni-

tude. For when apprehension has reached the point where the partial presentations of sensible intuition that were first apprehended are already beginning to be extinguished in the imagination, as it proceeds to apprehend further ones, the imagination then loses as much on the one side as it gains on the other; and so there is a maximum in comprehension that it cannot exceed.[72]

Kant is comparing and interlinking, or making an assemblage of, apprehension and comprehension where the latter translates *Zusammenfassung*, 'collecting together and holding together'.[73] The assemblage of an assemblage (comprehension is always already an assemblage per se) stretches the imagination to its limit, and Kant calls this limit 'sublime'; the paradox of crisis is that it can be measured retrospectively (or, what amounts to the same evasion of the present, as an anticipatory claim which Sluga calls 'at best conjectural'[74]), as an 'a priori' where crisis is an always present potentiality or *given* in human consciousness,[75] or as a fully recognized and apprehended experience. In the latter sense, the assemblage of an assemblage as given shape or registered by Benjamin, is 'das Jetzt der Erkennbarkeit.' For Husserl, to recognize Europe's crisis is to register an extensive sickness, a kind of trans-national ill health that cannot be healed by the 'humanistic disciplines'.[76] As with Kant's *Prolegomena*, Husserl's crisis lectures suggest that metaphysical approaches are virtually defunct and that only the sciences can perform a functional service. Yet Husserl's 'infinite task' is precisely that which fails to engage with the lived experience of crisis: it brackets not the everyday as such but the possibility that the everyday might be an explosive site of recognition and a moment of danger.

Direct your gaze away from the world – momentarily – to become a historical materialist. Politics, and politicians, have failed in the fight against Fascism. The meditative discipline of abstract thought is now needed, a process of turning *away from the world and its affairs*. Contemplate *the angel of history* horrified by the catastrophic events that we call progress – the storm that blows from Paradise is the catastrophic progress of mankind. How can this be? Our meditations on the concept of history should teach us to escape, extricate ourselves *from the snares in which the traitors have entangled* us; we are reminded that we represent *one-fifth of the last second of the last hour* of *the history of all organic life on earth* and that this reduction can be compared with the tremendous abbreviation that is now-time or a particular model of Messianic time. We are given, by Benjamin, riddles, aphorisms, prophetic texts and sombre analysis; we are given the historian as *prophet facing backwards*, able to penetrate the mysteries of the moment and to reveal the link between prophecy and the obligation of politics, where the politicians have to decide. Benjamin is subtly re-tooling German-Jewish philosophy in his final major text, wresting the moment as decision from Kierkegaard, Heidegger and Schmitt, placing it as a configuration that conjoins materialism and Messianism. The syntheses of Bloch and Rosenzweig are replaced with the explosive, anarchist energies of 'das Jetzt der Erkennbarkeit.' Benjamin's final text liberates history from the empty homogeneous *schema of progression* and unleashes the counterdestructive energies of historical materialism.[77]

Notes

1 On the terms 'recollection' and 'repetition', see the opening page of Kierkegaard's *Repetition: A Venture in Experimenting Psychology* (by 'Constantin Constantius'), in Søren Kierkegaard, *Fear and Trembling* and *Repetition*, trans. Howard V. Hong and Edna H. Hong, Princeton, New Jersey: Princeton University Press, 1983.
2 Benjamin, *The Arcades Project*, p. 456 [N7a,1]; Foster, *Compulsive Beauty*, p. 30.
3 Benjamin, *The Arcades Project*, p. 458 [N1,10].
4 Andrew Benjamin, *Present Hope: Philosophy, Architecture, Judaism*, London and New York: Routledge, 1997, p. 50.
5 Ibid., p. 44.
6 Benjamin, *The Arcades Project*, p. 474 [N9a,8].
7 A. Benjamin, *Present Hope: Philosophy, Architecture, Judaism*, p. 44.
8 Ibid.
9 Kierkegaard, *Fear and Trembling* and *Repetition*, p. 131; the Hongs point towards various translations of Leibniz's *Theodicy* on p. 363, note 5.
10 A. Benjamin, *Present Hope: Philosophy, Architecture, Judaism*, p. 49.
11 Ibid.
12 Ibid., p. 50.
13 Ibid., p. 53.
14 Benjamin, *The Arcades Project*, p. 474 [N9a,6].
15 Mendes-Flohr, *German Jews: A Dual Identity*, p. 86.
16 Michael Löwy, *Redemption and Utopia: Jewish Libertarian Thought in Central Europe: A Study in Elective Affinity*, London: Athlone, 1992, p. 124.
17 See, also, Rosenzweig, 'The New Thinking', *Philosophical and Theological Writings*, p. 114.
18 Benjamin, 'The Work of Art in the Age of its Technological Reproducibility', 'Second Version', *Selected Writings*, vol. iii: *1935–1938*, p. 107.
19 Ibid.; my emphasis.

20 Benjamin, 'Theories of German Fascism: On the Collection of Essays *War and Warriors*, edited by Ernst Jünger', *Selected Writings*, vol. ii: *1927–1934*, pp. 318–319.
21 Ibid., p. 320.
22 Ibid.
23 Safranski, *Martin Heidegger: Between Good and Evil*, p. 173.
24 Ibid.
25 Benjamin, 'A German Institute for Independent Research,' *Selected Writings*, vol. iii: *1935–1938*, p. 308.
26 Benjamin, 'On the Concept of History' and 'Paralipomena to "On the Concept of History"', *Selected Writings*, vol. iv: *1938–1940*, pp. 394–395 and 402.
27 Heidegger, *Nietzsche: Volumes I and II*, vol. ii, p. 41; see, also, Heidegger, *Being and Time*, p. 388.
28 Benjamin, 'Paralipomena to "On the Concept of History"', 'New Theses B', *Selected Writings*, vol. iv: *1938–1940*, p. 403.
29 Benjamin, *The Arcades Project*, 'First Sketches', p. 867 <Q°,21>.
30 Benjamin, 'Paralipomena to "On the Concept of History"', 'New Theses B', *Selected Writings*, vol. iv: *1938–1940*, p. 403.
31 Benjamin, *The Arcades Project*, p. 456 [N1,1]; p. 461 [N2,6].
32 Buck-Morss, *The Dialectics of Seeing: Walter Benjamin and The Arcades Project*, p. 245.
33 Benjamin, *The Arcades Project*, p. 486 [N18a,2]; quotation marks as in Benjamin's text.
34 Buck-Morss, *The Dialectics of Seeing: Walter Benjamin and The Arcades Project*, p. 245.
35 A. Benjamin, *Present Hope: Philosophy, Architecture, Judaism*, p. 57.
36 Ibid., p. 48.
37 Löwith, *Martin Heidegger and European Nihilism*, p. 221.
38 Ibid.
39 Ibid.
40 Ibid., p. 222.
41 Benjamin, 'Hitler's Diminished Masculinity', *Selected Writings*, vol. ii: *1927–1934*, p. 792.
42 Ibid.
43 Ibid.
44 Ibid., p. 793.
45 Buck-Morss, *The Dialectics of Seeing: Walter Benjamin and The Arcades Project*, p. 245.
46 Benjamin, 'Theory of Distraction', *Selected Writings*, vol. iii: *1935–1938*, p. 142.
47 Howard Eiland, 'Reception in Distraction', *boundary 2*, 30:1 (spring 2003), special issue: *Benjamin Now: Critical Encounters with 'The Arcades Project'*, 51–66; at 60.
48 Benjamin, 'Hitler's Diminished Masculinity', *Selected Writings*, vol. ii: *1927–1934*, p. 793.
49 Ibid., p. 792.
50 Eiland, 'Reception in Distraction', p. 63.
51 Benjamin, 'On the Concept of History', *Selected Writings*, vol. iv: *1938–1940*, p. 392; my emphasis.
52 Benjamin to Theodor W. Adorno, 2 August 1940, letter 332 in *The Correspondence of Walter Benjamin: 1910–1940*, p. 638.

53 Ibid.
54 Hans Sluga, *Heidegger's Crisis: Philosophy and Politics in Nazi Germany*, Cambridge, Massachusetts, and London, England: Harvard University Press, 1993, p. 7.
55 Husserl, *The Crisis of European Sciences and Transcendental Phenomenology*, p. 273.
56 Ibid.
57 Ibid.
58 Ibid., p. 274.
59 Ibid., p. 275.
60 Ibid., translator's introduction, pp. xxv–xxvi. See, also, Allan Megill on 'Heidegger and Crisis' in his *Prophets of Extremity: Nietzsche, Heidegger, Foucault, Derrida.*
61 Jacques Derrida, *The Other Heading: Reflections on Today's Europe*, trans. Pascale-Anne Brault and Michael B. Naas, Bloomington and Indianapolis: Indiana University Press, 1992, p. 33.
62 Benjamin, 'On the Concept of History', *Selected Writings*, vol. iv: *1938–1940*, p. 401.
63 Sluga, *Heidegger's Crisis: Philosophy and Politics in Nazi Germany*, p. 23.
64 Ibid., p. 65.
65 Ibid.
66 Jaspers, *Philosophy*, vol. i, p. 57.
67 Ibid., p. 58.
68 Ibid.
69 Sluga, *Heidegger's Crisis: Philosophy and Politics in Nazi Germany*, p. 65.
70 Kant, *Critique of Judgment*, p. 105.
71 Ibid., p. 107.
72 Ibid., p. 108.
73 Ibid., translator's footnote 14.
74 Sluga, *Heidegger's Crisis: Philosophy and Politics in Nazi Germany*, p. 65.
75 Ibid., p. 67.
76 Husserl, *The Crisis of European Sciences and Transcendental Phenomenology*, p. 270.
77 Benjamin, 'On the Concept of History', *Selected Writings*, vol. iv: *1938–1940*, section X, p. 393; section IX, p. 392; section X, p. 393; section XVIII, p. 396; Benjamin, 'Paralipomena to "On the Concept of History"', ibid., 'The Now of Recognizability', p. 405; 'The Dialectical Image', p. 406. See, also, Michael Löwy, *Redemption and Utopia: Jewish Libertarian Thought in Central Europe: A Study in Elective Affinity*, p. 125.

BIBLIOGRAPHY

Primary sources

Benjamin, Walter. *Gesammelte Schriften*, vols i–vii, ed. Rolf Tiedemann and Herman Schweppenhäuser, with the collaboration of Theodor Adorno and Gershom Scholem, Frankfurt am Main: Suhrkamp Verlag, 1972–89.

Selected works by Benjamin in translation (in chronological order of publication)

Illuminations, trans. Harry Zohn, ed. Hannah Arendt, London: Fontana, 1992 (first published in English 1968; first Fontana edition 1973).

The Correspondence of Walter Benjamin: 1910–1940, ed. and annotated by Gershom Scholem and Theodor W. Adorno, trans. Manfred R. Jacobson and Evelyn M. Jacobson, London and Chicago: The University of Chicago Press, 1994.

Selected Writings, vol. i: *1913–1926*, ed. Marcus Bullock and Michael W. Jennings, Cambridge, Massachusetts, and London, England: Belknap Press of Harvard University Press, 1996.

The Origin of German Tragic Drama, trans. John Osborne, London and New York: Verso, 1999.

Selected Writings, vol. ii: *1927–1934*, ed. Michael W. Jennings, Howard Eiland and Gary Smith, trans. Rodney Livingstone and others, Cambridge, Massachusetts, and London, England: Belknap Press of Harvard University Press, 1999.

The Arcades Project, trans. Howard Eiland and Kevin McLaughlin, Cambridge, Massachusetts, and London, England: Belknap Press of Harvard University Press, 1999.

Selected Writings, vol. iii: *1935–1938*, ed. Howard Eiland and Michael W. Jennings, trans. Edmund Jephcott, Howard Eiland and others, Cambridge, Massachusetts, and London, England: Belknap Press of Harvard University Press, 2002.

Selected Writings, vol. iv: *1938–1940*, ed. Howard Eiland and Michael W. Jennings, trans. Edmund Jephcott and others, Cambridge, Massachusetts, and London, England: Belknap Press of Harvard University Press, 2003.

Secondary sources

Adorno, Theodor W. *Prisms*, trans. Samuel and Shierry Weber, Cambridge, Massachusetts: MIT Press, 1997.

Arendt, Hannah, 'Editor's Note', in Benjamin, *Illuminations*.

Barthes, Roland. *Roland Barthes: Image, Music, Text*, trans. Stephen Heath, London: Fontana Press, 1977.

Baudrillard, Jean. *Symbolic Exchange and Death*, trans. Iain Hamilton Grant, London: Sage, 1993.

Baudrillard, Jean. *The System of Objects*, trans. James Benedict, London: Verso, 1996.

Baudrillard, Jean. *The Spirit of Terrorism*, trans. Chris Turner, London and New York: Verso, 2002.

Beckett, Samuel. *Proust and Three Dialogues with Georges Duthuit*, London: John Calder, 1999.

Benjamin, Andrew. *Present Hope: Philosophy, Architecture, Judaism*, London and New York: Routledge, 1997.

Benjamin, Andrew, and Peter Osborne, eds. *Walter Benjamin's Philosophy: Destruction and Experience*, Manchester: Clinamen Press, 2000.

Bennington, Geoffrey, with Jacques Derrida. *Jacques Derrida*, trans. Geoffrey Bennington, Chicago and London: The University of Chicago Press, 1993.

Berkowitz, Michael. *Zionist Culture and West European Jewry before the First World War*, Chapel Hill and London: The University of North Carolina Press, 1996.

Berkowitz, Peter. *Nietzsche: The Ethics of an Immoralist*, Cambridge, Massachusetts, and London, England: Harvard University Press, 1996.

Bernstein, J. M. *The Fate of Art: Aesthetic Alienation from Kant to Derrida and Adorno*, Cambridge: Polity, 1993.

Bloch, Ernst. *The Principle of Hope*, 3 vols, trans. Neville Plaice, Stephen Plaice and Paul Knight, Cambridge, Massachusetts: The MIT Press, 1995.

Bloch, Ernst. *The Spirit of Utopia*, trans. Anthony A. Nassar, Stanford, California: Stanford University Press, 2000.

Borch-Jacobsen, Mikkel. *The Freudian Subject: Language, Discourse, Society*, trans. Catherine Porter, Basingstoke and London: Macmillan, 1989.

boundary 2, 30:1 (spring 2003), special issue: *Benjamin Now: Critical Encounters with 'The Arcades Project'*, ed. Kevin McLaughlin and Philip Rosen.

Bowie, Andrew. *Aesthetics and Subjectivity: From Kant to Nietzsche*, Manchester: Manchester University Press, 1990.

Bradley, Fiona, ed. *Rachel Whiteread: Shedding Life*, London and Liverpool: Tate Gallery Liverpool, 1996–97.

Breton, André. 'Surrealist Situation of the Object', in *Manifestoes of Surrealism*, trans. Richard Seaver and Helen R. Lane, Ann Arbor: University of Michigan, 1972, pp. 255–278.

Britt, Brian. *Walter Benjamin and the Bible*, New York: Continuum, 1996.

Brodersen, Momme. *Walter Benjamin: A Biography*, trans. Malcolm R. Green and Ingrida Ligers, London and New York: Verso, 1997.

Bruggen, Coosje van. *Bruce Nauman*, New York: Rizzoli, 1988.

Buber, Martin. *Between Man and Man*, London and New York: Routledge, 2002.

Buck-Morss, Susan. *The Dialectics of Seeing: Walter Benjamin and The Arcades Project*, Cambridge, Massachusetts: MIT Press, 1999.

Burke, Edmund. *On the Sublime and Beautiful*, Charlottesville, Virginia: Ibis (no date); reprint of the 1812 edition.

Burleigh, Michael. *The Third Reich: A New History*, London: Macmillan, 2000.

Butler, Rex. *Jean Baudrillard: The Defence of the Real*, London: Sage, 1999.

Carr, David. Translator's introduction, in Husserl, *The Crisis of European Sciences and Transcendental Phenomenology*.

Caws, Mary Ann (ed.). *Manifesto: A Century of Isms*, Lincoln and London: University of Nebraska Press, 2001.

Caygill, Howard. *Walter Benjamin: The Colour of Experience*, London: Routledge, 1998.

Caygill, Howard. 'Benjamin, Heidegger and the Destruction of Tradition', in Andrew Benjamin and Osborne, eds. *Walter Benjamin's Philosophy: Destruction and Experience*, pp. 1–30.

Chénieux-Gendron, Jacqueline. *Surrealism*, trans. Vivian Folkenflik, New York: Columbia University Press, 1990.

Coe, Jonathan, 'Introduction' to B. S. Johnson, *The Unfortunates*.

Collins, Arthur. *Possible Experience: Understanding Kant's Critique of Pure Reason*, Berkeley, Los Angeles, and London: University of California Press, 1999.

Come, Arnold B. *Kierkegaard as Humanist: Discovering My Self*, London, Buffalo, Montreal and Kingston: McGill-Queen's University Press, 1995.

Cornwell, John. *Hitler's Pope: The Secret History of Pius XII*, London: Viking, 1999.

Critchley, Simon. *Very Little . . . Almost Nothing: Death, Philosophy, Literature*, London and New York: Routledge, 1997.

de Duve, Thierry. *Kant after Duchamp*, Cambridge, Massachusetts, and London, England: MIT Press, 1996.

Deleuze, Gilles. *Nietzsche and Philosophy*, trans. Hugh Tomlinson, London: Athlone, 1983.

Deleuze, Gilles. *The Fold: Leibniz and the Baroque*, trans. Tom Conley, London: Athlone, 2001.

Derrida, Jacques. *The Truth in Painting*, trans. Geoff Bennington and Ian McLeod, Chicago and London: The University of Chicago Press, 1978.

Derrida, Jacques. *Dissemination*, trans. Barbara Johnson, Chicago and London: The University of Chicago Press, 1981.

Derrida, Jacques. *The Other Heading: Reflections on Today's Europe*, trans. Pascale-Anne Brault and Michael B. Naas, Bloomington and Indianapolis: Indiana University Press, 1992.

Double take: Collective Memory and Current Art, London: South Bank Centre and Parkett, 1992.

Duchamp, Marcel. *À l'infinitif/In the Infinitive*, a typotranslation by Richard Hamilton and Ecke Bonk of Marcel Duchamp's *White Box*, Over Wallop, UK: The Typosophic Society, 1999.

Eiland, Howard. 'Reception in Distraction', *boundary 2*, 30:1 (spring 2003), special issue: *Benjamin Now: Critical Encounters with 'The Arcades Project'*, ed. Kevin McLaughlin and Philip Rosen 51–66.

Feliciano, Hector. *The Lost Museum: The Nazi Conspiracy to Steal the World's Greatest Works of Art*, New York: BasicBooks, 1997.

Fichte, J. G. *Science of Knowledge*, ed. and trans. Peter Heath and John Lachs, Cambridge: Cambridge University Press, 1982.

Fogelin, Robert J. *Wittgenstein* (second edition), London and New York: Routledge, 1995.

Foster, Hal. *Compulsive Beauty*, Cambridge, Massachusetts, and London, England: The MIT Press, 1993.

Foucault, Michel. *Language, Counter-Memory, Practice: Selected Essays and Interviews*, ed. Donald F. Bouchard, trans. Donald F. Bouchard and Sherry Simon, Ithaca, New York: Cornell University Press, 1988.

France, Anatole. *The Garden of Epicurus*, trans. Alfred Allinson, London: Bodley Head, 1926.

Frank, Manfred. *What is Neostructuralism?*, trans. Sabine Wilke and Richard Gray, Minneapolis: University of Minnesota Press, 1989.

Freud, Sigmund. *The Interpretation of Dreams*, trans. James Strachey, Harmondsworth, Middlesex: Penguin, 1986.

Gasché, Rodolphe. *The Tain of The Mirror: Derrida and the Philosophy Of Reflection*, Cambridge, Massachusetts, and London, England: Harvard University Press, 1986.

Gasché, Rodolphe. 'Objective Diversions: On some Kantian Themes in Benjamin's "The Work of Art in the Age of Mechanical Reproduction"', in A. Benjamin and Osborne, eds., *Walter Benjamin's Philosophy: Destruction and Experience*, pp. 180–201.

Gelber, Mark H. 'The first Issue of Martin Buber's German-Jewish Journal *Der Jude* Appears', in Gilman and Zipes, eds., *Yale Companion to Jewish Writing and Thought in German Culture, 1096–1996*, pp. 343–347.

Genette, Gérard. *Narrative Discourse*, Oxford: Basil Blackwell, 1986.

Gilloch, Graeme. *Walter Benjamin: Critical Constellations*, Cambridge: Polity, 2002.

Gilman, Sander L. and Jack Zipes, eds. *Yale Companion to Jewish Writing and Thought in German Culture, 1096–1996*, New Haven and London: Harvard University Press, 1997.

Glatzer, N. N. 'Foreword' to Rosenzweig, *The Star of Redemption*.

Goldsmith, Ulrich K. *Stefan George*, London and New York: Columbia University Press, 1970.

Green, Clifford J. *Bonhoeffer: A Theology of Sociality* (revised edition), Grand Rapids, Michigan, and Cambridge, UK: William B. Eerdmans, 1999.

Handelman, Susan. *Fragments of Redemption: Jewish Thought and Literary Theory in Benjamin, Scholem, and Levinas*, Bloomington: Indiana University Press, 1991.

Hanssen, Beatrice. *Walter Benjamin's Other History: Of Stones, Animals, Human Beings, and Angels*, Berkeley, Los Angeles and London: University of California Press, 1998.

Hansen, Miriam Bratu. 'Introduction' to Kracauer, *Theory of Film: The Redemption of Physical Reality*.

Hart, H. L. A. *The Concept of Law*, Oxford: Oxford University Press, 1997.

Hegel, G. W. F. *The Phenomenology of Spirit*, trans. A. V. Miller, Oxford: Oxford University Press, 1977.

Heidegger, Martin. 'The Origin of the Work of Art', in *Poetry, Language, Thought*, trans. Albert Hofstadter, New York: Harper and Row, 1971.

Heidegger, Martin. *Hegel's Phenomenology of Spirit*, trans. Parvis Emad and Kenneth Maly, Bloomington and Indianapolis: Indiana University Press, 1988.

Heidegger, Martin. *Being and Time*, trans. John Macquarrie and Edward Robinson, Oxford: Blackwell, 1990.

Heidegger, Martin. *Nietzsche: Volumes I and II* (*The Will to Power as Art* and *The Eternal Return of the Same*), trans. David Farrell Krell, San Francisco: HarperSanFrancisco, 1991.

Heidegger, Martin. *Nietzsche: Volumes III and IV* (*The Will to Power as Knowledge and as Metaphysics* and *Nihilism*), trans. David Farrell Krell, San Francisco: HarperSanFrancisco, 1991.

Hunsinger, George. *Kierkegaard, Heidegger, and the Concept of Death*, Stanford Honors Essay in Humanities, no. XII, Stanford, California: Stanford University Press, 1969.

Husserl, Edmund. *The Crisis of European Sciences and Transcendental Phenomenology*, trans. David Carr, Evanston: Northwestern University Press, 1970.

Hyppolite, Jean. *Genesis and Structure of Hegel's Phenomenology of Spirit*, trans. Samuel Cherniak and John Heckman, Evanston: Northwestern University Press, 1974.

Jacobs, Carol. *In the Language of Walter Benjamin*, Baltimore and London: The Johns Hopkins University Press, 1999.

Jacobson, Eric. *Metaphysics of the Profane: The Political Theology of Walter Benjamin and Gershom Scholem*, New York: Columbia University Press, 2003.

Jaspers, Karl. *Philosophy*, 3 vols, trans. E. B. Ashton, Chicago and London: The University of Chicago Press, 1969.

Johnson, B. S. *The Unfortunates*, London: Picador, 1999.

Kant, Immanuel. *Critique of Pure Reason*, trans. J. M. D. Meiklejohn, London: J. M. Dent, 1934.

Kant, Immanuel. *Kant's Critique of Practical Reason and Other Works on the Theory of Ethics*, trans. Thomas Kingsmill Abbott, London: Longmans, 1959.

Kant, Immanuel. *Prolegomena to any Future Metaphysics that will be Able to Present itself as a Science*, trans. Peter G. Lucas, Manchester: Manchester University Press, 1966.

Kant, Immanuel. *Critique of Judgment*, trans. Werner S. Pluhar, Indianapolis, Hackett, 1987.

Kermode, Frank. *The Genesis of Secrecy: On the Interpretation of Narrative*, Cambridge, Massachusetts, and London, England: Harvard University Press, 1979.

Kierkegaard, Søren. *Fear and Trembling* and *Repetition*, trans. Howard V. Hong and Edna H. Hong, Princeton, New Jersey: Princeton University Press, 1983.

Klossowski, Pierre. *Nietzsche and the Vicious Circle*, trans. Daniel W. Smith, London: Athlone and Chicago: The University of Chicago Press, 1997.

Kofman, Sarah. 'Explosion I: Of Nietzsche's *Ecce homo*', *Diacritics*, 24:4 (winter 1994), 50–70.

Kracauer, Sigfried. *Theory of Film: The Redemption of Physical Reality*, Princeton, New Jersey: Princeton University Press, 1997.

Krauss, Rosalind. 'X Marks the Spot', in Bradley, ed., *Rachel Whiteread: Shedding Life*, pp. 74–81.

Lane, Richard J. *Jean Baudrillard*, London and New York: Routledge, 2000.

Lane, Richard J. 'Beckett and Nietzsche: The Eternal Headache', in Lane, ed., *Beckett and Philosophy*, pp. 166–177.

Lane, Richard J., ed. *Beckett and Philosophy*, London: Palgrave, 2002.

Lane, Richard J. *Functions of the Derrida Archive: Philosophical Receptions*, Budapest: Akadémiai Kiadó, 2003.

Laqueur, Walter Z. *Young Germany: A History of the German Youth Movement*, London: Routledge, 1962.

Lefebvre, Henri. *Critique of Everyday Life*, trans. John Moore, London and New York: Verso, 1991 (first published 1947).

Leslie, Esther. 'Elemental: Walter Benjamin's *Arcades Project*', in Andrew Benjamin and Osborne, eds. *Walter Benjamin's Philosophy: Destruction and Experience*, appendix 2.

Lingwood, James. 'Introduction' to Lingwood, ed., *Rachel Whiteread: House*.

Lingwood, James, ed. *Rachel Whiteread: House*, London: Phaidon, 2000.

Livingston, Jane. 'Bruce Nauman', in Jane Livingston and Marcia Tucker, *Bruce Nauman: Work from 1965 to 1972*, Los Angeles: Los Angeles County Museum of Art, 1972, pp. 9–29.

Löwith, Karl. *Martin Heidegger and European Nihilism*, trans. Gary Steiner, Chichester and New York: Columbia University Press, 1995.

Löwy, Michael. *Redemption and Utopia: Jewish Libertarian Thought in Central Europe: A Study in Elective Affinity*, London: Athlone, 1992.

Lukács, Georg (György). *History and Class Consciousness: Studies in Marxist Dialectics*, trans. Rodney Livingstone, Cambridge, Massachusetts: The MIT Press, 1971.

Lyotard, Jean-François. *The Differend: Phrases in Dispute*, trans. Georges Van Den Abbeele, Manchester: Manchester University Press, 1988.

Marí, Bartomeu. 'The Art of the Intangible', in Bradley, ed., *Rachel Whiteread: Shedding Life*, pp. 61–73.

Massey, Doreen. 'Space-Time and the Politics of Location', in Lingwood, ed., *Rachel Whiteread: House*, pp. 34–49.

Megill, Allan. *Prophets of Extremity: Nietzsche, Heidegger, Foucault, Derrida*, Berkeley, Los Angeles and London, England: The University of California Press, 1985.

Mendes-Flohr, Paul. 'Franz Rosenzweig Writes the Essay "Atheistic Theology", which Critiques the Theology of his Day', in Gilman and Zipes, eds., *Yale Companion to Jewish Writing and Thought in German Culture, 1096–1996*, pp. 322–326.

Mendes-Flohr, Paul. *German Jews: A Dual Identity*, New Haven and London: Yale University Press, 1999.

Michalson, Gordon E., Jr. *Kant and the Problem of God*, Oxford: Blackwell, 1999.

Miles, Jack. *Christ: A Crisis in the Life of God*, London: William Heinemann, 2001.

Missac, Pierre. *Walter Benjamin's Passages*, trans. Shierry Weber Nicholsen, Cambridge, Massachusetts, and London, England: MIT Press, 1995.

Moses, Stéphane. 'Walter Benjamin and Franz Rosenzweig', in Gary Smith, ed. *Benjamin: Philosophy, Aesthetics, History*, Chicago and London: University of Chicago Press, 1989, pp. 228–246.

Nehamas, Alexander. *Nietzsche: Life as Literature*, Cambridge, Massachusetts, and London, England: Harvard University Press, 1985.

Nicholsen, Shierry Weber. *Exact Imagination, Late Work: On Adorno's Aesthetics*, Cambridge, Massachusetts, and London, England: MIT Press, 1997.

Nietzsche, Friedrich. *Twilight of the Idols and The Anti-Christ*, trans. R. J. Hollingdale, London: Penguin, 1990.

Nietzsche, Friedrich. *Daybreak: Thoughts on the Prejudices of Morality*, trans. R. J. Hollingdale, Cambridge: Cambridge University Press, 1991.

Osborne, Peter. 'Philosophizing Beyond Philosophy: Walter Benjamin Reviewed', in A. Benjamin and Osborne, eds. *Walter Benjamin's Philosophy: Destruction and Experience*, pp. 286–303.

Parini, Jay. *Benjamin's Crossing*, London: Anchor, 1998.

Pensky, Max. *Melancholy Dialectics: Walter Benjamin and the Play of Mourning*, Amherst: University of Massachusetts Press, 2001.

Pieper, Josef. *The End of Time: A Meditation on the Philosophy of History*, trans. Michael Bullock, San Francisco: Ignatius Press: 1999.

Popper, Karl. *The Open Society and its Enemies*, 2 vols, London: Routledge, 1999.

Rabinbach, Anson. 'Between Enlightenment and Apocalypse: Benjamin, Bloch and Modern German Jewish Messianism', *New German Critique*, 34 (winter 1985), 78–124.

'Rachel Whiteread', *Doubletake: Collective Memory and Current Art*, London: the South Bank Centre and Parkett, 1992.

Roberts, Richard J. *Hope and its Hieroglyph: A Critical Decipherment of Ernst Bloch's Principle of Hope*, Atlanta, Georgia: Scholars Press, 1990.

Rochlitz, Rainer. *The Disenchantment of Art: The Philosophy of Walter Benjamin*, trans. Jane Marie Todd, New York and London: Guilford Press, 1996.

Rosenzweig, Franz. *The Star of Redemption*, trans. William W. Hallo, London and Notre Dame: University of Notre Dame Press, 1985.

Rosenzweig, Franz. *Philosophical and Theological Writings*, trans. and ed., with notes and commentary, by Paul W. Franks and Michael L. Morgan, Indianapolis and Cambridge: Hackett, 2000.

Rubinstein, Ernest. *An Episode of Jewish Romanticism: Franz Rosenzweig's The Star of Redemption*, Albany: State University of New York Press, 1999.

Safranski, Rüdiger. *Martin Heidegger: Between Good and Evil*, trans. Ewald Osers, Cambridge, Massachusetts, and London, England: Harvard University Press, 1999.

Saussure, F. de. *Course in General Linguistics*, trans. Roy Harris, London: Duckworth, 1983.

Schmitt, Carl. *Political Theology: Four Chapters on the Doctrine of Sovereignty*, trans. George Schwab, Cambridge, Massachusetts, and London, England: MIT Press, 1985.

Scholem, Gershom. *On Jews and Judaism in Crisis: Selected Essays*, ed. Werner J. Dannhauser, New York: Schocken, 1976.

Scholem, Gershom. *Walter Benjamin: The Story of a Friendship*, trans. Harry Zohn, Philadelphia: Jewish Publication Society of America, 1981.

Shone, Richard. 'A Cast in Time', in Lingwood, ed., *Rachel Whiteread: House*, pp. 50–61.

Sluga, Hans. *Heidegger's Crisis: Philosophy and Politics in Nazi Germany*, Cambridge, Massachusetts, and London, England: Harvard University Press, 1993.

Smith, Gary, ed. *Benjamin: Philosophy, Aesthetics, History*, Chicago and London: University of Chicago Press, 1989.

Snyder, Joel. 'Benjamin on Reproducibility and Aura: A Reading of "The Work of Art in the Age of its Technical Reproducibility"', in Smith, ed., *Benjamin: Philosophy, Aesthetics, History*, pp. 158–174.

Spengler, Oswald. *The Decline of the West* (complete in 1 vol.), trans. Charles Francis Atkinson, London: George Allen and Unwin, 1926.

Stachura, Peter D. *The German Youth Movement 1900–1945*, London: Macmillan, 1981.

Steinberg, Michael P. 'Walter Benjamin Writes the Essays "Critique of Violence" and "The Task of the Translator", Treating the Subject of Messianism he Discussed with Gershom Scholem during the War', in Gilman and Zipes, eds., *Yale Companion to Jewish Writing and Thought in German Literature, 1096–1996*, pp. 401–411.

Steiner, George. 'Introduction' to Benjamin, *The Origin of German Tragic Drama*.

Stirk, S. D. *The Prussian Spirit: A Survey of German Literature and Politics, 1914–1940*, London: Faber and Faber, 1951.

Suarès, Carlos. *The Cipher of Genesis: The Original Code of the Qabala as Applied to the Scriptures*, Boulder and London: Shambhala, 1978.

Sussman, Henry. 'Between the Registers: The Allegory of Space in Walter Benjamin's *Arcades Project*,' *boundary 2*, 30:1 (spring 2003), special issue: *Benjamin Now: Critical Encounters with 'The Arcades Project'*, ed. Kevin McLaughlin and Philip Rosen, 169–190.

Taylor, Charles. *Hegel*, Cambridge: Cambridge University Press, 1989.

Tenbrock, Robert-Hermann. *A History of Germany*, trans. Paul J. Dine, München: Max Hueber Verlag, 1968.

Tew, Philip. 'The Lexicon of Youth in MacLaverty, Bolger, and Doyle: Theorizing Contemporary Irish Fiction via Lefebvre's *Tenth Prelude*', *Hungarian Journal of English and American Studies*, 5:1, 1999, 181–197.

Tew, Philip. *B. S. Johnson: A Critical Reading*, Manchester and New York: Manchester University Press, 2001.

Tew, Philip. 'Reconsidering Literary Interpretation', in José López and Garry Potter, eds., *After Postmodernism: An Introduction To Critical Realism*, London and New York: Athlone, 2001, pp. 196–205.

Thibault, Paul J. *Re-Reading Saussure: The Dynamics of Signs in Social Life*, London and New York: Routledge, 1997.

Tiedemann, Rolf. 'Historical Materialism or Political Messianism? An Interpretation of the Theses "On the Concept of History"', in Smith, ed., *Benjamin: Philosophy, Aesthetics, History*, pp. 175–209.

Tiedemann Rolf. 'Dialectics at a Standstill: Approaches to the *Passagen-Werk*', in Benjamin, *The Arcades Project*, pp. 929–945.

Weigel, Sigrid. *Body- and Image-Space: Re-Reading Walter Benjamin*, trans. Georgina Paul with Rachel McNicholl and Jeremy Gaines, London and New York: Routledge, 1996.

Wigley, Mark. 'The Domestication of the House: Deconstruction after Architecture', in Peter Brunette and David Wills, eds., *Deconstruction and the Visual Arts: Art, Media, Architecture*, Cambridge: Cambridge University Press, 1994, pp. 203–227.

Williams, John R. *The Life of Goethe*, Oxford: Blackwell, 2001.

Witte, Bernd. *Walter Benjamin: An Intellectual Biography*, trans. James Rolleston, Detroit: Wayne State University Press, 1997.

Wittgenstein, Ludwig. *Tractatus logico-philosophicus*, trans. D. F. Pears and B. F. McGuinness, London: Routledge, 1989.

Wittgenstein, Ludwig. *Philosophical Investigations*, trans. G. E. M. Anscombe, Oxford: Basil Blackwell, 1991.

Žižek, Slavoj. *The Ticklish Subject: The Absent Centre of Political Ontology*, London and New York: Verso, 1999.

INDEX